Stateville

Stateville
The Penitentiary in Mass Society

James B. Jacobs

The University of Chicago Press
Chicago and London

The University of Chicago Press, Chicago 60637
The University of Chicago Press, Ltd., London

Printed in the United States of America

90 89 88 87 86 85 84 987654

Library of Congress Cataloging in Publication Data

Jacobs, James B
Stateville.

(Studies in crime and justice)
Includes bibliographical references and index.
1. Illinois. State Penitentiary, Joliet. I. Title. II. Series.
HV9475.I32S824 365'.9773'25 76-22957

ISBN: 0-226-38977-4 (paper)

To My Mother and Father

Contents

Foreword

This is a historical and sociological study of a penitentiary; specifically, it presents fifty years of transformation and change of a large state prison. It is both a richly descriptive account and a powerfully trenchant analysis. The author has engaged in a careful historical examination of the archival records; he has pursued direct and prolonged participant observation with great skill; and, in addition, as a lawyer he has uniquely augmented his research by an elaborate assessment of the changing administrative and legal codes affecting the prison. Thus this book is a lasting contribution to the study of social institutions. But, in effect, it is also an analysis of contemporary society, since the prison and its internal life are a reflection of the state of the larger society. In the language of contemporary social science, this book is a contribution to macrosociology.

Sociologists have a rich tradition of exploring the social organization of the prison. The Chicago school of sociology was not limited to community studies; as in this case, it applied its perspective to a variety of institutions. Thus, this research builds on and enriches Donald Clemmer's pioneering book *The Prison Community,* published in 1940. The literature on prisons contains some of the most outstanding research monographs in sociology;

and let there be no misunderstanding: the vitality and the enduring core of sociology rest as much on its classic monographs as on its grand theories. For the individual sociologist, the prison is a manageable research site, one whose organization can be understood and mastered. At the same time, it is an encompassing and complex institution; it is an entity worthy of intensive research; to research a prison is to investigate a rather complete social system.

The intellectual power of this monograph results from James Jacobs's ability to use the prison as an indicator of the social organization and moral values of the larger society. This is best done by examining the prison on a trend basis over time. The internal social stratification of the prison has reflected and continues to reflect the stratification system of the outside society. The conception of prison management and the organizational goals of the prison in turn are outgrowths of the struggles and accommodations of civil society.

Because he presents an overview of the various "phases" of the institutional life of the prison during a half-century, Jacobs is able to record both the internal changes and the transformation of the larger society. Stateville is not necessarily the typical prison—there could be no single typical institution. But the trends in the history of Stateville are those which have operated throughout United States society. In the simplest terms, the prison has moved from an institution at the periphery of society, remote, isolated, with distinct boundaries, under the control of personalistic and authoritarian leadership. It was an organization with a strong emphasis on informal and interpersonal mechanisms of control. Over time, it has shifted more to the center of the larger society; its boundaries have become more permeable and its older control mechanisms have given way to more rational, bureaucratic, and legalistic arrangements.

Jacobs presents a developmental analysis in which a series of stages are identified that are common to social movement and institutional change. The "old order" of authoritarian control was followed by a period of mild reform, and mild reform only produced increased tension and hostility between prisoners and administration. The next phase was a more marked reform of the older system—which in turn produced more tension, disruption, and violence. In the pattern of the natural history of societal and institutional change, the subsequent phase was a counterreformation—a search for and the emergence of a new format of greater stability and mutual, if uneasy, acceptance by the contending parties.

There can be no doubt that a dedicated band of reformers initiated the efforts at institutional change. Among those who were active before and immediately after World War II were academic sociologists and their students who entered prison administration. Their contributions were important, but they were without deep or lasting influence. The changing mood in the nation—the increased emphasis after 1945 on "humanitarian" goals and the strong belief in the potentials of rehabilitation—served to keep alive the goals of transforming the prison. However, the popular movements and the agitations of the 1960s set the process of institutional change in motion. These social and political movements served to politicize the prisoners and increase the tensions between inmate and administration.

A variety of external groups entered the prison and sought to participate in the decision-making process. James Jacobs highlights the penetration of the prison in the 1960s and 1970s by Black Muslims, by street gangs of the city of Chicago, and by civil liberty and legal groups, as well as by educational and social welfare agencies. These kept up the pressure for change and heightened the internal tensions. But the basis of real transformation came from the judicial review of prison administration and prison procedures. In the late 1960s the courts started to apply their definition of due process and equal protection to the lives of the inmates. They sought to extend to the prisoner essential aspects of the rights of citizenship.

The result was the emergence of a new set of legalistic and bureaucratic rules and procedures for guiding the day-to-day activities of the prison administrators and their staff. Under these conditions, it was understandable that unionization of the guards took place, since they were searching for a set of rules and procedures as well as an occupational ideology to defend their position in the prison system. Out of the legalistic emphasis, a new equilibrium emerged, accompanied by strong administrative control and by a decline or a constriction of tension and violence in the prison. The new equilibrium was based on important elements of the rule of law, but it was also based on a rejection of some administrative practices of the period of marked reform.

James Jacobs makes use of the notion of mass society to analyze and understand the transformation of the prison. The term "mass society" refers to societal movements which seek to incorporate each and every person into the political and legal systems of society. Mass society, as used by James Jacobs, draws on a specific formulation of the term; it does not focus only on increase in scale and complexity and on the growth of impersonality in an advanced industrial society. It is rather a concern with the efforts to create a moral and legal system appropriate for contemporary society. The concept emphasizes the extension of the rights of citizenship throughout the social structure. Jacobs, as a legal scholar, is aware that the rights of citizenship—that is, particular elements—extend to the prison population as well. And the history of Stateville documents this transformation. A more legalistic, more bureaucratic prison system hardly creates a utopia, but it supplies a new basis for the social order of the prison.

Among the most brilliant aspects of the study is the analysis of the limitations and difficulties of the new organizational format. Stateville is still a prison. There are inherent limitations in the application of the rule of law to a prison setting. The guards and administrators find themselves under pressure to redefine their goals and practices, but it is easier to resist than to adapt.

But basically the application of the rule of law hardly guarantees that the prison will be more effective as an institution of rehabilitation or social education. It does mean that prisoners will existentially, and in the immediate moment, be treated more equitably and more humanely. The rule of law can at best create the preconditions for effective programs of rehabilitation and social education. But juridical review cannot guarantee them as an effective right, because there is not a foundation of knowledge on which to base such programs. At best, the juridical intrusion into the prison serves to permit the responsible penetration of external groups into the life of the prison and to increase the likelihood of contacts between the inmates and the agencies of the larger civil society. Attaining the major goal of reducing the size of the prisoner population depends, not on prison reform, but on a fundamental transformation of the agencies of education and employment which manage the transition from youth to adult status. But the broad sweep of Jacobs's analysis indicates that, in essence, the legal system—not the concept of the social sciences or psychiatry—has transformed the prison thus far. His analysis raises the persistent question of the extent to which limits have been reached in the effects of this particular approach.

There are those among the sociologists who assert with a shrill cry that there is a crisis in sociology. While it is not clear what is meant by this phrase, it does seem to imply that sociology has not been able to influence decisively the course of sociopolitical change. Only the philosopher kings among the sociologists could have expected it to do so. But if the phrase "crisis in sociology" has any real meaning, it implies that the intellectual standards of the discipline have been undermined or that its vitality—its ability to continue and to expand its intellectual traditions—has been shattered. In my view, volumes such as this by James Jacobs underline that there is no crisis in sociology. It is a rich and exciting study. It draws on a powerful intellectual heritage, and it is able to add the legal dimension to the participant observation study of social institutions. It is the grand tradition which declares that the work of a single man or woman can make a real contribution.

This study is a breath of fresh air in a period in which there is extensive debate about evaluation research and policy analysis. The conclusions of this book tell no one what is to be done. A body of data has been presented and a framework utilized for interpreting these findings. The reader is better informed, whether he be a professional prison administrator, a member of the citizen public, or a student of society. Being better informed, he himself can proceed to formulate his view and to make his decisions on a sounder basis and, it is hoped, more effectively. This is the ongoing task of social research on controversial topics, and this is what James Jacobs has admirably accomplished.

MORRIS JANOWITZ

Acknowledgments

This book grew out of my studies at the Law School and in the Department of Sociology at the University of Chicago. There are many faculty members at Chicago to whom I owe debts of gratitude, but there are three who stand out as requiring special acknowledgment.

From the summer of 1971, when I began as his research assistant, till the fall of 1975, when I left my postdoctoral fellowship at the Center for Studies in Criminal Justice to join the faculty at Cornell, Norval Morris was an enthusiastic and unswerving supporter of my evolving prison research. Throughout my highly rewarding association with the Center, of which he was codirector, Dean Morris was an inspiration as a teacher, scholar, and friend. He has been unsparing in his commitment to this project. To him and to the Center I also owe the encouragement which gave me the motivation and the resources to pursue my studies in the Department of Sociology—a decision which has greatly broadened and deepened my thinking about the matters presented in this book.

In my transition from law to sociology, no one was more instrumental than Barry Schwartz, who stimulated me in his classes and guided me through the sociological literatures on prison organization and street gangs. The intellectual heart of this book belongs to Morris Janowitz, chairman of my dissertation committee. I had already been studying Stateville for some time before I became one of Professor Janowitz's graduate students. My relationship with Janowitz was an intellectual summit of my years at the University of Chicago. Whatever insight lies in the pages between these covers I can trace to the discussions and critiques this teacher and scholar has devoted to my work.

Aside from the three mentioned above I should mention others with whom I was associated at the Center for Studies in Criminal Justice. Franklin Zimring, professor of law and codirector of the center, was a great supporter of this research not only—but not insubstantially—in making it financially possible. As a research associate at the center, Eric Steele was a daily source of intellectual stimulation. The center staff put up with me for years, with only an occasional complaint. I owe Ben Meeker, Helen Flint, Margaret Ochoa, Linda Sue Seth, Frieda Lancaster, and Ann Stern many many thanks. Appreciation is also expressed for the outstanding help of Liz Marx, my secretary at Cornell.

Such are my debts to the distinguished guardians and citizens of the university. But there are those in a very different but no less unique institution to whom I may owe even more in the execution of this research. There were prisoners at Stateville, who even while they were suffering the pains of their misfortune, were enthusiastic and diligent in their assistance and cooperation. I will single out Carlos Hernandez, Bobby Gore, Gregory Brown, Robert Pryor, and Timothy DeBerry for their help, but there were many others. Some of these individuals remain at Stateville and I cannot help but reflect upon their suffering as I acknowledge that without their assistance the book could not have been written.

On the prison staff side I received oustanding cooperation from two directors, Peter Bensinger and Alyn Sielaff; and from four Stateville wardens—Frank Pate, John Twomey, Joseph Cannon, and David Brierton. While at points I am explicitly or implicitly critical of various administrative judgments and decisions, I must emphasize how strong has been the commitment of all these individuals to the improvement of the prison system. No doubt few, if any, of us could withstand the scrutiny of retrospective analysis without faltering. These men are neither omniscient nor infallible, but their integrity has been of the highest order as has been their single-minded dedication to public service.

There were dozens of people in the various offices at Stateville who tolerated my curiosity, browsing, and searching; and who often called unknown documents, reports, and statistics to my attention. I must thank the entire Stateville staff and, in particular, Louis O'Shea, Robert Penrod, Daniel Bosse, Robert Kapture, Vernon Revis, and Bruce Hall. Standing out above all in his friendship and loyalty is that most remarkable former prison guard and former prison counselor Harold Retsky.

Finally I acknowledge only too well the patience of my family and friends who have listened for so long to what is now—for them—a very well-known history of Stateville.

Aerial view of Stateville
(*State of Illinois Department of Corrections photograph*)

Introduction

> The sociological point of view makes its appearance in historical investigation as soon as the historian turns from the study of periods to the study of institutions. The history of institutions, that is to say, the family, the church, economic institutions, political institutions, etc., leads inexorably to comparisons, classificatons, the formation of class names or concepts, and eventually to the formation of law. In the process, history becomes natural history, and natural history passes over into natural science. In short, history becomes sociology.
>
> Robert E. Park and Ernest W. Burgess
> *Introduction to the Science of Sociology* (1921)

The Chicago school of sociology emphasized the thorough empirical investigation of the social world in all its richness. Whether studying Chicago's Gold Coast, juvenile street gangs, or the real estate profession, the Chicago sociologists approached their subject with the commitment and fascination of naturalists. This commitment most often led to the detailed case study as the preferred strategy of research, although quantitative approaches also were used from the beginning. While the Chicago sociologists are lauded for getting close to their subjects, they were less attached to a particular methodology than to the institutions which they were studying.

Later sociologists continued to be concerned with the complexity of particular types of institutions rather than in the more abstract properties of formal organizations. In focusing on the historical evolution of institutions and on their articulation with the structure and culture of the larger society, this genre of studies draws as heavily on political sociology as on sociology of organization.

Among those "institutional analyses"[1] which illustrate this perspective, two of the most outstanding are Morris Janowitz's study of the American military (1960)[2] and Phillip Selznick's of the TVA (1949).[3] Janowitz demonstrated how a changing world order, nuclear weapons, professionalization, and changing bases of officer recruitment and socialization led to a transformation in military organization and in the military's relationship to the larger American society; most important was the military's more explicitly political role. Selznick's in-depth study of the TVA in its early years revealed how the original goals of the organization were displaced through the "co-optation" of various TVA departments by powerful national and local interests.

The present book is a case study and institutional analysis of Stateville Penitentiary, Illinois's largest maximum security prison located approximately thirty miles southwest of Chicago, the metropolis from which the great majority of its inmates have always been drawn. As home over the years to some of Chicago's most notorious gangsters and murderers and as a fiefdom over a quarter-century for one of the most powerful wardens in prison history, Stateville has enjoyed the notoriety of being one of the country's best-known penal institutions; like Attica, San Quentin, and Jackson, it is one of perhaps a dozen American megaprisons that informs the public's image of imprisonment. More important, Stateville's history reflects all the major societal changes of the last half-century.

In this analysis, I am interested, first, in plotting the changing integration of the prison with the larger society and, second, in showing how the changing relationship of the prison with the larger society is reflected in the changing patterns of authority within the prison. I draw on those studies dealing at the macrosociological level with the relationship between punishment and social structure; among the most outstanding of these are Rusche and Kirchheimer's *Punishment and Social Structure*[4] (which stresses economic variables) and Rothman's *Discovery of the Asylum*[5] (which stresses social and philosophical variables). But, more specifically, I build upon a distinguished tradition of sociological studies of the prison community.

None of these earlier studies has surpassed in imagination and sheer comprehensiveness Donald Clemmer's seminal case study of Illinois's "southern" maximum security prison at Menard.[6] Not since Clemmer has an American sociologist shown such sensitivity for the complex articulation of the prison with its local, regional and national environments. Clemmer hypothesized that "the prison is a microcosm of society." In the first edition of *The Prison Community* he emphasized the crucial importance of the social and economic milieu from which the prisoners were drawn. In attempting to explain prison society he pointed out the historically unique patterns of criminality generated by the Depression. Furthermore, Clemmer related the stratification and class divisions among the prisoners to external variables. The elite, Hoosier, and middle classes among the inmates each recruited and attracted criminals from different regions of the state and from different criminal subcultures. That Clemmer did not believe that the structure and form of the prison organization of his day would forever persist is clearly indicated in the preface to the 1958 edition.

> The data for *The Prison Community* were collected in the Depression years of the 1930's and throughout the book there are references to the fact that the culture of the prison reflected the American culture, for the prison was a culture within the larger one. Since then to employ just a few word symbols, we have seen World War II, urbanization, television, Korea, a peace time draft, rocketry, cold war, automation, sputnik, inflation and so on. It's a different world, and it is guided by legislators and administrators, operated by employees, and peopled by inmates who have, in varying degrees, been a part of this dynamic environment.[7]

In the 1950s and early 60s, selected research demonstrated that the relations of the actors within the prison had indeed changed over time as the relationship of the prison with the larger society changed. In particular, in Gresham Sykes's important study of the New Jersey maximum security prison there was full recognition of the importance of the prison's articulation with its environment.

> The prison is not an autonomous system of power; rather, it is an instrument of the State, shaped by its social environment, and we must keep this simple truth in mind if we are to understand the prison. It reacts to and is acted upon by the free community as various groups struggle to advance their interests. At certain times, as in the case of riots, the inmates can capture the attention of the public; and indeed, disturbances within the walls must often be viewed as highly dramatic efforts to communicate with the outside world; efforts in which confined criminals pass over

the heads of their captors to appeal to a new audience. At other times the flow of communications is reversed and the prison authorities find themselves receiving demands raised by a variety of business, political, religious, ethnic, and welfare interest groups. In addition, both the inmates and the custodians are drawn from the free community, whether voluntarily or involuntarily, and they bring with them the attitudes, beliefs and values of this larger world. The prison as a social system, does not exist in isolation any more than the criminal within the prison exists in isolation as an individual; and the institution and its setting are inextricably mixed despite the definite boundary of the wall.[8]

Sykes makes more than the obvious point that prisoners are never totally isolated. He sensitizes us to the fact that something important had changed since the time that Clemmer gathered his data at a rural southern Illinois Penitentiary in the 1930s. By the mid-1950s, prisoners were being drawn from a social world quite different from either the Coalville or Metro described by Clemmer. Since World War II the material and political expectations of prisoners, along with other marginal groups, had sharply risen. The "new" prisoners were confined at an institution that had become increasingly controversial and politicized. The wave of prison riots around the country in the early 1950s first evidenced the growing disjunction between the expectations of prisoners and a burgeoning reform movement and the "lag" in the prisoners' material and existential condition.

Richard McCleery, a political scientist, was the most directly concerned with exploring change over time within a maximum security prison.[9] His study of Oahu Penitentiary in Hawaii at the beginning and end of a decade (1945–55) during which control passed from the old conservative guards to the new liberal civilian reformers is a very important contribution to our study of the prison from the perspective of political sociology. Many of the trends McCleery documents in Hawaii did not occur in Illinois until fifteen or twenty years later, which indicates that ours is a highly differentiated society in which local and regional systems play a great role in mediating and even neutralizing national trends. McCleery's fine work demonstrates how competing groups outside the prison (governor, legislature, law enforcement agencies) articulate with factions inside the prison thereby contributing to the transformation of the inmate social system and to a shift in the basis of internal control.

In their effort to assess the impact of different organizational goals on inmate norms, attitudes and behaviors, Street, Vintner, and Perrow conducted a thorough comparative analysis of six midwestern juvenile institutions in the early 1960s.[10] Using data drawn from surveys of both inmates and staff, they showed the pervasive significance of treatment and custodial goals for the social organization of the prison community. But they also pointed out that organizational goals themselves are dependent upon: (1) the local community's acceptance of the institution, (2) the type of agency controlling the institution, and (3) the penal philosophy of the chief administrator himself. The six juvenile institutions ranged from public institutions (the most custodially-oriented) with no control over their inmate intake to private and parochial institutions (the most treatment-oriented) that were constrained with respect to intake by broad philosophical principles or by professional commitments. The private institution tended to be controlled by an elite which identified with the professional social workers and psychologists and was organized accordingly. The social organization of the prison was thus dependent upon the complex relationship of the institution and its elite to the organizational, political, and social environments.

In the years since the publication of the Street, Vintner, and Perrow work, several studies of maximum security prisons have demonstrated the significance of heightened race consciousness and ethnicity among the prisoners of the middle and late 1960s.[11] Most notable is *Hacks, Blacks and Cons,* in which Leo Carroll explores the hypothesis that, "as a result of humanitarian reforms within prisons and racial-ethnic social movements outside the prison, the structure of social relationships within prisons is increasingly taking on the character of race relations."[12] The proliferation of contacts between the prison and the outside facilitated the erosion of convict solidarity and stimulated the emergence among prisoners of "fragmented social organizations composed of numerous cliques with diverse normative and behavioral orientations."

The erosion of the barriers between prison and society since World War II needs to be understood historically and in terms of political and structural change. Edward Shils's interpretation of the dynamics of mass society provides a framework with which to examine the changing position of the prison and prisoner in the larger society.[13] Central to Shils's specialized use of the term "mass society" is the greater political, moral, and economic integration of the masses in the society's central institutional and value systems. Shils points to a heightened sensitivity on the part of the elite to the dignity and humanity of the masses.

> This [social] consensus has not, however, been unilaterally formed, and it is not sustained merely by the affirmation at the periphery of what emanates from the center, in which the mass has come to share the standards and beliefs of the elites. It consists also in the greater attachment of the center to the peripheral sectors of the society . . . the enhanced dignity of the mass—the belief that, in one way or another, *vox populi, vox dei*—is the source of the mass society. Both elites and the masses have received this into their judgment of themselves and the world; and, although they believe in much else and believe in this quite unequally, the maxim which locates the sacred in the mass of the population is the shaping force of the most recent development of society.[14]

Shils argues that, with the unfolding of mass society, the "charisma" of the society's center has diffused much more widely throughout society, touching the working class, women, youth, and ethnic groups "which have heretofore been in a disadvantageous position."[15] Throughout this book I document the progressive integration of the masses into the central institutional and value systems by tracing the movement of the prison's place in society from the periphery toward the center.

Fundamental to the realization of mass society is the extension of the rights of citizenship to heretofore marginal groups like racial minorities, the poor, and the incarcerated. The 1960s especially was a period of urban crisis, black militancy, student protest and of decade-long turmoil over the legitimacy of the Vietnam war. It is beyond the scope of this book to assess the impact of these societal trends on the daily behavior of the minority populations from which prisoners are disproportionately drawn, but I need only refer to the observations of the Kerner commission, the Eisenhower commission, and recent social commentaries to establish the increased politicization of American blacks and Latinos. Participation in riots, exposure to nationally recognized civil rights leaders, and a widely disseminated vocabulary of political and social protest became part of the life experience of many of those later confined in prison in the large industrial states during the late 1960s and 70s. Often the actors most directly involved in these political movements were themselves committed to prison and continued their struggle from behind the walls. Other prisoners could not remain totally unaffected by the presence in their midst of highly charismatic personalities who redefined their situation as that of "political prisoners."

Like other marginal groups in America, imprisoned felons in the post-World War II years have come to make increasing claims to the rights of citizenship. The rise in the material expectations of prisoners (reaching a climax in the prison riots of 1952-53) and the later intensification of rights consciousness (crystallizing in prison uprisings in California and New York in 1970-71) should be seen as consequences of the progressive realization of mass society. Just as blacks demanded social and political equalities in the 1950s, so too did prisoners of that decade and the next press for a redefinition of their situation within society. Most significant was the identification made by prisoners with the social and then political struggle of other marginal groups, e.g., blacks, Chicanos, radicals.

During this same period when the claims of marginal groups spread from the streets into the prisons, there was also increased legitimation of prison reform; public opinion polls began to show that the majority of Americans now accepted rehabilitation as the purpose of imprisonment.[16] The prison reform movement gained strength and legitimacy in the late 1960s as middle-class activists and drug users came increasingly into contact with the prison. The same energies that were tapped for the civil rights of blacks and against the Vietnam war were also channeled toward the prisons.

Ties between the prison and the central political institutions of society also proliferated in the mid-60s. The founding of the Law Enforcement Assistance Administration (LEAA) in 1968 made millions of dollars available for prison studies and for the development of model programs to deal with the confined. One result was to bring the prison closer to the federal governmental bureaucracy.

Much of what the government has done has been in collaboration with colleges and universities. As more and more LEAA money has become available for research, criminal justice departments and criminology curricula have become institutionalized in junior colleges, colleges, and universities across the country. The number of degree programs multiplied from 50 in 1960 to at least 660 in 1975.[17] Professional and academic journals on the subject have also proliferated. New professional and paraprofessional careers like counseling and rehabilitation have been established. Some students and graduates of such programs are teaching courses for college credit to prisoners behind the walls; others are moving into new prison administrative positions.

Prison administrators have become increasingly professionalized. Many of those now entering the field were initiated through academic study rather than having come up through the ranks. In 1965 every warden in Illinois had come up through the system; none had a college degree. By 1974 there was not a single warden who started as a guard, and six of the eight held master's degrees.

Various interest groups in the society are solely committed to lobbying for the rights of prisoners. While New York's Fortune Society and Illinois's John Howard Association are two of the best known, hundreds of ad hoc groups have sprung into existence. The ex-offender movement has even begun to become established. In California, groups of ex-offenders, under the leadership of ex-offender and prison sociologist John Irwin, have formed a prisoners' union and similar developments have occurred elsewhere.

Prisoners are no longer isolated from developments in the outside community. Daily newspapers make their way into the prison, including many copies of the radical underground press. In addition, inmates have access to the news over the radio and especially over the television. In some prisons, including Stateville since 1975, each inmate can have a television set of his own. In other prisons, TV sets are placed in areas of work assignments and on the galleries.

Media coverage of prison matters has sharply increased in recent years, reflecting the fact that the prison has become a central issue of concern in American society. Prisoners are thus provided with limited access to the public through which they can state their grievances. In several instances of prison rebellions, inmates have asked for press conferences and/or press and television coverage. At Pautuxet Institute in Maryland, in 1973, prisoners seized hostages in order to get a press conference. The role of the media at Attica has been a subject of voluminous debate.

The federal courts' abandonment of the "hands off" doctrine was the most important development in the prison's environment. Until the mid-1960s the convicted man sent to prison lost all his constitutional and legal rights, experiencing a "civil death" which redefined the convict as "a slave of the state."[18] He might use habeas corpus procedures to complain of irregularities at his trial and the *fact* of his confinement but not to complain of the *manner* of his confinement. Courts left prison affairs to the discretion of the administrators. By and large, the prisoner was shut off from the courts and placed outside the protection of the rule of law.

The extension of the rule of law into the prison was a natural outgrowth of the judicial activism of the sixties under the leadership of the Warren Court and of the "legal revolution" that brought fuller rights of citizenship to racial minorities, the poor, the illegitimate, and the criminal defendant. The federal judicial system, which had become increasingly active in protecting the rights of minorities through expansive interpretations of the U.S. Constitution, also became more sensitive to the plight of those behind bars.

An expanded interpretation of the scope of habeas corpus, along with §1983 of the Civil Rights Act, have provided prisoners powerful procedural tools with which they can complain of administrative abuses. In the past few years, federal and state courts have scrutinized every aspect of the prison regime and have issued injunctions and declaratory judgments affecting discipline, good time, living conditions, health care, censorship, restrictions on religion and speech, and access to the courts. In a few spectacular cases, prisons and entire prison systems have been declared unconstitutional, establishing the principle that the constitution, the rule of law, and due process embrace the convict, except in those instances where prison authorities can show compelling reasons to deny basic freedoms.

Representatives of the mainstream legal community have become increasingly interested in prison matters and thus strengthened the prison reform movement. Two presidential crime commissions made up predominantly of lawyers proclaimed the need to revamp the entire prison system. The American Bar Association's Commission on Corrections added its substantial support to the calls for prison reform. Seminars on prisoner's rights litigation are annually sponsored by the American Bar Association.

During the sixties, legal aid groups funded by the Office of Economic Opportunity brought idealistic young attorneys into constant combat with the prison authorities. A number of "radical law collectives" in various cities enthusiastically launched themselves into prison reform litigation as part of their efforts to bring about institutional reform of American society in general. These law collectives began in the mid-sixties' antiwar movement and broadened their interest to prisons as their own members were increasingly threatened with arrest and incarceration. Following the Attica riots, lawyers flocked to that prison in order to protect individual prisoners from reprisals and, in some cases, to evidence their solidarity with prisoners. Radical lawyers and politically-conscious inmates support one another's definition of prison as an arena in the battle between the establishment and revolutionary forces. The days of the jailhouse lawyer struggling alone to find an avenue to the courts are fading into memory.

The realization of mass society as expressed by such trends as the growth of prisoners' rights and the intrusion of juridical norms into the prison has provided the impetus toward the transformation of institutional authority and administration. When the prison was an autonomous institution located at society's periphery and beyond the ken of the courts and other core institutional systems, there was no need for the system of internal authority to become rationalized. It was only when outside interest groups began making demands on the prison and holding the administrators accountable for their decisions that traditional authoritarian systems of institutional authority became untenable. The decline of institutional authority and the pervasive violence which filled the vacuum in turn intensified the pressure for bureaucratization and a restoration of control.

Rational-legal bureaucracy, according to Max Weber, was the most efficient system of administration given the macrostructural conditions existing at the time. But Weber was also careful to point out the presence of various countertrends and internal inconsistencies and limits in the movement toward increased bureaucratization. While my analysis of Stateville traces the movement from charismatic to traditional to rational-legal forms of authority and to ever-increasing bureaucratization, I attempt to go beyond a simplistic unilinear statement. I approach the prison as an organization in action, in dynamic relationship with its political, moral, and institutional environments. At any point in time, various pressures and criss-crossing strains are evident; there is no inevitable or predetermined outcome.

I The Authoritarian Regime

Warden Joseph E. Ragen (*Acme Newspictures*)

1 The Search for a Stable Equilibrium, 1925–36

Above all the cells were clean and airy. Indeed, it was the cleanliness and airiness that impressed me most about Stateville as a whole. What a contrast to the grimy, gloomy, forbidding surroundings of the old prison! Here the eye could wander hundreds of yards in one direction before being stopped by the barrier of the prison wall. From my high cell on the fourth gallery I could look over the wall to the rolling farmland beyond.

Nathan Leopold
Life Plus Ninety-nine Years

At the turn of the century the state of Illinois begat some of the most intense criminal justice reform efforts in the United States. One such effort was the construction of Stateville Penitentiary in order to ameliorate the deplorable conditions at the old Joliet prison. As for other reforms, we may note that in 1897 Illinois became one of the first states to adopt the indeterminate sentence, and in 1899, as a result of the state's Juvenile Court Act, the first juvenile court in the country was established in Illinois.[1]

During the first year of Governor Charles Deenen's administration (1905), widespread agitation against the conditions in the old Joliet prison (built in 1860) attracted the attention of the citizens of Illinois. Investigations resulted in severe criticism of the state for maintaining "brutal and inhumane conditions."[2] The state legislature quickly responded. In 1907, sixty-five acres were purchased in Lockport, across the river and six and one-half miles northwest of the old Joliet prison, as the site for a new, reform era penitentiary. A three-man legislative committee was sent to Europe to survey prison planning abroad. The committee was most impressed by the panopticon model laid out by the English utilitarian philosopher Jeremy Bentham in the nineteenth century.[3] The panopticon differed from the traditional Auburn and Philadelphia prisons in its circular design so that, in theory, a single guard standing in the center of a round cell house could see clearly into every cell. The circular cell houses were placed like satellites around a huge central dining hall, to which they were connected by tunnels (spokes). A guard standing in the center of the dining room could, by rotating 360 degrees, look down each tunnel into each of the round houses.[4]

Stateville officially opened on 9 March 1925. Although located several miles from its sister prison in Joliet, both institutions were administered by a single warden whose main office was soon permanently moved to Stateville. The four "round houses" (each with four tiers of exterior cells) maximized air and light and boasted such conveniences as flush toilets. (The old Joliet prison made do with slop buckets until it was finally remodeled in 1956). Instead of completing the two remaining round houses during a period of economic depression, the state chose to construct the largest rectangular cell house (B) in existence. B House contained 600 cells and, by 1932, 1,300 inmates. While Stateville had been built in order to relieve the overcrowding at the Joliet prison, by 1935 it held almost 4,000 inmates and the Joliet prison population had not been reduced. The overcrowding was not alleviated until the late 1960s, when a different moral climate favorable to probation and other "diversion" programs had achieved wide public acceptance (see table 1).[5]

Beyond affecting the very decision to build Stateville, the reform energies of the period touched the prison in several ways. The Illinois Division of the State Criminologist was established in 1917. The state criminologist and his staff were charged with responsibility for "diagnostic evaluation" of the felon upon his entrance into the prison system and with treating mental problems among the prisoners. That the first state criminologist, Herman Adler (professor of psychiatry at Harvard Medical School), was a psychiatrist, indicates that the medical model was introduced early into the Illinois prisons. However, from the beginning the Division of the Criminologist maintained a multidisciplinary approach. Social histories, psychological testing, and psychiatric interviews were all used in the preparation of reports which advised the Parole Board on the background of each offender.

The Division of the Criminologist included the research-oriented Institute for Juvenile Research as well as the Joliet Diagnostic Depot (across the street from the old Joliet prison). The fact that the Division of the Criminologist was established independent of the Stateville/Joliet organization demonstrates from the outset the organizational strategy used to blunt the blade of reform. Over the years, reforms which have introduced into the prison new roles and personnel have been consistently accompanied by the establishment of new departments with narrow responsibility. Such departments have generally been isolated from the locus of decision making rather than integrating professionals into the chain of command.

In its first decade, Stateville was weakly integrated with its institutional environment. Local autonomy was almost complete, but certain decisions, like the expansion or creation of new prison industries, could only be made by the Department of Public Welfare in Springfield. Before 1917, each Illinois prison was run independently by the warden and a board of trustees which exercised little or no control. In 1917, the Illinois prisons were placed under the Department of Public Welfare with the Superintendent of Prisons having nominal supervisory authority over the system. In practice, local autonomy prevailed almost totally, and the superintendent exercised little decision-making authority. In 1933, the Illinois prisons were coordinated under the Classification Act into the Illinois State Penitentiary, the intention being that each institution would serve a different "type" of offender.

Here was another example of how the prison system could be parceled out to different interest groups simultaneously. The Classification Act was consistent with the belief of "professionals" and reformers that inmates should be separated according to their treatment needs. But the professionals and reformers were given no authority either over prison programs or over prison transfers. At best, the criminologist's staff at the Diagnostic Depot could "recommend" institutional placement, but in general the professionals were unfamiliar with the programs available at the different prisons. In fact, the prisons might be distinguished from one another at any point in time only by the strictness with which inmates were being controlled. Perhaps the most significant effect of the Classification Act was to transform a prison "system" whose institutions were autonomous into a hierarchically organized prison system where the possibility of transfer from one prison to another reinforced social control for the prison system as a whole.[6] In addition, social control was bolstered in 1920 when the legislature approved the Progressive Merit System, which tied "good time" deductions from the prisoner's sentence to overall participation and conformity to the institutional programs.

During Stateville's first decade, there were no institutionalized pressure groups or watchdog agencies impinging upon the prison. The most significant outside pressures came from a press that became increasingly concerned about "coddling criminals" as the violence on the streets during the Depression years continued to rise. Escapes, riots, and general violence periodically alerted press attention. Intellectuals related to the prison segmentally and intermittently. Nathan Leopold reports assisting one of Clifford Shaw's graduate students in a study of a professional criminal career. (In exchange for the assistance, the researcher supplied tailormade cigarettes on the sly.) The same convict also describes visits from Professors Burgess and Sutherland of the University of Chicago's Department of Sociology.[7]

The 1928 Clabaugh commission,[8] charged with evaluating the parole system and the indeterminate sentence law, is itself an example of intellectuals' interacting with the prison. The members of the commission were Judge Andrew A. Bruce, who taught at Northwestern University Law School, Albert S. Horno, dean of the University of Illinois College of Law, and Ernest W. Burgess, of the University of Chicago's Department of Sociology. John Landesco (later to achieve fame with his publication of *Organized Crime in Chicago*) was a young research assistant employed by the commission. The recommendations of the commission resulted in the creation of the Office of the Sociologist-Actuary in 1933, after the inauguration of the scholarly and reform-minded governor Henry Horner. This position established a "foot in the door" at Stateville for academics that was to last for decades, although, as with the state criminologist, the sociologist-actuary was not integrated within the Stateville administration but was under the separate authority of the Parole and Pardon Board. The sociologist-actuary and his staff, located at Stateville, pioneered in the development of parole prediction tables, which brought worldwide attention to the Illinois prison system. (The office was abolished in 1967, when the duties of the sociologist-actuary were incorporated into the Division of the Criminologist.)

It is a telling commentary on the organization's ability to isolate and restrict intellectual roles that men of the caliber of Ferris Laune (sociologist-actuary) and Saul Alinsky and Donald Clemmer (state criminologists) could be present at the Stateville/Joliet prisons and have no impact whatever on day-to-day operations. The narrow definition of their research roles prevented their attention from straying to questions about the daily regimen.

For decades, the intellectuals interacted with inmates rather than with officials. Essentially, their presence represented a formal co-optation of the reform elements of the society.[9] The 1937 Illinois Prison Inquiry Commission noted in the foreword to its report:

> State officials seem not to fully realize that university people can be utilized to the advantage of the officials themselves. University people are interested in social questions and will no doubt continue to visit penal and correctional institutions for factual materials. The question is, will the officials continue to look upon them as nuisances, or can these officials be brought to an understanding of the fact that university instructors and their students are capable of making valuable contributions toward the administration of public questions. It seems likely that the university men would embrace the opportunity to work for the officials and to work with them.[10]

The prison was most closely tied to the partisan political system through both the staff and inmates. The spirit of reform in Illinois led to the passage of the Civil Service Law in 1905 and to its extension to all positions and places in state service by amendments in 1907 and 1911. Public interest waned in the next decade. In 1917, the Buck Amendment practically destroyed the significance of all previous civil service legislation. Besides adding new exemptions to the law, the Buck Amendment (1) gave the removing officer power to discharge an employee upon the mere charge that it was good for the service; (2) eliminated the opportunity for a hearing before the Civil Service Commission unless the employee stated that his discharge was due to political, racial, or religious reasons, and (3) gave the appointing officer power to make renewable temporary appointments.

Tension between the spoils system and civil service reform

had profound consequences for the social organization of the prison.[11] The Clabaugh commission bristled with criticism of pervasive partisan politics in the penitentiaries: "As it is now, our wardens and prison officers are often appointed solely for political reasons and with little regard to their qualifications."[12] The early wardens too were political appointees, usually chosen from the ranks of local sheriffs. Under Illinois law a sheriff could not run for two successive terms. In some counties, wardenships alternated between sheriff and deputy; in others, between sheriff and prison official if both belonged to the party in power. Elmer Greene, for example, former sheriff of Lake County, became the Stateville/Joliet warden in 1926. As sheriff he had earned the indebtedness of Governor Len Small by helping the latter sway public opinion in Waukegan, where Small had been tried (and found innocent) of converting public funds to his own use. (The governor was later indicted for bribing the jury but was again acquitted.)

As warden, Greene considered it a matter of course to require employees to contribute to the governor's political party and to the payment of the $650,000 judgment that had been entered against Small in a related civil suit. The Catholic chaplain's first paycheck at Stateville in 1928 contained a bill for $5 labeled a "contribution" to that judgment. When Small was replaced in Springfield by Governor Louis Emmerson, Major Henry Hill was appointed warden. He too was without previous prison experience. When approached early in his term by the Catholic chaplain with a warning that a riot was imminent, Hill replied, "I can handle it. If there's trouble, I'll kill 'em."[13]

The Illinois Prison Inquiry Commission, appointed by reform governor Henry Horner after the sensational killing of Richard Loeb at Stateville in 1936, was even more pessimistic about the effect of the spoils system on the prison's ability to accomplish its goals.

> The success or failure of a sound prison program rests upon the personnel selected to administer the system. The practice seems to be that with each new incoming administration, the personnel of our prison changes. This is due largely to the fact that a great number of positions in the penal system become available for political patronage regardless of the individual qualifications for the job. As a result, one can scan the pages of Illinois history and

find that in nearly every administration there has been some major uprising in the penal system, riots causing a loss of many lives, and the destruction of much state property.[14]

The guards were as closely tied to the political scene as were the senior administrators. Their jobs were allocated by patronage and were lost when the governorship passed into the hands of the rival political party. Not only was job security nonexistent, but wages were barely above subsistence. The 1928 Clabaugh commission noted:

The position of the guard is well-nigh intolerable. His salary is ridiculously low, far less than that which can be earned by even the most incompetent mechanic. His hours of labor are very long—sometimes sixteen hours a day, and he himself is a prisoner. His isolation is almost complete, as under the rules which exist at Joliet, at any rate, he is not allowed to talk with prisoners.[15]

The guards were so poorly treated, according to Chaplain Eligius Weir, that until Warden Joseph Ragen was appointed in late 1935, there were only enough beds in the guards' quarters to accommodate half the men. When one shift was relieved, it would literally take over the bed and bedding of the shift coming on duty. Not only were the guards underpaid; they worked twelve (sometimes sixteen) hours per day six days per week in a situation of chronic understaffing. On average, 225 guards (divided between two shifts) were available to guard 3,400 inmates (1:15), compared with the current 400 guards divided among three shifts for 1,500 inmates, (1:3.75). Once again, the Clabaugh commission report illuminates the guards' plight:

The guards are on the twelve hour system. Every regulation enforced upon prisoners is a constraint upon the guard; he is under constant tension, further irritated by minute encroachment from an idle and sometimes ill-humored convict group. The life of the guard, except for his privilege of leaving at night after his twelve hour shift, is in many cases more unpleasant than that of the convict. . . .

The guards are politically appointed, untrained for their work by even an institutional school of instruction, with no assurance of tenure or pension, underpaid, many physically unfit for the crises (escapes, mutiny, pursuit and suppression), inexperienced in prison conditions; many of them [are] called "hayseeds" by the finished Chicago criminal.[16]

The very high levels of idleness, violence, and escape that marked this period have to be considered, in part, as a consequence of the spoils system (see table 2). Since state government was organized not so much to provide service as to provide employment in order to reinforce political constituencies, the organization was naturally plagued by inefficiency.[17]

Many of the personnel were replaced whenever an election changed the party or faction within the party that controlled the governor's office and those who survived sacrificed their rank. At any one time, only a small cadre of trained guards was present to run the industries or to look after security properly. Rules were made up on the spot to minimize the guard's work. Discipline was arbitrary and capricious. Lockup in solitary confinement was accompanied by "stringing up," which required the inmate to stand handcuffed to the bars eight hours a day for as long as fifteen days, sometimes longer.[18] During the ordeal, he was sustained on one slice of bread and one glass of water a day.

Aside from the wardens and guards, there were few other employees at Stateville. In 1936, the entire noninmate clerical staff consisted of the business manager, chief clerk, comptroller, record clerk, credit clerk and storekeeper. The only way such an immense institution could function was for inmates to fill clerical positions throughout the prison. This gave certain inmates powerful leverage to bargain (explicitly and implicitly) for privileges.

The prison was not left solely in the hands of the paramilitary hierarchical organization. Even in 1936, Stateville had a newly appointed director of education, a director of industries, several chaplains, and enough medical personnel to run a hospital. The Clabaugh commission expressed concern, however, that these professionals tended to become too "institutionalized," concerning themselves primarily with issues of custody at the expense of their professional responsibilities.[19]

Those reforms that were instituted during Stateville's first decade, like the opening of the commissary in 1930 and the provision of radios in 1931, came through informal bargaining by the Catholic chaplain who, according to his own report and Leopold's, was the prisoner's primary advocate. Warden Hill provided the commissary and radios as part of a deal with Father Weir, whereby the chaplain promised to use his best efforts to talk the inmates out of their intention to kill an unpopular guard. Such reforms as these were not institutionalized and could be dissolved through the same processes by which they were created. There were no formal mechanisms by which prisoners might make requests or complaints to the administration. The prison operated largely on the strength of tradition; it was a kind of feudal system.

Leopold describes a status system among the inmates rooted in the offense for which the inmate was convicted.[20] The murderers and robbers held the highest status; the "rape-o's" and "sex fiends" the lowest. Leopold speculates that the low status of the forgers, con men, and embezzlers, was probably based less on the nature of those crimes than on lower-class offenders' resentment of middle-class offenders. Paralleling the status hierarchy based upon offenses was the hierarchical system of prison roles. Many studies of prison organization have described these roles, which range from the low-status "rat," who is universally despised, to the high-status "right guy" (of which Leopold presents himself as an example), who is universally admired.

The rat and the right guy were socio-emotional roles functionally related to the peculiar problems of imprisonment. The very low standard of living (even "tailormade" cigarettes were contraband) and the other deprivations attendant upon imprisonment generated a functional distributive system with roles organized around the supplying of food, liquor, sex, information, and money. Prison rackets, especially gambling, flourished. Warden Ragen is said to have collected fifteen thousand dollars in cash in 1936 turned in by inmates to be held in account for them when he declared that he would confiscate all cash not turned over.[21]

Over and against the interlocking status system and roles were both primary and secondary ties sometimes imported from the street and sometimes indigenous to the prison itself. Ethnic loyalties played the same role in 1936 that racial solidarities do today. The formation of homogeneous ethnic cliques inside Stateville was reinforced by primary groups imported from the streets.

Upon taking over the job as warden at Stateville [writes Gladys Erickson], Joe Ragen soon discovered that three powerful gangs dominated the prison. One composed chiefly of Irishmen was led by Daniel Rooney. Another captained by Frank Covelli was for Italians only. And the third, the Powerhouse Outfit, was made up of a motley assortment of desperados under the thumb of Marty

Durkin and Rocco Rotunna. There were eight or nine lesser gangs, and all of these warred among themselves—and preyed on the unorganized inmates who were not fortunate enough to have an affiliation. The gangs maintained their power through strong arm methods. Knifings, sluggings and assaults were common daily occurrences throughout the prison. Gang members bullied the guards and made no pretense at recognizing any authority among the lesser prison personnel.[22]

Not only did the partisan political system penetrate the prison through the staff, it was also reflected in the inmate social system. Nathan Leopold observed that

many of the Jewish inmates came from the West Side of Chicago; many had friends high in the council of the 24th Ward Democratic Club, which was, at the moment, at its political zenith. Some of the boys asked their friends in the organization to help in the celebration [of Passover]. Not only did they contribute generously in the form of money and food, but they obtained permission from Warden Whipp to bring down some vaudeville acts to entertain at dinner.

We were permitted on several occasions to remain in the general dining room as late as midnight. Sometimes the warden and his wife and other officials would be our guests at dinner. The men were permitted to talk and visit with their friends from the outside, and the entertainers put on their acts.[23]

And Ragen's biographer points out:

Many of the inmates had strong political connections. Whenever a politician wished to confer with one of his incarcerated constituents, he simply arranged in advance to have him transferred to the farm, where visiting was easy and private. Other politicians arranged to send entertainers, male and female, into the prison yard to bring some measure of cheer to favored groups of inmates.[24]

The period between 1925 and 1932 was marked by violence among inmates and between inmates and staff. Although accurate statistics are not available, there is good reason to believe that the absence of a capable administration made this period as lawless and violent as the period 1969–75, when for different reasons the formal organization collapsed. Father Weir reports several instances where gang members were simply released from isolation when gang leaders walked to the corner (isolation unit) and personally intimidated the deputy warden.[25] In addition, gang leaders set up shacks on the yard and sold young offenders as homosexual prostitutes. Gambling flourished throughout the prison.

In 1926, seven inmates took the deputy warden hostage and stabbed him to death when he refused, at knife point, to cooperate in their escape. In 1927 there erupted a serious riot at the old prison. In March of 1931, another riot at the old prison was precipitated by an event inmates called the "Washington's Birthday Massacre." Father Weir recalls that, according to the inmates' version of the events, the administration had been tipped off that an escape attempt by three notorious inmates was imminent.[26] Instead of foiling the escape before it materialized, the officials set up a trap outside the walls and killed all three inmates as they went over the top. A coroner's jury absolved the prison authorities of all blame despite some public support for the prisoners' claims.[27]

The ensuing riot at the old prison was followed four days later by a much larger riot at Stateville. Five hundred thousand dollars worth of damage resulted from the rampaging and burning. One inmate was killed in the retaking of the prison. The entire prison was placed on "lockup" for seven months, an administrative strategy later to become a tradition at Stateville in times of crisis. Soon thereafter, Warden Hill was replaced by Warden (Colonel) Frank Whipp, characterized by Chaplain Weir as "a bigoted [against Catholics] and ignorant man without any real interest in the prison."

As the Depression deepened on the outside, the shops and industries stopped functioning, the staff retreated to the walls, and formal organization, which had previously governed every aspect of inmate life, became relaxed. But after 1932 the violence diminished. Leopold describes this period as follows.

> The next four years, from 1932–1936, were, in many ways, the best I have known in prison. Not for me personally, but for the institution in general. If the two or three years before the riot [of 1932] were the Wild West Days, this period could be called the Golden Age. Hobbies flourished among the men; discipline was at its least stringent. For example, there was yard every day now instead of once a week, and the men were permitted to go to the yard any time they were not actually working. Rules like the one requiring lines to march in strict military cadence were relaxed or not enforced. There was a general spirit of informality. The

> garden plots were going full blast; athletics of all kinds were encouraged. There were handball courts all around the prison, and everywhere you could see fellows dressed only in shorts and shoes engrossed in hot games. Naturally, everyone was suntanned. Sunbathing became a hobby.[28]

We may hypothesize that the absence of effective control was caused by the lack of a trained or career-oriented staff coupled with overcrowding and pervasive idleness. The decrease in violence against the staff can be explained by the withdrawal of the guards from actively attempting to enforce the rules, and, indirectly, by the misery of the Depression out on the streets, which attenuated the inmates' frustration at parole policies.[29]

The Depression also encompassed Stateville. The number of prisoners increased inexorably, creating a situation of unemployment and idleness that paralleled conditions on the streets. Even the limited market of state agencies using prison industrial products cut back upon purchases. Idleness resulted from the political situation in the state as well as from the generally depressed national economic situation after 1929. In that year the Illinois legislature, responding to the widespread unemployment on the streets, killed the last of the labor contracts by which private contractors could come into the prisons in order to carry out private projects by use of prison labor.[30] Overcrowding was a major problem. Cells in the round house built for a single individual were holding three men. A prison built for a maximum capacity of 1,800 inmates was pressed to hold 3,500. There were no programs to speak of. Loeb and Leopold inaugurated a correspondence school, which they ran on their own time out of their cells. This supplemented a fourth grade school system staffed by inmate teachers. With respect to inmate employment in useful activities, the Clabaugh commission found that 85 percent of the Stateville inmates were idle in 1927. The situation had not improved by 1936.

> Notwithstanding the development of the Stateville branch, it failed to keep pace with the increase in the prison population, and both the new and old prisons are today seriously overcrowded, and the amount of idleness is shocking, giving rise to discontent, conspiracies and bad conduct among the prisoners themselves.[31]

We may conclude that the failure to establish a stable social order at Stateville between 1925 and 1936 reflects the organization's inability to settle on a goal or set of goals that could have led to the development of a professional, career-oriented staff. Wardens could not expect to prolong their tenure by successfully managing prison crises. The influence on the prison of the partisan political system had to be reduced before a stable social order could be achieved.

Illinois National Guardsmen at Stateville, March 1931 (*Acme Newspictures*)

2 Emergence of Personal Dominance, 1936–61

> Just as nature, without the right to make laws and enforce them, could accomplish nothing good for nature's world, so would the warden of a penitentiary without the right to make rules and enforce them, be unable to accomplish anything for the good of the institution as a whole. But nature does have her laws and they are strictly obeyed. And the order in nature is the duplicate of that order that nature's Creator had in mind for nature. In the mind of a penitentiary warden there is a certain order which should prevail throughout the whole institution, from the next highest ranking official to the lowest inmate.
>
> Joseph E. Ragen and Charles Finstone
> *Inside the World's Toughest Prison*

The years 1936–61 were most obviously marked by the establishment of an authoritarian prison regime under the growing personal dominance of Warden Joseph Ragen. So unassailable did the Ragen system become that it was disturbed neither by the post-World War II pressures toward prison reform nor by the prison violence of the 1950s. Ragen's goal of creating a stable social order at Stateville depended upon gaining a large measure of economic, political, and moral autonomy. The absence of interference by outside forces enabled him to develop his authoritarian system of internal order which reached its full elaboration by the early 1950s.

Ragen was aided by World War II, which diverted attention from the prisons by creating an employment boom which undermined the prison's significance as an instrument of patronage. The prison organization achieved a stable goal in providing secure and economical custody for offenders. Beyond that, the emergence of a career-oriented elite at the prison provided Stateville a purpose independent of its instrumental goals. For its top staff, Stateville became an institution whose survival was valued for the occupational and moral status which it conferred.

Like his predecessors, Joseph E. Ragen was a former sheriff

from a small, rural Illinois town. He was appointed warden of Stateville in 1936 as a consequence of a crisis in control behind the prison's walls which threatened to erupt into a full-scale political scandal.[1] Although his ninth-grade education, lack of verbal finesse, according to the Chicago press of the time, and provincial background made him an unlikely candidate to succeed in managing the Stateville/Joliet inmates,[2] his reputation as a strict disciplinarian while warden of Menard[3] made him attractive to a Depression society alarmed by rising crime rates, gang violence, and prison escapes.

Joe Ragen's thirty-year "rule" of Stateville was based upon the patriarchal authority that he achieved. In the vocabulary of both employees and inmates, "he ran it." The "old boss" devoted his life to perfecting the world's most orderly prison regime. He exercised personal control over every detail, no matter how insignificant. He tolerated challenges neither by inmates nor by employees nor by outside interest groups. He cultivated an image which made him seem invincible to his subordinates as well as to the prisoners.

In the course of thirty years he transformed Stateville into an efficient paramilitary organization famous and infamous throughout the world; a "must" on any foreign penologist's tour of the United States. Ragen himself was well known and well integrated into national prison circles, counting leading prison officials across the country among his closest personal friends. In 1951 he was elected president of the American Correctional Association.[4] Frequently he was invited to other states to consult on prison matters. One long-time staff member recalls that Ragen boasted at the end of his career that he had been called upon to investigate fifty-seven different prisons. His national connections and reputation were important resources in maintaining Stateville's political autonomy.

Ragen was a complex individual and prison administrator. He was feared and respected, beloved and despised. He inspired intense loyalty among the elite who were close to him, but many among the rank and file deeply resented his authoritarian, arbitrary leadership. Sociologists who worked at Stateville at the time remember Ragen as a strict old-style disciplinarian, while key administrators still refer to him as a penologist and a humanitarian. All agree that Stateville was his sole interest and that as warden he was seemingly omniscient with respect to every detail.[5]

He demanded absolute personal loyalty. In the Officer's Rule Book, employees were presented with the following homily:

> If you work for a man, in Heaven's name work for him. If he pays you wages that supply your bread and butter, work for him, speak well of him, and stand by him, and stand by the institution he represents.
>
> If put to a pinch, a pound of loyalty is worth a pound of cleverness; if you must vilify, condemn or eternally disparage, resign your position.
>
> But as long as you are a part of the institution, do not condemn it. If you do you are loosening the tendrils that hold you to the institution, and the first high wind that comes along, you will be uprooted and blown away, and probably you will never know why.[6]

In exchange for the loyalty of the employee to the warden, the warden was obliged to the employee:

> It has been shown previously that the warden of a penitentiary is responsible to the people of the state for the conduct of employees under him. It has also been demonstrated that, in order to insure the maximum efficiency of his officers, the warden must demand of them adherence to certain rules and regulations. In other words the officers have definite duties, and in satisfying those duties, they are justifying the faith placed in them by the warden. . . . An enlightened warden will see that his officers are treated justly with all the consideration they deserve, and it behooves the officers working under such a warden to evidence their appreciation by doing their duty to him as well as he has done his to them.[7]

Donald Clemmer pointed out that Ragen fired a guard for brutality at Menard,[8] but many informants also insist that he often turned his back on beatings at Stateville. He would castigate guards for referring to inmates as "sons-of-bitches" but he would do so himself in the next breath. While many of the inmates may have seethed with bitterness, an equal number preferred doing time at Stateville because "you knew where you stood."

Ragen maintained "that if you stress the small things, you will never have to worry about the big ones." Thus, under his fully elaborated system of administration the inmates were subjected to intense supervision under innumerable rules blanketing every aspect of prison life. While many inmates suffered emotionally and psychologically from this intense supervision, they were physically safer, better fed, and provided with more programs than inmates of most other prisons of the period. In comparison with other prisons of the forties and fifties, Stateville had less violence, more industry, and less corruption. When prison riots touched almost every major prison across the country in the early 1950s, Stateville continued to run smoothly.

Ragen trained a whole generation of employees who for years held leadership positions at Stateville and throughout the Illinois prisons. When he took over management of the entire Illinois prison system as director of public safety in 1961, he appointed Stateville captains and administrators as wardens at Stateville, Pontiac, Vandalia, and Vienna. He made his personal secretary warden of the women's prison at Dwight. One cannot hope to understand the goals, strains, and conflicts in the Illinois prisons today without assessing the Ragen legacy.

In place of a system where order was based upon the rule of inmate bosses and gang leaders, Ragen established a patriarchal organization based upon his own charismatic authority. Later the perfection and perpetuation of this organization became a goal in itself.[9] Under Ragen, Stateville was transformed from an organization without a stable goal to an institution infused with independent moral value. Stateville was Joseph Ragen's answer to *Walden Two.* Every person and every object had its place. From the award-winning gardens to the clocklike regularity of the movement of prisoners in precise formations from assignment to assignment, the prison reflected its warden's zeal for order and harmony. Indeed, Ragen and the organization's elite looked on the prison as morally superior to the outside society with its petty politics and debilitating corruption.

The single most important barrier to the triumph of Ragen's system of personal dominance was the intrusion of the partisan political system. With respect to the staff this meant that the civil service and a career-oriented professional elite had to prevail over the spoils systems. With respect to the inmates, favoritism based upon outside status or attachments had to be replaced by a status system completely articulated with the closed world of the prison.

Ragen resigned his position as did all his top assistants in 1941, when a Republican (Dwight Greene) won the governorship.[10] But in 1942 the sensational Toughy-Banghart-Darlak escape mobilized public opinion and the press to call for the resignation of the new warden, E. M. Stubblefield. Ragen's subsequent return under a Republican administration marked a transition in the history of Illinois prisons. A public organization which heretofore existed primarily as a tool of the political party in power was beginning to emerge as an apolitical pre-bureaucratic organization which carried on for the material and moral benefit of a controlling elite.

One of the conditions Ragen imposed upon Governor Greene upon reassuming the wardenship in 1942 was that political influence on hiring and promotions would have to cease. With each succeeding administration, Ragen renewed this demand and tightened his control. While nominally a Democrat, he tried to establish a politically independent position. Although largely successful, he was never completely able to eliminate all politics from the prison. The position of superintendent of industries, for example, was a political appointment until Ragen put one of his own people in the position in 1957. Ragen acquiesced in hiring guards sent to him by politicians. But, except during the Great Depression and a few periods of recession, guard positions were going begging and political influence was not needed. This was particularly true for southern Illinoisans, those most likely to be recommended by politicians. What Ragen did ensure from the beginning was that, once hired, no one would be forced to resign because of a change in political control in Springfield.

During the next twenty years Ragen neutralized Illinois's partisan political structure by building an independent basis of support, in part through calculated public relations. Serving under Republicans and Democrats alike, he became independent of political control much as J. Edgar Hoover did at the FBI. Like Hoover, Ragen, in the eyes of the public and of his staff, came to embody the values of his organization.

State legislators were invited to the prison regularly for tours and banquets. The Stateville "chicken fry" constituted an institution in Illinois politics. This picnic, served by inmates at the minimum security farm, was regularly attended by 800–1,000 people drawn from all over the state. The annual American Legion banquet and show at Stateville was consistently attended by more than 1,000 legionnaires.

More important, Ragen satisfied the legislature by military discipline, few escapes, no riots, and by turning back part of his budget each year. The press, which was early critical of Ragen, soon was impressed by his relentless discipline. Over the course of the next twenty-five years Ragen cemented his relationship with the press into a virtual alliance. The support which the conservative Chicago papers (especially the *Tribune*) gave to the tough law-and-order warden effectively blunted whatever infrequent criticism might come from the ranks of academic specialists and reformers.

Perhaps the most poignant illustration of the articulation between press and prison is the ten-part series on Ragen and Stateville published by the *Chicago Tribune* in July 1955 and subsequently reprinted as a pamphlet by the John Howard Association (a comment on the success of Ragen's cooptation of that "prison reform organization"). The *Tribune* introduced this series with accolades for Ragen even at a time when reformers, including many liberal prison officials around the country, identified "Ragenism" with repression.

> The remarkable story of Joseph P. Ragen and the two penitentiaries he runs—Stateville and Joliet—will be told in a series of articles starting in tomorrow's Sunday Tribune. Ragen is known as the outstanding prison administrator in the United States. Stateville and Joliet, among the worst penitentiaries in the country when he took charge twenty years ago, have become models for the nation. The governors of a dozen other states have summoned him to make surveys and recommendations for reorganizing their prisons.

Ragen's relationship with the conservative Chicago press was rooted in compatible social and moral philosophies, but was also cultivated by public relations. Scrupulously honest with respect to private gain from his public trust, Ragen was lavish in the use of public funds to embellish the reputation of the institution which he administered. (One is tempted to conclude that Ragen saw this as a moral obligation.) Favorite reporters were often given private tours and sumptuous dinners at Stateville. The Ragens were frequent and extravagant hosts in their suite in the administration building.

Of the reporters, Gladys Erickson of the *Tribune* and Charles Finstone of the *American* (married to each other) were most closely allied to Ragen. The former was allowed free access to the prison (extraordinary at the time for a woman), and was rewarded for her early support of Ragen by being given the scoop on the only escape, as well as some exclusive interviews, and later by being chosen to write the warden's biography.[11] Finstone collaborated with Ragen on an 800-page manual on how to administer "the world's toughest prison" published toward the end of Ragen's career.[12]

Ragen distrusted "outsiders," by whom he meant anyone who did not work directly for him. He neutralized those outsiders who worked in one capacity or another at or around the prison by narrowly circumscribing their roles or by completely coopting them. His assistant wardens had, of course, risen through the ranks. Anyone who worked in the "back" wore a uniform. His superintendent of education, one of a handful of college-educated employees, was made to serve an apprenticeship as a guard for six months before assuming his responsibilities. Ragen did not share authority with any subordinates, least of all with "civilians." The decision-making structure revolved around the morning captains' meeting attended by three or four captains and two assistant wardens. After Ragen had been briefed, he conducted, accompanied by his two boxer dogs, his personal inspection of Stateville and the other Joliet prisons.

Professionals in the Division of the Criminologist were neutralized through administrative segmentation and cooptation. Upon commitment, inmates spent six weeks at the Joliet Reception and Diagnostic Depot, where they were given batteries of psychological and sociological tests, presumably so that they could be "classified" and their prison careers rationally planned. Recommendations were then made as to the best "program" for the inmate. This system was pointed to all over the country as a progressive reform in the treatment and classification of offenders. Even Ragen boasted of its operation.[13] In practice, Stateville disregarded the sociologists' and psychologists' recommendations and substituted its own system of classifying inmates, which served to maximize control and conformity. "Fish" (newly committed inmates) were assigned to the most arduous assignment, the coal pile or the rock quarry. By conformity to rules and regulations and by diligent work they might rise to a better job. The threat of demotion likewise served to reinforce conformity on the good jobs.

State criminologist Roy Barrick, whose incumbency almost precisely paralleled that of Ragen (1942-61), was in complete agreement with Warden Ragen about the desirability of limiting the criminologist to an advisory role.

> The criminologist and his staff are not delegated with administrative responsibilities in the prisons. They do not have to do with the custody, discipline, treatment, or parole of prisoners. An advisory relationship is maintained with the Director, the Superintendent of Prisons, the Attorney General, the Parole and Pardon Board, and the Wardens and their staffs. Recommendations are offered as to the segregation, assignments, training, and treatment of inmates for the consideration of prison officials, but the Criminologist and his staff do not execute their recommendations, since this is an administrative matter. Experience has demonstrated that an advisory relationship is a sound principle upon which to conduct the professional program, for it gives emphasis to the educational objectives of classification.[14]

The only "outsiders" with legitimate access to the prison were the chaplains, doctors, and the two sociologist-actuaries employed by the Parole Board. Hans W. Mattick, one of the sociologist-actuaries who worked at Stateville in the early fifties (Daniel Glaser was the other) recalls that during the entire three years of his employment there, he was "shaken down" (searched) at the gate house every day and made to pass through the electric eye and the gate designated for visitors. By way of contrast, any new guard after a week's indoctrination was passed through the employee's gate on the other side, without an electric eye and with only a cursory visual inspection by the gatekeeper.

The "shakedown" invariably included the requirement that Mattick remove his outer sport coat and empty his briefcase. He was then "patted down," the contents of his brief case were inspected, and a thorough search of the pockets and linings of his sport coat was conducted.[15] On several occasions Mattick learned that his office itself was "shaken down" and that the officers conducting the search strenuously objected when they found the files and desk locked. When Mattick told Ragen that the records of the office were the property of the Parole Board and the board's authorization was required before the shakedown squad would be permitted to search the desks and files, Ragen was "displeased." In such an atmosphere of distrust and disapproval, Mattick reports that he was constantly concerned with being "set up" by having contraband "planted" in his office or briefcase or on his person by the agents of Ragen. The painstaking care with which he documented the date and source of every piece of paper he handled and carried into or out of Stateville testifies to the hostile climate under which such "outsiders" worked. Distrust engendered distrust and few professionals could tolerate more than a year or two in the Office of the Sociologist-Actuary at Stateville. Mattick lasted three years before he left to become the assistant warden of the Cook County Jail.[16]

Until Ragen's departure in 1961, there was almost no interaction between outside groups concerned about prison conditions and Stateville. Ragen turned down a federal grant in 1956 for guard training because he did not want anyone inside the prison who did not work for him. University people were most certainly not welcome other than to make an occasional tour or infrequent survey. The John Howard Association, under weak leadership, was allowed infrequent access to the prison in exchange for regular support of Ragen policies. The cordiality of Ragen's relationship with the John Howard Association was revealed in a May 1955 prison bulletin wherein Ragen recalled "the efforts John Howard has made on behalf of inmates" and asked for blood donations for the ailing president of that organization. The TV College, started in 1956 in cooperation with a nearby junior college, necessarily brought a small number of teachers to the prison but only when it was necessary to administer examinations. The only outside group consistently given the "privilege" of coming inside with a program for the convicts was Alcoholics Anonymous, itself headed by a Stateville sergeant designated by Ragen.

Ragen's Stateville was an autonomous institution accountable neither to other public agencies nor to the public at large.[17] Although the Joliet prisons which Ragen administered were nominally under the control of the Department of Public Safety (organized in 1941), in reality Ragen had absolute autonomy in directing every detail of the Stateville routine. The director of public safety was Ragen's boss in name only. This position remained a political plum until Ragen himself took the job in 1961, and the directors rarely, if ever, even visited Stateville. When they did, it was merely a social occasion.

Nor was Ragen accountable for his actions before the courts.

His only defeat in this area occurred shortly after he returned to Stateville in 1942. Judge Barnes of the Federal District Court of the Northern District of Illinois admonished Ragen in open court that he could not interfere with prisoners who wanted to send habeas corpus petitions to the federal courts "even if they are written on toilet paper."[18] Other than this single decision, Ragen never lost an important case before the courts, which granted the broadest discretion to prison administration.

Where previously those inmates skilled in drawing up habeas corpus petitions served as jailhouse lawyers for hundreds of clients within the prison, upon assuming the position of Stateville warden Ragen announced that no inmate could aid in the preparation of another's legal work and subsequently threw several of the leading "lawyers" into segregation. Inmates were almost completely shut off from the courts. Records are not available for the number of lawsuits filed against the Stateville administration prior to 1954, but between 1954 and 1961 only twenty-one law suits were filed against Ragen as warden of Stateville and only four were ever carried to the point of a written court decision (see table 3). Of these four, three were *pro se* actions indicating the lack of outside legal help then available to inmate writ writers. The only suit with outside legal assistance was brought in 1949 by several former jailhouse lawyers complaining of wide abuses throughout the administration of the prison.[19] In affirming the lower court's dismissal of the inmates' action, the Seventh Circuit Court of Appeals held that "the government of the United States is not concerned with, nor has it power to control or regulate the internal discipline of penal institutions of its constituent states." In the three later decisions complaining of brutality,[20] interference with the mails,[21] and destruction of property,[22] the federal courts ruled against the inmates and reiterated their commitment to maintaining a "hands off" approach to matters of penal administration.

By neutralizing the outside forces that threatened interference in internal administration, Ragen was free to construct an authoritarian system encompassing both staff and inmates. While to the outsider Stateville appeared to be a smooth-running paramilitary organization which ran according to the comprehensive system of rules and regulations, the insider experienced a highly authoritarian system where informal influence was rooted in ethnic ties, religious affiliations, and particularistic relationships. There was constant competition to gain greater proximity to the charismatic leader. Paralleling the formal system of comprehensive rules, regulations, and sanctions was an informal system resting upon gossip, rumor, friendship, backbiting, and informing.

The captains maintained fiefdoms held together by personal loyalties and commitments. The rivalry among the captains for Ragen's approval spilled over to the lieutenants, who, like the captains, cultivated informers among the inmates in the intense competition to supply more extensive and more detailed information up the chain of command. The relentless pursuit of information was the means by which even potential threats to the system could be squelched. The goal was always to be one step ahead of the inmates, thereby perpetuating the myth of the administration's omniscience. Informers were the backbone of the system. Ragen's most oft-quoted maxim was, "Whenever you see three inmates standing together, two of them are mine."

The lieutenants were the linchpins of the organization. They functioned as a police force which carried out law enforcement, order maintenance, and service functions. They mediated between the administrators and captains on the one hand and the inmates and line employees on the other. Entering a work area, they would disseminate information, discipline guards and inmates, and, with a certain "noblesse oblige," respond to requests for favors that might be accomplished "up front."

Sergeants were placed in charge of cell houses and at the key gates. Promotions were slow. Many employees, even after twenty years, never rose above the rank of guard. Those destined for high position were spotted by Ragen early in their careers and groomed for rank. Turnover among the line employees was very high due to the low wages and rigid discipline.[23] The Stateville culture and tradition was carried most prominently by a small number of long-time, higher-echelon staff (lieutenants and above) and high-status inmates.

In the name of the greater good, all kinds of individual prerogatives might be trampled. Neither guards nor inmates had any protection against arbitrary administrative action. To Ragen, Stateville constituted the ultimate moral order, and its employees were expected to embody its values. In his manual outlining their responsibilities, Ragen was as much concerned with guards' behavior off the job as on. He warned guards against becoming indebted to local merchants or in any other way reflecting badly on the prison. For adulterous relations or frequenting houses of prostitution or taverns with unsavory reputations, they were threatened with dismissal.

Guards, like inmates, were "written up" and given pink disciplinary slips ("pinkies") for such misdeeds as "maintaining a dirty assignment," "reading the newspaper," or "failing to salute a captain." During this period anybody could "write up" anybody else and was encouraged to do so. Failure to write up a violation was itself a violation. It was common for "kites" (notes smuggled to captains or to the outside) to be written by inmates against guards. Enough tickets (disciplinary reports) and pink slips resulted in arbitrary suspensions without pay or even in dismissal. The atmosphere of insecurity and distrust well served Ragen's strategy of divide and conquer. Perhaps some indication of Ragen's rigorous supervision of his staff can be gleaned from the following employee bulletin dated 27 January 1955.

Upon entering the hospital at the Joliet Branch on January 19, I found Sergeant Frank Riley at the desk, and I have never failed to find him at the desk upon entering the hospital, which is an indication he does not leave his desk too much. There seemed to be a lot of turmoil when I walked in. Upon visiting the second and third floors, I found bedding equipment, dirty clothes, and the place looked anything but being in shipshape condition. Mr. Riley has been warned of his lack of supervision by the Chief Guard and other supervising officers at the Joliet Branch, but he seems to refuse responsibility. For this violation and others, he is being demoted from Guard Sergeant to Guard. Officer Burton is being suspended for one (1) day for not having the second and third floors properly supervised and in proper condition for visitors.

Guards worked six days a week, eight hours a day, until Ragen left Stateville in 1961. Wages were low and overtime was not allowed. When the chief guard required an employee to work extra hours, the employee was legally entitled to an equivalent amount of compensatory time off. But it was standard procedure for employees to accumulate hundreds of hours of uncompensated overtime without ever being allowed a day off.

Ragen recruited guards exclusively from rural southern Illinois.[24] While civil service requirements enhanced Ragen's independence from the partisan political system, they never limited his administrative prerogatives, since chronic understaffing nearly always left the organization free to engage in "direct hire." Lieutenants and officers were sent in teams to southern Illinois, Missouri, and Kentucky to find good prospects. The guards themselves were not attracted to Stateville by any special desire to work in a prison, but left their homes to escape a dismal economic situation that has plagued southern Illinois for decades. These rural guards constituted a culturally homogeneous work force which reinforced the prison's isolation from its surrounding environs. Many of the guards maintained farms, residences, and sometimes their families "down south" and visited home whenever possible. While in Joliet, they lived at the officers' barracks, which physically separated them from their neighbors and reinforced their solidarity with one another. (Those who lived there at the time estimate between one-fourth and one-third of all the guards lived in the barracks.) Ragen also constructed a trailer park (in 1953) for married guards. Senior guards and the assistant wardens lived a kind of baronial existence, with anything between one and five inmate houseboys and yardmen, in state-owned houses on the prison's property outside the walls.[25]

The officers' barracks and the trailer camp were as vulnerable to "shakedowns" as were the inmates' cells. The captains (or Ragen himself) might raid the barracks at any time during the day or night in order to search for contraband like alcohol or radios or to expose any gambling that might be occurring. An 11:00 P.M. curfew at the barracks was rigidly enforced. When Ragen was dissatisfied with the cleanliness or orderliness of the barracks, he would cut off the water or electricity. The situation persisted long after Ragen's departure under the caretaker regime of his top assistant and chosen successor, Frank Pate.

In the late 1950s, an employees' association began to develop at Stateville underground, because Ragen would no more recognize organizations among employees than he would among inmates. He maintained an open door to speak with any one individually, but would not accept those who purported to speak on behalf of others. Discussion of "controversial" topics while on duty was against the rules.

> There are rules of long standing in the institution that no controversial subjects are to be discussed while on the institution property. Neither will there be any solicitations made by any employee on state property. . . . Under no circumstances is anyone to violate the above mentioned rules, and if they do they can expect to be disciplined. (Bulletin no. 196, September 24, 1955)

Sensitive to the relationship between basic services (especially food) and inmate morale, Ragen stressed that the inmates were entitled to good food, clean clothing, and satisfactory housing. (At every meal a lieutenant had to sign a statement that he had tasted the food and found it fit). Beyond these essentials, Ragen emphasized that inmates were entitled to nothing. Any other things given them were "privileges granted by the officials of the institution and the Department of Public Safety." One long-term inmate described his orientation into this system as follows:

> On February 10, 1949, the new arrivals at Stateville were taken to the "Jug" [later the isolation unit] for an orientation lecture. I was told, in effect, *these walls are our walls; you will stay off our walls . . . or we will most certainly blow you away.* And I was told, too, that everything in the universe was a privilege. Work was a privilege, communication with family and friends was a privilege, and even the spending of one's own money was a privilege. At Stateville prison, even the grass was sacred: *Stay off our grass or we will put your stinkin' self in the hole.*[26]

The Ragen system was based upon internal security so intense that the ultimate perimeter security would never need to be tested. The kinds of restrictions on inmate freedoms which were imposed in the name of security often seem rather far removed from immediate security needs; although scenarios could always be constructed whereby, for example, an inmate who left food on his plate could be said to be challenging authority in a way that, left unpunished, might result in widespread rebellion. Ragen himself bragged that Stateville was the "tightest prison in the United States" (Leopold adds "so tight it cracks"). Few inmates would disagree. During his twenty-five-year tenure as warden, there were no riots, not a single escape from behind the walls, and only two guards and three inmates killed. Whether this security system was a byproduct of the maintenance of order, or whether the achievement of order was the primary goal, it is clear that a highly predictable routine which reinforced inmate and staff expectations was the consequence.

The formal organization of the prison was built around comprehensive prescriptive and proscriptive sets of rules and regulations and punishment for their infraction. It was practically impossible for an inmate to abide by all the rules and regulations.[27] Failure to button a shirt or to salute a white cap (captain) was reason enough to be brought before the disciplinary captain. "Silent insolence" was an actionable offense. At "the corner" (the captain's office) the disciplinary captain gave the accused rule violator Hobson's choice. The inmate might admit to the rule infraction and "take his weight" (take the blame) or try to dispute the "ticket" and thereby be found guilty of calling a guard a liar, itself a violation of the rules. In either event, he would do time in the "hole" (the isolation unit) or suffer a privilege denial (yard, commissary, earphones).[28]

While Ragen eliminated the practice of "stringing inmates up" at isolation, he did require them to stand silently at attention inside the isolation cell eight hours per day. In the late 1950s, as the nationwide trend toward increased concern for prisoners gained strength, the standing also was abandoned.

The multitude of rules made it a certainty that any inmate could be found guilty of a rule violation at any time and thus could be placed in isolation. Not, of course, that a violation had to be found to remove a "no good son-of-a-bitch" or an "agitator" or a "troublemaker" from the population. In the 1954–55 *Annual Report of the Department of Public Safety,* Ragen pointed out, "we have found that segregation of a very small percentage of nonconformants has added to the more efficient operation of the institution program."[29]

While Ragen stated that no inmate should be treated differently than any other, discipline was so strict that the organization could only function if innumerable exceptions were made. The captains' clerks couldn't be "busted" and there were other "untouchables" throughout the prison whose inviolability was based upon stooling, indispensability, or personal relationships with the staff. This led to an arbitrary system of justice, whereby overlooking infractions was a reciprocity for certain inmate compliance, particularly the supplying of information.[30] Under such circumstances, it is not suprising that identifying, avoiding, and punishing "rats" became the central theme of the inmate social system.

So effective was this system of arbitrary discipline and harassment of troublemakers that on any given day there were only 25–30 disciplinary tickets for a population of 3,500; thirty-two cells were sufficient to segregate all serious and chronic troublemakers. It was arbitrary coercion and relentless supervision coupled with a meaningful "reward system" that ensured maintenance of order and control.

The reward system was a much more effective mechanism of social control during the Ragen era than it is today. There was a much greater disparity in the living conditions between the best-off and the worst-off inmates. Prisoners in Illinois faced extremely long prison terms throughout the 1940s and 1950s. Crowded conditions meant that the average inmate was confined with two other men in a tiny cell from 3:00 P.M. to 7:00 A.M. Those inmates with jobs in the administration building could be given "night details" in order to keep up with their paper work. Thus, they could remain in the comfortable offices sometimes until late evening. These "up front" positions as well as the jobs of clerks and runners carried with them the opportunity for many illegitimate "scores" within the prison as well. Former sociologist-actuary Lloyd Ohlin explains that while he was employed at Stateville some of the inmates who worked for him kept a still going (unbeknown to him) in the file cabinet.[31] In addition they used to steal Parole Board decisions and sell them to the inmates in the back before they were officially announced. He concludes that for inmates with good jobs the Stateville system was not oppressive.

Ohlin's successor in office, Daniel Glaser, has pointed out that the old cons knew how much they could get away with.[32] "In the hospital where our offices were located there was regular transmission of food from the officers' mess to the inmates working elsewhere in the building, generally carried by the porters, and elaborate reciprocities of exchange in services or contraband were continually being fulfilled by the inmates. A little hair oil from the officers' barbershop was a major exchange item in our building."

Ragen and his top staff made it a practice to offer many of the top jobs to inmate leaders and toughs. Vernon Revis, a Ragen protégé for many years and eventually superintendent and assistant warden, explains how he approached a "tough son-of-a-bitch" who had just been released from isolation for refusing to work and asked him how he would like to be his personal clerk. Apparently such situations were common. The Catholic chaplain during Ragen's tenure has noted that Ragen only chose murderers for his clerks. Glaser points out that Ragen picked "square john" type inmates to do the mail censoring, housing them and feeding them in the basement of the administration building completely apart from the others. Other tough inmates were coopted as nurses in the detention hospital, where they celled as well as worked in comparative comfort.

In a tribute to Stateville's disciplinary system, the *Chicago Tribune* reporters in 1955 observed:

> Discipline at Joliet-Stateville is not merely strict; like security, it is absolute. Not even the slightest infraction of the rules is tolerated. The inmates march to and from work, meals, the bathhouse, the barber shop, the commissary, in a column of two's and they march in step. Profane or abusive language to employees or other inmates is not tolerated. Neither is insolence.[33]

The silent system was enforced in the dining room and while marching in lines. The entire prison functioned with Prussian punctuality. It is frequently said that you could set your watch by the movements of the lines of prisoners. The strictness of the system caused difficulties for many inmates, although to be sure this strictness protected inmates from many of the physical depredations common at other prisons dominated by "barn bosses." Going "stir bugs" was an everyday occurrence at Stateville during the Ragen years, as is indicated by the number of transfers to the Psychiatric Division (see table 4). According to notorious Chicago gangster Roger Touhy:

> You should know the record of insanity that has resulted from the routine established by rules. What a bad effect all those rules—rules—rules have on men, particularly the young men who come down here. They can't take it.[34]

"Going stir bugs"—a paranoid condition wherein the inmate feels that he is being watched from every post and plotted against in every conversation—has been described to me by several old-timers.[35] Whether "stir bugs" is a condition of actual psychological deterioration or a strategy to escape the mainline population or some combination of the two is not of great importance here. Requests for transfer to the more relaxed atmosphere of Menard, either as mental patients or as members of its general population, were very frequent despite the hardship that the distance made for visitors.[36]

In the mid-1950s a greater societal acceptance of the legitimacy of prison reform moved Ragen to redefine his system of total control as "rehabilitation." Both the *Tribune* articles of 1955 and *Inside the World's Toughest Prison* (1962) are replete with references to Ragen as a "penologist" and a humanist. According to Ragen himself,

There is so much good in the worst of us. . . . Rehabilitation takes as its major premise the thesis that ignorance is the root of all evil, that if man is equally familiar with right and wrong, he will in the majority of instances choose the former. Most of the men in prison have a corrupted courage. They dared to rebel against an unsupportable environment, but they were mentally and spiritually untrained to prosecute the rebellion morally. It has for years been admitted that slums constitute the most insidious social menace known, and the greatest task of the penologist lies in counteracting the influence of the slums. Something like ninety percent of all prison populations in this country are recruited from the marginal and sub-marginal sections of the large cities. The prison authorities must take this chronically underprivileged mass of humanity and place it on the path of morality.[37]

The change in the philosophical justification of the same prison system is explained by the increasing prominence being given to prison reform by professional administrators and academics after World War II and following the wave of prison riots in the early 1950s. If Stateville was to maintain its preeminence, then its basis of order would have to claim legitimacy within the vocabulary of the mainstream of "enlightened" opinion about the purpose of prison. About Ragen's reaction to the reform movement, Daniel Glaser recalls:

Rehabilitation to him was the number of inmates in school, and during his ACA term and thereafter in the early 1950's he rapidly increased the size of the academic and vocational schools, which were conspicuously located for visitors and kept brightly painted—as was the entire prison. . . . There was always at least one guard in the school and no students were there more than a few hours each day, so his figures for the number of students enrolled in school compared to the numbers at many other prisons made it look favorable. The vocational school was oriented to personal service for staff in repairing cars and radios, appliances and typewriters, and tended to keep as its inmate crew mainly inmates who already had some training or were master craftsmen from the outside. Staff would bring in rundown autos, radios and appliances, pay for parts and supplies including a little surplus of these for the school, and get the labor done free by the inmates. Several staff members told me of buying rundown or wrecked autos or appliances, getting them fixed at "the joint" and selling them for a profit. The elite staff of Ragen's favorites seemed to have the inside run on these and other fringe benefits from inmate labor and prison facilities.[38]

That so many penal practices over the years could be established in the name of rehabilitation is a tribute to the ambiguity of that term. Ragen reasoned that the strictness of the Stateville regime would coerce the inmate into a conformity that would ultimately produce a respect for the rules. Through obedience to prison rules, the inmate would be resocialized. Ragen was not without outstanding examples of reformed ex-offenders to "prove" the success of his system.

While the Works Progress Administration and the Civilian Conservation Corps were creating jobs for the unemployed on the outside, Ragen put as many Stateville inmates to work as possible restoring the prison grounds with no better tools than kitchen pans and bare hands with which to carry dirt.[39] A cardinal principle of Ragenism from the beginning and for the next twenty-five years was to keep every inmate working, even if it entailed certain diseconomies and featherbedding. The warden believed that, by working the men, conspiracies for escape and disruption would be minimized. All inmates were assigned to jobs essential to the operation of the prison (clerks, maintenance, laundry, dining room, etc.) or to prison industries where, according to Ragen, an inmate could learn a marketable trade like sheet metal or furniture making.[40] The industries were a source of great pride to Ragen. They were at the heart of his "rehabilitation program" and he showed slides of the industries whenever he spoke to community groups. Even at the height of the system, however, it is unlikely that more than 20 percent of the population was assigned to industries.[41] The industries also served primarily to reinforce control by keeping inmates busy rather than providing job training. One veteran of the Ragen years recalls:

> I was assigned to work in the Tailor Shop where, for roughly twenty months, I watched hustlers, pimps, burglars, gunmen, and killers at work sewing hems on little red flags. I could not then and I can not now seriously entertain the notion that any of these vocational *trainees* would long work as a seamstress in the "free world." I had no enthusiasm at all for the work of sewing buttons onto jockey shorts. I was rescued from that line of privileged help by being "fired" from the Tailor Shop and reassigned to work in the so-called Vocational School.[42]

While ostensibly the assignments hummed with activity, they were plagued by featherbedding caused by the fact that Stateville, throughout the Ragen era, held twice the number of inmates designated as maximum capacity. Perhaps no better symbol of the Ragen regime can be described than the coal pile to which all "fish" were assigned for six months and to which those inmates who "required" punishment were sent. The Stateville coal pile is legend among those old-timers unfortunate enough to recall the experience. In *Next Time is for Life,* Paul Warren provides a poignant description of the Stateville coal pile.

> In a line of men I had wheeled a wheelbarrel down a narrow strip of cement walk to a coal pile. When my wheelbarrel was filled I bent over, took hold of the steel handles and lifted. Christ, it weighed a ton! Straining with all my might, I managed to pick it up, turn around with it and start up the walk. A few steps and the wheelbarrel began to tip. I spread my legs and pulled at the lowering handle. It was too much. I let go and the load of coal spilled over the ground.... All morning I struggled with that wheelbarrel. I learned to stall when the guard wasn't looking. On the pretense of tying a shoelace, I rested a moment. I brushed my face and felt the coal dust scratch. The dust and sweat had mixed to form a mud. Every step was painful; my sore muscles were stretched beyond endurance.[43]

The coal pile was actually a series of coal piles. A train dumped the coal into the prison yard where it was shoveled into wheelbarrows and carried to one pile after another and stacked in perfect pyramids. The process was repeated until the coal ended up at the powerhouse. The work was draining (for the guards as well) during both the hot and cold months, and its very existence helped to stimulate the intense competition for the better jobs among the inmates.

Illinois prisoners were serving far longer prison terms in the 1940s and 1950s than they are today. Of the indeterminate sentences, 36.8 percent were one-to-life in 1934–42, but only 0.4 percent were one-to-life in 1973. Likewise 36.9 percent of the determinate sentences in 1957 were more than twenty years while only 3.4 percent of the minimum sentences in 1973 were greater than twenty years. In addition, the great liberalization of the good time and parole laws has had an even more important effect on actual time served. In any case, a 1960 nationwide sample found that Illinois prisoners were serving the second-longest prison terms in the country.[44] The lengthy sentences and the differential desirability of various jobs created an inmate social system organized according to occupational status. Much jockeying for the better jobs occurred, thus reinforcing the vitality of the "rat" system. If a high-status inmate could be dethroned, his position would, of course, become available. To a great extent, occupational mobility depended upon the identification of deviants.

Those inmates in key positions who were able to maneuver cell and job assignments achieved high status within the inmate social system.[45] The important point to keep in mind when we compare the inmate social system of Ragen's era with the present is that, during Ragen's day, power and prestige were attached to one's position in the formal organization, while at present they are independent of formal organizational status. This is not to say that informal affective ties did not bind inmates together during those years. Upon his appointment to Stateville, Ragen's initial task was to win back control of the prison from the ethnic gangs which were in virtual control. The Italians (associated with Taylor Street in Chicago) maintained especially strong solidarity throughout the 1950s and were sometimes able to assert their influence in strong-arming weaker inmates and controlling some of the better jobs. While the blacks constituted almost 50 percent of the population by the mid-1950s, racial identity at the time was a weak basis for action, and blacks asserted an influence far less than their numbers.

The inmate social system tended to be stable due to the very long prison terms and comparatively low turnover. In the early 1950s Stateville received less than 1,000 new inmates per year, while today almost 2,400 are admitted annually. One former guard notes that out of 150 inmates he had supervised in the furniture factory, 50 had served more than twenty calendar years.

The inmate social system at Stateville during the 1940s and 1950s approximated that described by Sykes and Messinger for other penitentiaries[46] except that there was no prisoner ideological solidarity. The prestige structure based upon offense was carried over from earlier decades. The inmate code, even if honored more in the breach, provided an ordering of relationships among "cons". Both inmates and guards who lived through the Ragen years report that theft between inmates was practically nonexistent. What fights there were involved individual grudges, most often gambling.

A thriving black market in coffee, cigarettes, and "hooch" provided some relief from the Spartan existence. While Ragen removed $15,000 in currency from the prison in his first few years, he by no means eliminated the trafficking of guards or the numbers racket and other forms of gambling.

Nevertheless, inmates during the Ragen years were poor. All who had the funds and desire to trade could be accommodated at the commissary, open just four and a half days each week. Today, with a 60 percent smaller population, there are more inmate customers at the commissary each week than there were twenty years ago. The income of inmates today primarily derives from money sent in from the streets—a source of income quite uncommon twenty years ago.

Fraternization between guards and inmates during Ragen's administration was a violation for both castes. No more interaction than was necessary to carry out work assignments was to be tolerated. Relations between guards and inmates were impersonal and ritualized. The rules were known and accepted by all participants. As long as the inmate did not challenge authority directly, he might engage in black market trade without serious repercussion. He could, of course, expect periodically to be busted for contraband, purged from his assignment, and sent to the "hole" and back to the coal pile, but these were the pitfalls upon which expectations were built. ("You get me this time, but think of all the times I beat you.") In six months to a year, the inmate might have a new position and might once more be involved in black market activity.

More extreme was the punishment inflicted upon those few inmates who dared to directly challenge Ragen's authority by complaining to the outside, attempting escape, defying an officer, or organizing concerted opposition to the regime. Such individuals could expect to be beaten by the captains and lieutenants or by their specially selected inmate helpers.

All inmate communications with the outside were rigorously controlled and censored.

> Inmates are permitted to write one letter each week, on Sunday, to their friends and relatives. These letters must be respectful and decent in every way, containing no solicitations or remarks derogatory to the institution. Close censorship is maintained over outgoing mail as well as incoming, and accurate records are kept in both instances.[47]

Ragen told inmates not to complain to outsiders about the prison or to act in any other way so as to bring criticism upon the institution. He argued that criticism could only result in a negative reaction against ex-convicts and thus redound to the detriment of prisons and prisoners. For the offense of criticizing Stateville to visitors or in letters, an inmate could expect to be "purged" from his job after doing seven days in the hole (isolation).

There was little possibility of organized resistance. The efforts of jailhouse lawyers to take Ragen to task before the courts resulted in their transfer from the mainline population to segregation for years on end. Inmates who challenged the system could be "salted away" in segregation for as long as a decade. One of Ragen's most rebellious inmates, Major Price (who had savagely attacked two guards in the 1940s and proclaimed himself to be a communist) was kept in segregation for twelve years. Another "troublemaker" and future leader of the Stateville Black Muslims, Thomas X. Cooper, spent ten years in segregation. Jailhouse lawyer Maurice Meyers was thrown in segregation for a year and told he would never be released until he returned records smuggled out of the prison in order to blackmail Ragen into allowing inmate commissary funds to be used for a legal assistance program.

Both isolation (short-term punishment) and segregation (long-term punishment) units were located in the same building. The isolation cells were larger, often holding as many as six (sometimes more) inmates and were constructed with heavy steel doors which blocked the prisoners completely from view of those passing the cells. Aside from being in the special wing, segregation cells were more like ordinary cells, containing one or two prisoners. However, the prisoners were continuously confined to their cells and were always under intense surveillance. Inmates so confined were served their meals in their cells, had no recreation, and were escorted by two guards to the shower once a week.

Thus, in 1961, when Ragen left Stateville, his system of charismatic dominance was unassailable. To the Illinois public, press, and politicians Joe Ragen was "Mr. Prison" in Illinois. In the last half-dozen years of his wardenship he codified the entire administrative system. Stateville was carefully prepared for the transition from a charismatic to a traditional system of authority. In Frank Pate, his assistant warden, Ragen had a thoroughly loyal and like-minded successor. Yet on the national scene it was clear that the type of regime exemplified by Ragen and his generation was passing. At the National Institute of Corrections, the influential Howard Gill used Stateville as an example of what was wrong with the American prison system. In his seminars he referred to Stateville as a "monolithic monstrosity."

The great jump in the material expectations of the inmates was still a few years off. The civil rights movement was gaining momentum on the streets, and at Stateville the inmate majority had already passed to the blacks, although this was never acknowledged. In 1960 there was some trouble with self-proclaimed Black Muslims, but they were easily dealt with in segregation. Change would, no doubt, have buffeted Stateville even had Ragen stayed on, but his departure added the problem of organizational succession to a host of other strains that found their source in developments occurring in the 1960s in American society at large.

3 Challenge to Institutional Authority, 1961–70

> While walking inmate Washington to isolation he said, "The next time you walk me, you'll have to fight me to get me out, you better bring your army because I'll have mine, you whites and those bogus niggers are thru running this country, you know that don't you? This persecution of us Muslims will have to stop. . . ."
>
> Disciplinary ticket, 17 October 65

From 1961 to 1970 the authoritarian system of personal dominance inherited by Ragen's hand-picked successors was undermined as the prison became less able to dominate its relations with the outside. Staff reaction to the loss of institutional autonomy, the emergence of racial consciousness, and the penetration of juridical norms, was a consistent strategy of resistance. Until 1970, this all-out effort to maintain the old equilibrium was successful in preserving the basic structure of the social organization, but it led directly to a sudden and complete organizational collapse after 1970. By resisting even the most limited changes in the sixties, the tradition bearers of the prison's goals and values hastened their own demise.

Joseph P. Ragen left Stateville in 1961 to become director of public safety, but his departure for Springfield was hardly fateful for the administration of the prison. In the late 1950s, the Ragen system had been codified. The inmate rule book was expanded; a 132-page manual of "Rules and Regulations" describing the proper functioning of every employee's post and position was published. Copies of the relevant descriptions from the latter document were placed on every assignment. In his last years at Stateville, Ragen even took to memorializing various sectors of the prison (as well as the state-owned houses) with plaques dedicated to top members of the ruling elite.

Until Ragen's final retirement from public life in 1965, Stateville continued to be run by the same rules and by the same elite as it had for the previous three decades. Even while he was in Springfield, Ragen's superordinate goal was managing Stateville and the Joliet prisons. During those four years, he maintained his home and his family at Stateville and spent three or four days a week at the prison making tours, interviewing segregation cases, and directing activity as he had been accustomed in the past.

Frank Pate succeeded Ragen as warden. Pate had begun as a guard at Stateville in 1939, had served as chief guard and most recently as assistant warden. He was personally devoted to Ragen. The assistant wardens who served Pate were also longtime Ragen protégés who had come up through the ranks.[1] There was complete continuity between regimes.

However, Pate neither sought nor exercised the charismatic authority of the Old Boss. In part this was due to his long years of collegial association with the men over whom he now had command. This is not to say, however, that Pate did not claim deference and the emoluments of office. The prison remained an imperatively coordinated paramilitary organization, which required its warden to personify its goals and values. But, in practice, the administration of the prison drifted into collegial rule. The very fact that the warden's role had reverted to a bureaucratic "office" is indication of the transition from a charismatic to a traditional system of authority; a transition accompanied by ritualization and organizational strain.[2]

Furthermore, Warden Pate had to contend with Director Ragen until 1965. Heretofore, the director of public safety had been a political appointee. While Ragen always maintained a correct formal relationship with his nominal superior, neither the director of public safety nor the superintendent of prisons had ever interfered with Ragen's management of the Illinois prisons. The day Ragen became director, the autonomy of the local warden began to erode, a trend that has continued irreversibly to the present. Ragen increasingly demanded reports from "his" penitentiaries, and he personally intervened in routine decision making. According to Pate, "you couldn't even promote a man [inmate] in grade [i.e. from a low to a higher security classification] without Ragen's approving it." He further recalls that staff frequently complained, "That's not the way the old boss did it." A former inmate who worked as a domestic in the warden's house both in Ragen's and in Pate's regime recalls that Pate was expected to place a daily telephone call to his predecessor. Subordinates understood that Pate "wasn't running it" and sometimes went over his head to Ragen on important issues.[3] For the first time in decades, lines of authority were amorphous, confused, and contradictory. The carefully constructed organization entered a period of drift.

Nor did Pate enjoy his predecessor's prestige statewide or nationally. Ragen had never included his protégés in his out-of-state consultations and site visits, nor were they invited to the private parties where politicians and the press were entertained. Interestingly enough, the lack of a national perspective is cited by several longtime employees as the major difference between Ragen and Pate. The more parochial perspective at Stateville prevailed at precisely the time that outside forces were generating strains for the prison's internal organization. Without a leader of national or even statewide prominence, Stateville was less able to protect the sanctity of its boundaries.[4]

In 1965, after an acute illness and an apparent mental breakdown, Joe Ragen was forced to resign as director of public safety. Governor Otto Kerner appointed Warden Ross Randolph of Menard to replace him. For years there had been an intense rivalry between Ragen and Randolph for preeminence in Illinois corrections. Each was openly critical of the other's style of administration. It is said that Randolph's laxness never ceased to annoy Ragen. Ragen's lockups and strict discipline were sharply criticized by Randolph, who himself was becoming a national figure in corrections by the mid-1950s.

Ross Randolph had followed a somewhat unconventional career in the Illinois prison system. He held a college degree and began his prison career as a schoolteacher at Pontiac, later joining the FBI before his appointment as warden of Pontiac by Governor Adlai Stevenson. Randolph was transferred to Menard following the bloody riot of 1952 (which called an embarrassed Stevenson back from the presidential campaign trail). Randolph managed a much more relaxed prison by not insisting upon the enforcement of the myriad petty rules which Ragen insisted on, and he received favorable scores from reformers when compared with his Joliet rival. Unlike Ragen he was quite active in the local Chester community[5] and was skilled in his relations with powerful downstate politicians. He was also comfortable with academicians and had early in his regime invited Southern Illinois University classes into Menard. The well-known prison reformer Meryl Alexander, then on the faculty of SIU between his rise to assistant director of the United States Bureau of Prisons and his subsequent appointment as director, was a close friend of Randolph's and applauded his appointment as Ragen's successor in the Department of Public Safety.

As director, Randolph continued to centralize prison administration at the expense of local autonomy. "Civilians" were introduced into Stateville's administration. George Stampar, a Ragen appointee as supervisor of parole services and a Ragen protégé, was made Stateville assistant warden in 1965. Stampar was the first individual with a college degree (a master's in sociology) and the first "outsider" to be appointed into the Stateville chain of command. In his early years, he encountered "total resistance" to his attempts to liberalize some of the old rules.[6]

Two civilian educators were appointed in 1968. While Stateville had had civilian school administrators for many years, the Randolph appointees moved to professionalize the educational program by eliminating such corruption as the sale (for a carton of cigarettes) of General Education Diplomas (for high school equivalency) by the inmate instructors. They also unsuccessfully pressed Warden Pate to assign the educational program a higher priority so that its operation would not be disrupted whenever there was a need for extra hands in the industries.

Randolph made various moves to liberalize the Stateville regime. The first, and symbolically the most important, was his "easing" of the inmate dress code. Almost immediately after taking office, Randolph permitted the inmates to take off their caps if they chose to do so during the hot summer months. Even today this decision is recalled with emotional anguish by Stateville guards and administrators. Later he allowed talking in the dining room and while marching in line. Stateville officials were quick to predict that "capitulation" on the dress code would mean more demands and further capitulation. The next summer, inmates were allowed to take off their shirts on the recreation yards. Later, when the order was reversed, "it was impossible to get them back on." Pate and his top staff were frustrated and demoralized. The authoritarian system was being undermined by the prison's own central office for reasons attributed to jealousy and politics. The Pate regime became increasingly defensive and ritualistic. Each liberalization of the rules was resisted, finally accommodated, and then held out as the farthest step which could be taken before "giving the prison away."

Randolph introduced outsiders to Stateville as he had been accustomed to doing at Menard. Between 1965 and 1970, various entertainment groups were allowed behind the walls for the first time. Where Ragen had absolutely refused to accept any federal grants for fear of losing control over the programs which they would implement, Randolph welcomed the first federal monies being made available through the Law Enforcement Assistance Administration. Outside groups (e.g., Northern Illinois University) were permitted to bring educational courses into Stateville, despite Warden Pate's fear that the individuals sponsoring such programs had their own selfish (and sinister) motives.[7]

Randolph also eased some of the restrictions on employees. By 1966, the income of Illinois guards had probably fallen the farthest behind private industry since the 1920s. Turnover soared (see table 5). While Randolph could not increase pay scales, he did eliminate the practice of placing tickets in the guard's personnel folder for such offenses as "having a dirty assignment." The old elite which ran Stateville chafed at this relaxation of the rules and considered it the beginning of the "employees all going to hell."

Between 1961 and 1965, an underground union of employees with approximately fifty members existed at Stateville. It was completely resisted by Warden Pate and the administration. In fact, a sergeant was ordered to join, and his wages were paid for by the institution in order to report on its activities.[8] Randolph permitted the union to surface and officially recognized it in 1967, allowing checkoffs for union dues to be made from the payroll. Ironically, the union grew during this period because of the fear that Randolph was going to replace all the Ragen people. In 1967, the employees' union voted to join a national union, the American Federation of State, County, and Municipal Employees (AFSME), and the membership began slowly to identify with the mainstream American labor movement.

Randolph now had the power to reverse the long trend of inter-institutional transfers whereby Stateville was able to exile its inmate troublemakers to Menard. In 1964, when Ragen was director of public safety, Stateville-Menard transfers prevailed over Menard-Stateville transfers by a ratio of 5 to 1; by 1966, Randolph had reduced that ratio to 1.5 to 1.

Far more fateful for Stateville's organization than Ragen's departure as warden was the passage of Illinois's new criminal code, which adopted the Model Penal Code of the American Law Institute. The legal reformers completely revamped the substantive criminal law and included a section on sentencing and parole which made offenders serving life sentences (whether indeterminate or determinate) eligible for parole after twenty years, minus time off for good behavior. In short, after eleven years and three months, a felon sentenced to life might be paroled.[9]

This legal reform, which was effective 1 January 1962, immediately had a dramatic impact upon a prison where hundreds of felons were serving flat sentences of ninety-nine years or more and were not eligible for parole until one-third of the sentence had been served.[10] The assistant warden estimates that "approximately three hundred old-timers went to the Parole Board in 1962 and 80–95 percent were let out."[11] This estimate is consistent with the parole figures for the Joliet complex as a whole for that year. In 1961, there were 739 paroles (from Stateville, Joliet, and the Honor Farm). In 1962, there were 1,046 paroles. The figure has remained at close to or above 1,000 ever since.

The parole of so many old cons in the early 1960s had important consequences for the entire prison organization. Because the industries were paying jobs, old cons with years of experience were concentrated there. Over the years these men had become skilled in their jobs. Some had been on the job since the equipment had been installed. The supervisor of the furniture factory at the time recalls that more than half of his men were released on parole between 1962 and 1964. When these inmates were paroled, civilians had to be hired as instructors and supervisors. The prison industries, once the pride of the Ragen system, never again showed a profit. Even in a period of rising inflation, the dollar volume of sales decreased steadily after 1964 (see table 6). The same was true for the Honor Farm, which had consistently bred prize herds and had shown a profit in every year until the late 1960s.

Scores of civilians were added to the Record Office, General Office, Chief Clerk's Office, and the Bureau of Identification to take the place of the old-timer inmate clerks. Heretofore, the entire administration of the prison from accounting tasks to record keeping was made possible by using inmates under the direction of a single (or perhaps two) civilians in each office. With the parole of many clerks and bookkeepers, there occurred a crisis in administration. From 1962 to the present, one can see a steady decline in the number of inmates filling positions of responsibility within the formal organization. One of the ironies of the past decade has been the decline of inmate incumbency of responsible organizational positions (as teachers, vocational instructors, accountants, clerks, etc.) at the same time that the reformers advanced a philosophy of rehabilitation.

The parole of the old cons, the rising proportion of minority inmates, and the increasing inmate turnover (see table 7) all contributed to the demise of the traditional inmate social system. Some of the best jobs in the prison were abolished. Shorter prison terms gave less reason to find a good job. The "rat" system died when the old cons left. The intricate accommodation system that had joined guards and inmates together deteriorated. New racial consciousness made cooperation between guards and inmates more problematic. The few privileges that once attracted inmate cooperation became fewer and less valued. The booming economy on the outside pumped more money into prisoners' hands than ever before.[12]

While the Pate regime faithfully carried on the Ragen legacy, the inmate population no longer fully acquiesced in the legitimacy of official authority. The racial composition of the inmate population had already changed to a black majority in the mid-1950s, coinciding with the emergence of the civil rights movement on the streets (see table 8). The civil rights movement contributed directly to politicizing the inmates at Stateville. To be sure, both black numerical superiority inside the prison and the example of black civil rights activity on the streets were factors facilitating the rise of black nationalism and the organization of the Black Muslims, whose activities directly challenged the traditional relationship between keeper and kept.[13]

The Black Muslims were a nationalistic religious movement with an eschatology based upon the "chosenness" of the black race and the perniciousness of "white devils." The Muslims urged upon angry, disillusioned, and frustrated "so-called Negroes" a positive collective identity based upon moral superiority. For the first time, they linked the prisoners' situation to the struggles of other marginal groups in the society.

The movement was supported by symbolism (the scimitar and tusk crossed as swords) and by a myth of creation (the primacy of black people), armageddon (delayed by Allah from 1917 to 1984) and messianic resurrection (in the form of Elijah Muhammad). No more fertile ground for the movement could be found than the prison, where a majority black population existed under the authoritarian rule of a homogeneous southern white cadre of guards.

It is impossible to understand the vehemence and determination with which the prison resisted every Muslim demand, no matter how insignificant, except by understanding that what seemed to be at stake was the very survival of the authoritarian regime. Permitting Muslims to possess a copy of the Quran did not on its face threaten prison security, but recognition of the Muslims as a bona fide religious group,[14] entitled to all the deference and legitimacy of the traditional religions, was perceived as a grave threat to the moral order of the prison and to the Ragen world.

The Muslims called the prison racist, discriminatory, and repressive. They linked its inherent defects to the basic illegitimacy of the white government that ruled America. The Muslims posed a greater threat to the prison organization than earlier ethnic gangs. Their fervent hatred of the white race escalated the traditional boundaries of conflict between guards and inmates and was an especially emotional issue for the white guard force drawn from southern Illinois's rigid caste system.

While Ragenism never blatently supported racism, blacks were expected to occupy a lower caste and conduct themselves with an appropriate "Uncle Tomism." Until 1962, few black inmates held good jobs and no black employees were in positions of responsibility. Cell assignments and special details were strictly segregated.

The Muslims' definition of their situation as requiring organization, group participation, and communion challenged the basic tenets of traditional penal administration—that all inmates are equal, that no inmate speaks for any other inmate, and that an inmate must do his own time. While the Italians from Taylor Street in the 1950s might have maneuvered to obtain a good job or the best prison "hooch," they did not define the prison as a communal experience.

Early in the 1960s, Muslims began huddling together on the recreation yards, carrying on teachings, prayer, proselytizing, and other organizational activities. From the outset they attracted some of the prison's most persistent and belligerent "troublemakers." Whether troublemakers were attracted to Muslimism or whether attraction to Muslimism automatically defined an inmate as a troublemaker is difficult to resolve when posed in this way. The Muslims offered legitimacy and significance to the frustration, bitterness, and egotism of some of Stateville's most recalcitrant inmates. The officials countered by purging Muslims from their jobs, blocking their legitimate prison activities, and suppressing them whenever possible. Not surprisingly, many of the leaders ended up in segregation.

The Black Muslims surfaced as a problem for prison officials at Stateville in 1960, although a few scattered disciplinary reports identify Muslim inmates as early as 1957. An internal memorandum dated 23 March 1960 lists fifty-eight Stateville inmates as having had at some point an affiliation with Islamism, Muhammadism, or Muslimism. By 1965 the number was 175, of whom 100 were listed as still being at Stateville. On 26 July 1960 the first collective Muslim disturbance occurred within the segregation unit.

> At 2 p.m. the above date, after placing the lower east section of the Segregation on Isolation the inmates on the upper east side started a disturbance, yelling and shaking the doors to their cells. I sent officer ——— and he and captain ——— came over and went on the gallery to see what the trouble was. The inmates demanded to see Warden Ragen, claiming they were being mistreated by having their Moslem writings taken from them, also they claimed inmate ——— was the cause of all the trouble.

The organizational development of the Muslims was accompanied by a politicization of the relations between inmates and officials and among the inmates themselves. Unlike the ethnic "gangs" of the 1950s, the Muslims articulated their prison concerns in the vocabulary of political and social protest. Claiming that they were being discriminated against on the basis of race and religion, they invoked their ideology to resist "repression." In June of 1964, six Muslims in segregation presented Stateville officials with the first written inmate demands in the history of the penitentiary.

1. We demand the use of the Chapel for Islamic religious services once to two times a week.
2. We demand that Arabic books and African historical books be put on the High School curriculum.
3. We demand to purchase the Holy Quran and all other Islamic religious *periodicals*.
4. We demand the right to contact our spiritual advisors and religious ministers, particularly: Honorable Mahmoud Shawarihi, Deputy Director of the Islamic Federation of the United States and Canada.
5. We demand that a religious minister for Muhammad's Temple No. 2 be allowed to hold religious services once to two times a week in the Stateville and Joliet prison chapels.
6. We demand to have one to two meals a day cooked Kosher Stylo within the prison by one of our cooks.
7. We demand that Muslims whatever their locations be allowed to attend religious services.
8. We demand the right to say our Salates (prayers) on time at the prescribed time from five to seven times a day (together whenever and wherever a Muslim can be found).
9. We demand to attain and to purchase Muslim's newspapers and magazines.
10. We demand the right to correspond by mail with any Imam within an Islamic Capital, National or international.
11. We demand the suppression, and "*Genocide*" oppression of the Islamic religion be stopped forthwith, now, and forevermore.
12. We demand that religious persecution, intolerance and special punishment be stopped now, immediately, and forevermore.
13. We demand that any Islamic program, including "Muhammad Speaks" be added to radio-T.V. activities in Stateville and Joliet Prisons and to embrace all Penitentiaries within the State of Illinois.
14. We demand the right to purchase and attain Islamic religious

emblems and symbols as other inmates are allowed to purchase by and through their reverend, priest and rabbi.

The demands indicate the uniqueness of the Muslim movement behind the walls. They do not merely ask the officials to more faithfully carry out their duties, i.e., better food, more recreation, fairer parole decisions. These demands assert rights and freedoms inconsistent with traditional definitions of imprisonment and require a radically new relationship between the prison castes. To meet the demands would have required the administration to disregard a definition of inmates as a degraded caste that must be made to accept the inferiority of its place. Coming from inmates, especially black inmates who, particularly, were expected to "know their place," these demands challenged the Ragen *Weltanschauung* which depicted the "good inmate" as passive, obedient, humble, and morally inferior.

Shortly after the presentation of the demands, Stateville experienced its first collective violence in more than thirty years. The inmates of the segregation unit, incited by the Muslims' leadership, burned their cells, broke up their sinks and toilets, threw food and missiles at guards and embarked upon a hunger strike for a period of several days. While the insurrection was contained within the segregation unit, it introduced an era in Stateville where mass confrontation with authority became a possibility.

For the Muslims, organizing was not simply a means to achieve certain advantages in the prisons. It was an end in itself. While Muslim leaders wrote frequently to the warden that their religion demanded their obedience to authority, their organizational activities and desire for communion necessarily brought them into conflict with the traditional system of authority. On the recreation yards, the Muslims clustered together in defiance of the prisons' rules.[15] In most cases they dispersed when ordered to do so, but confrontations were not uncommon. In his reports to the warden the disciplinary captain described a pattern of defiance ranging from refusing orders to cursing, spitting at, and striking guards.

This episode [on 6 November 1965] began when Officer E. G. approached a large group of inmates who were congregated on the yard. This was the only large gathering of inmates on the yard at the time and as Mr. G. neared, he stated that he could hear small parts of a conversation, which he lists as being: "Yes I heard that they cut out their tongues last week," and "The white man wasn't anything but a devil," and "The white man was really holding the black man down." Mr. G. states that he did not know which of the inmates in the group had made the statements, however, Mr. G. states that there were several white inmates within hearing distance of this group and to prevent what could have caused a racial disturbance of some degree, he (Mr. G.) ordered the group to disperse.

The inmates in this group refused to obey Mr. G.'s order and at this point I would like to stress that all these inmates, with the exception of three, were known by this office as claiming to be followers of the Black Muslim Sect within the institution and after being brought to the Isolation Unit these three inmates claimed that they too were Black Muslims. Inmate W. informed Officer G. that he was not going to move and inmate J. then told the group that Mr. G. was the same officer who had asked him (J.) for his name and number a few days before. Then looking directly at Officer G., inmate J. stated "you're nothing but a white nigger." . . .

The Muslims were also unique among prisoner groups in their vigorous recruitment of membership. Defining themselves as a movement, they preached their doctrine on the recreation yards, on the industrial assignments, and inside the cell houses. Internal memoranda from the period (obviously collected with an eye toward the litigation) include numerous letters from inmates complaining of harassment by Muslim proselytizers.

This is in regards of a matter which I feel you should check into.

I am assigned to Tailor Shop, North Wing, working on the pocket line, I do my work as best I can, under present conditions.

My complaint is as follows:

I have two fellow inmates working on the line with myself and another inmate making the count be four (4), 3 colored fellows and myself white.

Two of these fellows are constantly casting remarks about the White man in America being a Devil and indirectly this is a threat, not only to me, but also any colored fellow that's not of the *Muslim* faith.

Twice I have prevented Inmate L. from attacking these *Muslims.*

He and I both have repeatedly requested to the floor man to move us to another line to avoid trouble.

The Black Muslims not only made demands of the Stateville administration and the Department of Public Safety, but they complained to the courts as well. By framing their grievances as violations of classic constitutional guarantees, they were able to mobilize support within the liberal establishment, particularly the Chicago Loop law firm of Jenner and Block, and the American Civil Liberties Union.

Muslim leader Thomas Cooper filed his original *pro se* suit against Warden Pate in 1962 from his segregation cell, alleging under section 1983 of the Civil Rights Act that his confinement in segregation was retribution for his religious beliefs. He claimed that he was being unconstitutionally denied access to the Quran, Muslim literature (particularly *Muhammad Speaks*) and the Muslim clergy. During the next five years of Stateville's most famous legal battle, Cooper received assistance from LaSalle Street Lawyers, the ACLU and Elijah Muhammad, who wrote to inform Cooper that he had hired an attorney named Edward Jacko "to protect the interests of Cooper and the Nation."

Cooper's original writ was dismissed by the Federal District Court for failure to state a cause of action. The ruling was affirmed by the Seventh Circuit Federal Court of Appeals.[16] But in a historic *per curiam* decision, the Supreme Court of the United States reversed the lower courts and ordered the district court to hold a trial on Cooper's complaints.[17]

The trial (held in April 1965) forced Director Ragen and Warden Pate to justify their refusal to recognize the Muslims as a religious group. On this issue they were on weak ground. They could make no rational argument for allowing Christian inmates to read the Bible but for refusing to allow Muslim inmates the Quran or for refusing Muslim inmates Arabic documents while Jewish inmates were allowed Hebrew literature.

Arguing that any concessions to the Muslims, no matter how slight, would lead to chaos within the prison, the director and warden appeared capricious and arbitrary before the courts and the public. The trial was given television news coverage and was widely reported in the press. To the inmate population, the picture of Cooper and Pate testifying against one another as equal adversaries did much to increase the Muslims' prestige and to intensify the challenge to the traditional status of prisoners.

Judge Austin's memorandum opinion, upheld on appeal,[18]

constituted a partial victory for the Muslims. Judge Austin ordered that Muslims be allowed access to the Quran, that they be allowed communication and visits with Muslim ministers, and that they be allowed to attend Muslim religious services. On the other complaints, the judge refused to allow Muslims to receive contemporary Muslim literature (like *Muhammad Speaks*) or Arabic textbooks and refused to order Cooper released from segregation.

Throughout the five years of litigation (and even afterward), Warden Pate and his captains were determined to expose the Muslims as traditional "troublemakers" who were transparently disguising their true intention to destroy the order of the prison under patently absurd claims of constitutional rights. The organization's elite denied any social or political significance to Muslim activities. The segregation rebellion of 1964 was dismissed as an attempt to get publicity in order to "embarrass and harass the administration." So concerned was the administration with public reaction that lieutenants were required to turn in their blackjacks during the trial to minimize the possibility of any claims of brutality. (They never got them back.)

The prison administration adopted the posture that any concession to the Muslims would totally undermine prison discipline. The comprehensive "Muslim file" was filled with letters from Pate to state's attorney Thomas Decker calling the latter's attention to newspapers articles from all over the country which reported unfavorably on Muslim activities on the streets or in other prisons. Letters passed along criticisms of the Muslims by other wardens, and included a resolution by the American Correctional Association urging the Muslims' suppression as well as reports of disciplinary infractions involving Muslim inmates at Stateville. Director Ragen wrote to U.S. Attorney General Ramsey Clark on 7 May 1964:

> It would be impossible for me to stress too strongly the importance of the [Cooper] case to the penitentiary system. There is absolutely no question but that the Black Muslims are dedicated to destroying discipline and authority in the prison system. Any concession is a step toward chaos.

Warden Pate answered an interrogatory in connection with *Cooper* v. *Pate* on 17 September 1964 in similar fashion:

> The prison has been fertile field for converting prisoners to the Black Muslim Sect. Their policy of Black Supremacy appeals to the non-conformists and agitators in the penal institution because they realize that their disciplinary record is so poor and they have no justification for their conduct, therefore they align themselves with an organization such as the Black Muslims and then claim because they are members or sympathizers the officials are persecuting them and that the majority of their disciplinary reports are false or exaggerated.

The Stateville administrators implored those individuals outside the prison to whom the prison had become increasingly accountable to accept their definition of the situation. The definition of the Muslims as a group unalterably opposed to prison authority apparently was held by the "professional" staff in the Office of the Criminologist, as is evident in the following memorandum reporting on a classification interview.

> During the course of classification interviews the inmate was very polite, answering most questions with "sir" and in a very quiet, responsive manner. He told me that since 1957 he has been a member of the Black Muslims, has attended the Temple regularly and has followed the precepts concerning abstinence from drinking and narcotics, as well as the dietary rules. He added, however, that he was not one of the militant persons, stated that he knew of the suit which has been filed but in his opinion nothing would come of it and it was the wrong way to act. He also stated that he knew he was in prison, that the Black Muslim religion was not accepted and that he fully intended to make the best of this, make no demands and practice whatever he felt necessary alone and bothering no one.
>
> He seems sincere in his statements but this was discussed with the State Criminologist and it was felt that if the inmate has had a seven-year connection with the Black Muslims he may well be giving lip service to his intentions or may even represent the new tack that the Muslims are to present if they intend to "pull in their horns" prior to any forthcoming senatorial investigation.

Conflict with the Muslims was always most intense in the segregation unit, where the Muslim leaders were concentrated.[19] The 1965 memorandum opinion in *Cooper* v. *Pate* only heightened the conflict between Muslims and officials. Both sides appealed the district court's ruling, and the administration continued to compile its evidence on Muslim disruptiveness. On 30 July 1965, Warden Pate wrote to the Illinois attorney general.

Through our Senior Captains I have been advised that those inmates who are followers of the Elijah Muhammeds [sic] and who adhere to the Black Muslim Sect have been subjecting our officers to the following:
Being cursed at; Threatening; Being spit upon.

There have been several instances of disobeying orders and disrespect towards the officers, insolence, etc.—the violations are relatively of the same nature. It has been increasing and is widespread throughout the institution. More and more of this information is being received daily.

I believe these incidents show the utter contempt the Black Muslims, as a whole, have for the rules and regulations of the institution. Especially the attitude towards the officers who endeavor to enforce the rules. We are of the opinion that we will have further problems with the Black Muslims after we implement Article 4 of the Judgement Order issued by Judge Austin. We feel that the tolerance of the non-followers of the Elijah Mohammeds will become more and more less tolerant of their preaching and attempting to strong-arm them into joining the movement. . . .

This information is being sent to you in order to keep your office informed of the developments which resulted due to the recent case of Cooper vs myself. I will endeavor to keep you informed of any future information I receive from our officers concerning this sect.

Cooper's own disciplinary record was obviously embellished by the administration for purposes of discrediting him with respect to his lawsuit. Submitted as "Deposition Exhibit B" in connection with *Cooper* v. *Pate* is a disciplinary record consisting of eighty-seven tickets between 26 February 1953 and 9 February 1965. Fourteen of these tickets were given out between May 1964 and February 1965 for the same offense of "contacting other inmates through the pipes in the Segregation Unit plumbing system." In order to get this information against Cooper, an officer was daily ordered to the basement of the segregation unit, where, by keeping an ear to the plumbing, he could "tap" the conversations being carried out by the inmates who emptied the water out of their commodes in order to talk to one another over the pipes.

In 1966, rumors of an imminent Muslim takeover of B house generated a considerable internal administrative correspondence. While the cell house takeover did not materialize, the Muslims did organize a hunger strike in July 1966, and continued to be sent to isolation for flouting authority, which offense included possession and distribution of contraband Muslim literature.[20]

The Muslim problem as perceived by the administration became utterly intolerable by late 1966. As if to vindicate their judgment on the Muslim issue despite the court ruling, every Muslim infraction of the rules was carefully recorded. A random sample of fifty days of disciplinary records for various years between 1946 and 1970 shows six times more "assaults on officers" in 1966 than in any other year. Also revealed is the highest number of "challenges to authority," which include assaulting officers, throwing feces, attempting escape, breaking up cells, insubordination, demanding to be escorted to isolation, and violating a privilege denial (see table 9). That 1966 was actually the most violent year in Stateville's history is not consistent with the recall of any informant or any other corroborating evidence. There are no filed accident reports of guards being seriously injured. All administrators and guards today agree that violence did not reach alarming proportions at Stateville till 1969. Yet the "assaults on officers" in 1970, possibly the most explosive year in the history of Stateville, are only one-fifth of the 1966 number. The most likely explanation for the wave of assaults in 1966 is that a change in the reporting system occurred. These crime statistics were "manufactured" either consciously or unconsciously in the aftermath of the Cooper trial as a response to the intervention of the courts on behalf of the Muslims.

After 1966, the Muslim problem subsided somewhat, although as late as 1968 the assistant warden of the old prison wrote to Warden Pate that the Muslims "were up to something big" and that he had therefore "locked up" their six main leaders. Muslim disputes with the administration and litigation with respect to literature and diet, and other matters continues to the present.[21]

Ironically, Elijah Muhammad did not send a Muslim minister to the Joliet inmates and was even slow in responding to their request for one. One Stateville captain maintains that "the word came down in 1968 following the [Martin Luther] King riots from Elijah Muhammad to follow all the rules and regulations and not make waves." Perhaps at a time when the Muslims on the streets were moving to consolidate their economic gains, the prison mosques were becoming something of an embarrassment. In any case it is not uncommon today to hear guards refer to Muslims as "some of our best inmates."[22] One industrial supervisor stated that he "couldn't run his shop if it weren't for the Muslims."

While the Muslims' activities undoubtedly affected the atmosphere of the entire prison, especially relations among the black inmates, their impact upon the day-to-day life of the prison must be placed in proper perspective. Muslim organizing often went on covertly, out of the sight of the majority of inmates. Of an inmate population in excess of three thousand, the Muslims probably never numbered more than one hundred, and many of their most dramatic challenges to authority were concentrated within the segregation unit. Only rumors of rebellion inside the unit filtered out to the general population.

The average white inmate saw perhaps a half-dozen or a dozen Muslim inmates in his cell house or huddling together on the recreation yards. The grapevine carried the word from time to time that the Muslims were "organizing something big" and going to the courts. The racial situation at the prison among the inmates persisted as it had for decades. Cells were segregated and the races were kept separate on the tiers.[23] On the assignments, blacks and whites worked on different work crews. The isolation punishment cells were completely segregated. When moving through the prison in their lines, the whites always paired up together at the front of the lines and the blacks fell into place behind. Whites continued to hold the best jobs in the prison, particularly in the administration building, where the few black inmates were usually employed as janitors. While there were occasional mutterings of "white devil" and occasional instances of blacks breaking into the front of the lines, racial confrontation per se was avoided at least until 1969.

The whites and blacks organized themselves into separate social systems, mixing together only on the ball field, in infrequent work situations, or in black market business deals. Social relations among the whites continued to take into account the offense for which the prisoner had been committed, the murderers and thieves conceiving of themselves as an elite group from which "rape-o's," child molestors, and stool pigeons were excluded.

The solidly white guard force was not for the most part openly racist although white inmates recall that when the blacks were not around the guards spoke of "having walked some nigger." According to white and black inmate informants, a few of the guards wore Ku Klux Klan rings, but they were a small and insignificant faction.[24] Stateville has never generated the kinds of complaints about gross brutalities that have arisen in other penitentiaries, though the captains and lieutenants were never reluctant to "fight" an inmate who threatened trouble. An insightful white informant from the period estimates that one such "fight" would occur each week. The precipitating event was most usually an inmate threat, verbal or otherwise, to an officer. Lieutenants and captains felt relatively unrestrained in subduing the inmate, usually in his cell, at the isolation unit, or in detention hospital. Looking back on the pre-1969 period, many of the captains speak openly about the "good old days" when they could "teach an inmate some respect" without fear of the courts or of the censorship of civilian outsiders.

Thus, between 1961 and 1970, Stateville experienced a period of limited change. The loss of a warden who could command absolute authority, the loss of local autonomy, heightened race consciousness among blacks, and the penetration of legal norms exposed severe strains in the authoritarian system. The incapacity of the Pate regime to adapt to the changing relationship of the prison to the outside made the violent changes after 1970 all the more sudden and cataclysmic.

II The Search for a New Equilibrium

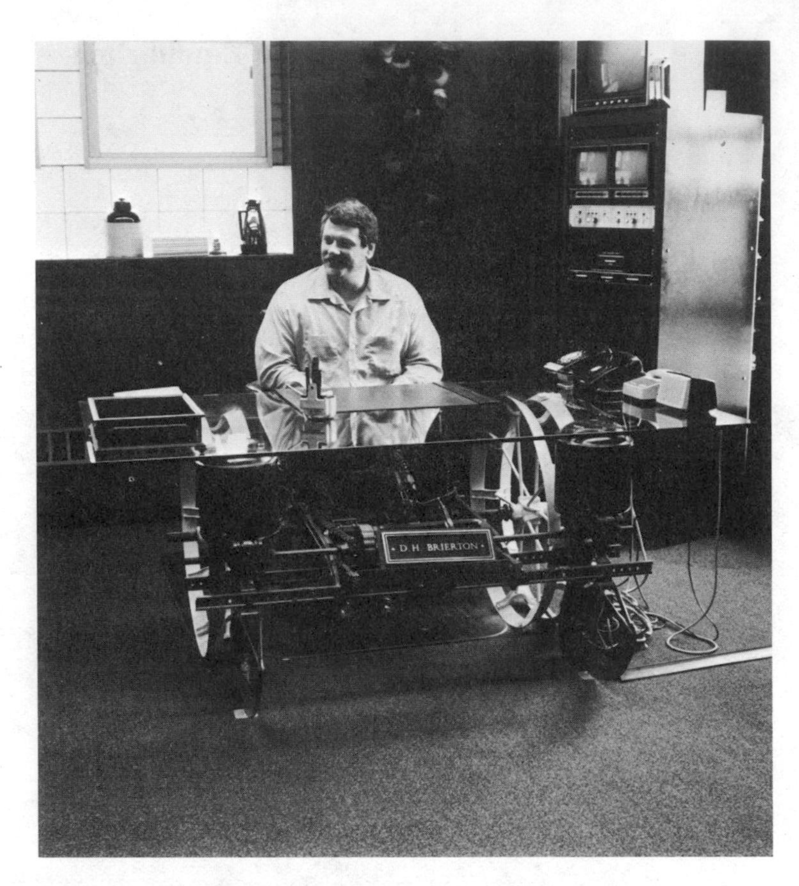

Warden David Brierton

4 Emergence of a Professional Administration, 1970–75

The history of adult correctional services in Illinois reflects the maintenance of essentially independent, parochially operated institutions, a phenomenon which has given rise to excessively provincial attitudes in the administration of our facilities. Much of this can be blamed on the fact that, heretofore, we have existed as a relatively subordinate adjunct to the Departments of State whose salient responsibilities were other than the administration of correctional services. The 76th General Assembly acknowledged that the rehabilitation of criminal offenders could not become an effective reality while functioning as a satellite enterprise, and thus created the new Department of Corrections.

John Twomey, *State of Illinois, Department of Corrections, Five Year Plan: Adult Division*

Stateville's transformation from a patriarchal organization based upon traditional authority to a rational-legal bureaucracy was powered by three main sources. The first was the creation of the Illinois Department of Corrections, which has centralized specialized resources and ultimate authority in a burgeoning and professionally oriented central administration located in Springfield. The central office has virtually eliminated local autonomy by usurping the prerogative of formulating policy, by promulgating comprehensive rules and regulations, and by demanding ever increasing reports on more and more details of day-to-day activities at the local prisons.

The second source was the emergence of a highly educated elite occupying the top administrative positions. This elite does not share the homogeneity of the guard force, nor does it view Stateville as an institution with an independent moral value over and above its instrumental function in the criminal justice system. It has brought to the prison the values and attitudes of the American university and embodies within it an ethos of public service. While it is true that under the "rehabilitative" regimes of Pate's two immediate successors, John Twomey and

Joseph Cannon, bureaucratization was stimulated only marginally, the proliferation of administrative tasks and positions held by those with university credentials laid the groundwork for the explicit bureaucratization that has been carried out by Warden David Brierton since December 1975.

The third pressure toward bureaucratization has come from the injection into the organization of a large number of civilians filling specialized treatment roles. The presence of teachers and counselors on a day-to-day basis at Stateville led to an administrative and moral division of labor which more narrowly specified duties and responsibilities of the entire staff. Furthermore, the civilians' persistent criticisms of the patriarchal regime ultimately elicited greater attention to the processes of decision and rule making.

The Demise of Local Autonomy

With Ragen gone, political intervention into the Illinois prisons (but only at the highest levels) was resumed. Governor Richard Ogilvie, a Republican, took office in January 1969. Ross Randolph, a Democrat, resigned as director of public safety and was replaced by a downstate Republican sheriff (as acting director). The new governor appointed an important backer and member of his transition team, thirty-three-year-old Peter Bensinger, scion of one of the wealthiest Republican families in Illinois, to head the Youth Commission (a subdepartment within the Department of Public Safety) and to chair a task force to review the entire penal system.

While the task force was composed mainly of Illinois prison people (among them Warden Frank Pate), it also included many of the treatment people in the system, like state criminologist Arthur Huffman and Menard sociologist John Twomey. In addition, academic specialists were invited to serve on the task force. Norval Morris (University of Chicago Law School), Meryl Alexander and Tom Eynon (both of Southern Illinois University) all participated. After a year-long study the task force called for a total revamping of Illinois's adult and juvenile prisons, the establishment of community-based facilities, and the reorganization of Illinois' juvenile and adult prison facilities into a separate Department of Corrections.

Ogilvie chose Peter Bensinger to be the first director of the new department, which came into being in 1970. If Ross Randolph's appointment to Public Safety came as a shock to Stateville after Ragen's departure, it was at least softened by the fact that Randolph was "a prison man" with thirty years in Illinois prisons. Bensinger, however, was young, Yale-educated, and a former European sales manager for the Brunswick Corporation. Stateville staff recognized in his appointment the triumph of liberalism that Ragen had predicted and for so long forestalled.

Bensinger took over a prison system that had been physically, fiscally, and organizationally deteriorating for a decade. The fiscal base was poor. Salaries of all staff were terribly low. Turnover in 1969 was at an all-time high. The inmates were becoming more rebellious with the influx of Chicago street gangs which were carving up the prisons into turfs, carrying on gang rivalries, and intimidating the staffs.

In the course of the next three years, the Bensinger administration created a powerful, active, central Springfield administration. Personnel assigned to the Springfield central office increased from 71 in 1965, to 191 in 1972.[1] The fiscal base of the prison system increased from $56 million to $79 million. Salaries for guards rose almost 30 percent. Federal grants to the department multiplied from $1.7 million in fiscal year 1971 to $5.6 million in 1974 to $10.6 million in 1976.

Bensinger's reform program, which relied upon the advice of academic experts, American Correctional Association standards, and the treatment people in his own department, demonstrated primary concern with increasing the "respect," "dignity," and "status" of the prisoner. Almost at once Bensinger doubled (to $50) the "gate money" given to an inmate when he left prison. Subsequently, he doubled (to two) the number of letters that inmates were permitted to mail each week, and he virtually eliminated censorship of outgoing mail. For the first time, inmates of Illinois prisons were allowed to order *Playboy*. Sunday visiting was initiated, and all prisons were ordered to release inmates from their cells in the evening during the warm weather for night yard.

Interests outside the prison were cultivated. Bensinger sponsored entertainment programs for the inmates: Peter, Paul and Mary, Marcel Marceau, and many black musical groups. The introduction of college courses sponsored by Northern Illinois University, Lewis College, Joliet Junior College, and Northwestern University was facilitated. The director cooperated with the black civil rights group Operation Push, and permitted its representative, Dorothy Mason (over the protest of many of the Ragen people), regular visits with as many inmates as wished to see her. The new director formed strong ties with the academic community, particularly with Norval Morris. Under Bensinger's personal authorization the first stage of my own research was carried out at Stateville during the summer of 1972.

Bensinger also placed outsiders on the staffs of the local prisons. One of his earliest decisions was to hire civilian counselors. In addition, civilians were for the first time hired as teachers rather than as educational administrators. Group therapy was implemented by contracting for the services of outside psychologists and social workers.

The director of the Department of Corrections cultivated the press as Ragen had done in earlier years as warden of Stateville. Bensinger institutionalized this relationship by the full-time appointment of an information officer who regularly prepared and distributed press releases on happenings in the department. The results in general were very successful; press coverage was generally favorable.[2] The highly visible reforms, coupled with personal charisma and outstanding public relations, contributed to Bensinger's election as president of the American Association of Directors of Correction and smoothed the way for his later political career.[3] The fact that in 1970 Bensinger even saw prison work as a potential springboard into statewide elective office is a comment on the prison's changing position in mass society.

Contrary to the staff's view of Stateville's mission as unique, Bensinger issued directives which applied with equal force to all Illinois prisons. Assistant Director Bud Monahan was frequently criticized for reversing Stateville administrators on matters of employees' discipline. Even when the central office agreed with the institutions on a disciplinary matter, guards were increasingly disposed to take their cases before the Civil Service Commission. Relations between guards and administration became increasingly subject to written rules and rational authority. Some top guards believed that the institution had lost its authority to discipline its own staff members. Old-time "Ragenites" argued that without such authority it would be impossible to control the inmates.

To critics, the Illinois prisons seemed at long last to be catching up with those of the rest of the country. To old-time institution people, Bensinger was "permissive" and his changes left no doubt that he was "for the inmate." To the inmates, Bensinger was, in the words of one Stateville administrator, "a savior who would free them." Expectations soared. Inmates began to exploit a split between the liberal Bensinger and the conservative "Ragenites" at Stateville. Stateville guards and administrators were told by inmates that they were acting contrary to the director's orders and philosophy. The central office increasingly was defined by Stateville staff as an outside force meddling with something they didn't know anything about. Particular hostility was leveled against Bud Monahan, who, because he had risen from the Youth Commission, was presumed to know nothing about adult maximum security prisons. There was widespread cynicism about the competence of college-educated "professionals" and "so-called experts."

Furthermore, the liberal reforms themselves contained contradictions and limitations. Inmates in the Illinois prisons were not a monolithic group. There was more that divided than united them according to their own definition of the situation. Liberal regulations that attempted to ameliorate the intensity of authoritarian control may have reduced suffering for some segments of the prisoner population while increasing it for a substantial number of other inmates, who became easy prey for aggressive and gang-oriented inmates. All of Illinois prisons suffered from the lockups, administrative disruption, and deteriorating physical conditions.

A special committee headed by an eminent Chicago attorney, Maurice Wexler, was appointed by Governor Ogilvie at the request of Bensinger to draft the nation's first Unified Code of Corrections.[4] The code provided a legislative mandate for a separate Department of Corrections (which, as we have seen, had come into being in 1970) with an Adult Division and a Juvenile Division each to be administered by an assistant director. The fact that the prison had become less of a peripheral institution and one that was now to be tied more closely to society's core institutional system was recognized in the provision setting up an Adult Advisory Board and a Juvenile Advisory Board, each composed of nine persons with "demonstrated interest in and knowledge of adult and juvenile correctional work" to be appointed by the governor.[5] Since its inception the Adult Advisory Board has been dominated by academic specialists like Norval Morris, Hans Mattick, and Tom Eynon.

The code provided direct impetus for the bureaucratization of the new department. Provision was made for staff training and development, for a separate program of research and long-range planning, and for a grievance mechanism whereby the prisoners could complain of their institutional treatment. Most important was the requirement in several provisions that the department maintain written records.

> The Department shall maintain records of the examination, assignment, transfer, discipline of committed persons and what grievances, if any, are made in each of its institutions, facilities, and programs. The record shall contain the name of the persons involved, the time, date, place and purpose of the procedure, the decision and the basis therefore, and any review of the decision made.[6]

The code went far in inaugurating a new relationship between prisoners and prison authorities. In the place of absolute authority and unreviewable discretion the new Unified Code of Corrections announced a more contractual, abstract, and legalistic relationship between the prisoners and their wardens. Various provisions made it clear that the prisoners were entitled to a certain standard of living conditions, medical care, disciplinary procedures and work opportunities. The code provided a rule of law to which prisoners could appeal the decisions of their immediate superiors. This amounted to a redefinition of the statuses of the institutional participants.

The code states that the "Department shall promulgate Rules and Regulations in conformity with this Code." Bensinger's Springfield staff drafted a comprehensive volume of administrative regulations to implement the code provisions. Three meals a day and a mattress were to be provided for inmates in isolation. A three-man disciplinary committee was to replace the traditional authority of the captain to run the disciplinary court. Another committee took over the assignment captain's role in making work assignments. The administrative regulations provided standards for censorship, allowed for access to law books, and prescribed conditions in isolation. The unprincipled and unreviewable discretion of the past was for the first time narrowed by rule making.

While Bensinger participated in drafting the Unified Code of Corrections and supervised the writing of the Administrative Regulations, his administration was far from successful in implementing them. In part, this failure is attributable to Bensinger's inexperience and the brevity of his tenure as director. While Bensinger went far in casting major policies for the department, he often deferred to the judgment of his wardens when it came to deciding whether, when, and how a particular reform could be implemented. Having no intimate experience with daily prison routine, the director of the Department of Corrections had no standard by which to judge whether a lockup was necessary, whether gang leaders were too dangerous to be left in the population, or whether employee morale was so low as to jeopardize a new program. Sensitive to the deeply imbedded resistance to change among large segments of the staff, Bensinger did not sweep out the old-line employees, who he sometimes feared might actively mobilize their resistance.

By 1972, when the Administrative Regulations were completed (the code was formally passed in July), the familiar gap between formalized rules and working procedures became apparent. The rules were simply not followed. Employees in the mail office, for example, continued to operate much as they always had.[7] In some instances the staff simply found strategies to circumvent the rules. Instead of providing an inmate a hearing within seventy-two hours of an alleged disciplinary violation, new forms of "pretrial detention" were developed at Stateville. In clear violation of the letter and spirit of the rules, inmates "under investigation" were placed indefinitely and without hearings in lockup.

Thus, the first reform administration of Peter Bensinger created inexorable pressure toward bureaucratization. It did so by strictly limiting local autonomy through the strengthening of central authority and by establishing universalistic criteria against which administrative action could be evaluated. These developments did not all occur at once, nor were they implemented without considerable strains at the local level. The Bensinger reforms completed the undermining of the authoritarian system of personal dominance but did not replace it with a viable model of administration at the local level.

The Separation of Administration from Custody

Frustration had mounted continuously for Frank Pate since Ragen's departure from the Department of Public Safety in 1965. First he had to contend with the activities of the Muslims and, beginning in 1969, with the rebellious Chicago gangs. Second, he had to contend with pressures emanating from the increasingly active and policy-oriented Springfield office. Pate resented the fact that Randolph had eliminated Stateville's prerogative to transfer inmates at will to Menard, had discontinued the use of "pink slips" as a disciplinary mechanism for employees, had recognized the union, had permitted talking in the dining room, and had relaxed the dress code.

Pate's greatest frustration came from having to take into account outside forces sharply critical of Stateville. The once cozy relationship with the John Howard Association broke down as the leadership in that organization passed to more militant individuals. The academic community, minority groups, and, most important, the courts were attacking him. He was tired and disgusted after losing the *Cooper* case. Each victory stimulated more lawsuits. Each new attack seemed to threaten the traditional basis of his authority still further.

The appointment of Bensinger as Director of the new Department of Corrections placed new strains on the warden's role. Pate had been invited to participate in the 1969 task force. Having no more than a high school education and having spent most of his adult life at Stateville, it is not unlikely that he was uncomfortable in conference with the Yale-educated Bensinger and with the highly educated treatment people like Leo Meyer, John Twomey, and Arthur Huffman (not to mention Meryl Alexander, Norval Morris, and Karl Menninger).

Bensinger, anxious to establish his credibility as a "reformer" with the press and the minority community, pushed a whole series of reforms on Pate that violated "the way things had been done" at Stateville for decades. All of his reforms were unpalatable to Pate. To his closest aides and friends, Frank Pate admitted that he could no longer handle the job, and in the fall of 1970 he resigned.

Director Bensinger chose John Twomey to become the new warden of the Stateville/Joliet complex. Twomey had come up through the system as a prison sociologist at Menard and had served Bensinger briefly as chief of program services for the new department. He was an "intellectual" in prison circles, holding a master's degree and having completed all but his dissertation for the Ph.D. degree in the Department of Sociology at Southern Illinois University. At the time of his appointment he was thirty-two years old.

While he was without a firm conceptual model for administering Stateville, Twomey did adhere roughly to a human relations model of formal organization. He believed that most problems that emerged in the prison were caused by failure in communication, and he stressed nothing so much as "talking out" problems. He believed that the problems of a prison were the problems of people. He interpreted the challenges to effective administration in terms of personal difficulties in "gaining acceptance," "establishing his image," and "maintaining credibility." Perhaps there exists no more poignant illustration of Twomey's management style than Bulletin no. 206, issued 14 December 1971.

> During the past month this institution has been officially visited by members of the state legislature and various state departments who have the responsibility to inspect facilities under the Department of Corrections.
>
> In every instance, these individuals have been sharply critical of the lack of cleanliness and good housekeeping in all areas. I have been aware of this problem myself over the past year and I have tried suggesting, hinting, encouraging, chiding, and complimenting—all to no avail. I am left with no alternative but to order that proper standards of cleanliness be maintained and to enforce that order.

The human relations approach was not inconsistent with the world view of the old Ragenites.[8] They agreed with Twomey that, to accomplish goals, you had to "win over the staff" and "earn the confidence" of key individuals. Day-to-day management of the prison required the judgment of experience and intuition. They held to a view of Stateville as a unique mysterious institution whose ways might only be revealed to an outsider in the course of years.

Pate's resignation left Assistant Warden Vern Revis as the titular head of the remaining Ragenites. Revis continued to wield enormous personal influence over the custodial ranks, but the control of the institution was clearly passing to the new generation of college-educated "civilians."[9] While the remaining Ragenites did not actively subvert the new reform program by precipitating confrontation and violence, they did resist every liberalization of the rules and persistently presented the situation at Stateville in a way that defined change as impossible. "How can we bring in programs when the place is going to blow any day?" "How can we allow all these legal groups in here when the turnover among guards is so high and the manpower situation so critical that we can't even get inmates out of the cell houses?" The Ragenites actually did not see any possible way to bring about change without "giving the place away." If a change was implemented without disastrous consequences, the Ragenites would predict that the next inmate demand would certainly precipitate disaster. It is only by understanding their commitment to the old authoritarian system and to the definition of the prison as constantly being on the verge of collapse that one can understand the impact this group has had on the prison since 1970.

Twomey's appointment as "chief administrator" was traumatic for the custody staff. In the beginning, rumors abounded that he was a radical from Berkeley who was going to fire most of the staff. The young warden's early actions did little to allay the fears. With Norval Morris standing beside him as guest speaker at a Stateville high school graduation ceremony shortly after his appointment, Twomey announced to the inmates, "I am here to serve you." This statement rapidly reverberated around the institution reinforcing the opinion that the new administration was "pro-inmate" and "anti-staff."

Twomey initiated an institutional radio program in which he answered inmates' questions and spoke of his "philosophy." He encouraged inmates to correspond with him, at once ratifying their status as legitimate participants in the organization and undermining the chain of command. Twomey advocated a rehabilitative ideology which defined "inmates as men" and held that they were "redeemable." The Ragenites were much more cynical. They viewed inmates as a separate species and saw their job as carrying out a holding action for society.

The single decision made by Twomey which most embittered the custodial force was to cease coercing inmates who refused voluntarily to be "walked" to the isolation unit. With gang violence increasing inside the prison, Twomey decided that if an inmate would not go peaceably it was a mistake to drag him forcibly off his assignment, and especially from his cell in front of his gang associates and other inmates. Instead, Twomey ordered that such a recalcitrant inmate would be "dead-locked" in his cell the next time he returned to it and kept there indefinitely until he decided voluntarily to go to isolation. The custodial force saw this as the epitome of Bensinger/Twomey "permissiveness." They argued that if they were not given free rein to coerce a belligerent inmate to go to isolation, their authority would be totally undermined. This was an especially salient issue for the lieutenants, who operated as the police force within the penitentiary.

While the upper-echelon guards were alienated by the "no fight" policy, the rank-and-file guards were angered by Twomey's decision to take away their discretionary authority to have an inmate walked from an assignment at any time. Under Ragen the staff had operated according to a strict caste system. In principle, no member of the staff was questioned by any other for his handling of an inmate. This meant that if any guard wanted an inmate walked from his assignment for any reason, he need merely call a lieutenant and the inmate would be walked; the guard's judgment would not be questioned.

It was the increasing number of confrontations between groups of gang members and guards on the yard and on the assignments, threatening to make Stateville another Attica, that prompted Twomey's order. In the future, guards would not have absolute authority to have an inmate walked. The decision would be made in fact, and not just nominally, by lieutenants and captains. Eventually the emerging union (discussed at length in chapter 7) forced Twomey to rescind this order; but while it was in effect—and even after it was reversed—it served to mobilize the rank and file against the warden.

Twomey never overcame what he defined as his "image problem." He became progressively withdrawn from his staff. For advice, he turned to "civilians" (the nonuniformed staff). In place of the daily captains' meetings, Twomey set up his own kitchen cabinet. He relied particularly on an administrative assistant, Frank Mueller (formerly of the Youth Division) and on his long-time friend and colleague from Menard days, Leo Meyer (a psychologist). For the captains who once made and interpreted policy, access to the warden became increasingly restricted. The formulation of policy became increasingly separate from its implementation.

There was no table of organization nor line of authority which reflected what was happening. Where authority was vested, it was without responsibility. There were four or five assistant wardens. All but George Stampar were holdovers from Ragen days. Each assistant warden carved out his own idiosyncratic role. When a staff member needed to have a decision made, he could go to any one of these assistant wardens and try to gain approval.

The establishment of a kitchen cabinet meant that for the first time in Stateville's history, the administration and the custodial force were distinct. Stampar (superintendent of the minimum security unit), Daniel Bosse, Mueller, Meyer, and (special counselor) Warren Wolls were probably the most influential men around Twomey, and none of them had been prison guards. All held college degrees, and Stampar, Meyer, and Wolls had master's degrees. A definite split emerged within the organization between the old-timers who went to assistant wardens Vernon Revis, Lewis Lence, or Ernie Morris with any problems, and the new civilian employees who looked to Twomey for leadership. The situation was fragmented further by the counselors' alienation from both custody and administration.

After the "I'm here to serve you" speech, Twomey gained some popularity with the inmates, who were quick to exploit the situation. They would tell the counselors, teachers, and other outsiders that the old Ragenites were subverting the new liberal program. This interpretation of the situation was immediately presented to me by the gang leaders when I entered the prison in June 1972. Inmates would sometimes belligerently confront the custodial staff with the argument that their action was illegal according to Springfield or Warden Twomey. All the actors in the situation braced themselves for a split between treatment-oriented and custody-oriented staff, and the self-fulfilling prophesy was set in motion.

Twomey was labeled "Mr. Effective Immediately" by the inmates. Scores of bulletins were issued from his office but were seldom implemented. Often this was not because the custody staff were in open rebellion but because they were too disorganized to carry out directives. From the assistant wardens down to the line officers, job responsibilities were not clearly spelled out. People were still operating by tradition. The old tradition bearers would pass along by word of mouth the way things had to be done, and this is how they *were* done, regardless of sporadic bulletins to the contrary. Line officers continued to act as they had always acted and to take their orders from the same people.

Staff demoralization and disorganization resulted in the demise of security within the prison. Violence escalated. The last escape from behind Stateville's walls had occurred in 1942, when Roger Touhy and his cohorts commandeered a truck and used a ladder to go over the wall. Between 1971 and 1972, four inmates escaped from Stateville, three walked out together in disguise through the front gate, and one left in a metal cabinet with a shipment of furniture. The old Ragenites saw their world collapsing around them.

The disorganization was so great that the capacity to complete basic tasks was reduced. Inmates did not get showers; the food areas did not get cleaned; lawyers were made to wait hours because tickets could not get delivered. The following reply by the special counselor to an inmate grievance illustrates the organizational crisis.

> To. Benjamin F.
>
> This memo is to inform you that Warden Twomey received your note requesting a personal interview that you sent him on Feb. 20. Working out of the Warden's office in the area of inmate related problems, he asked that I see you and try to assist you with this problem. On March 1, I sent a ticket to interview you at the Sociologist's Office. When you did not arrive, I called B House only to learn that there were insufficient correctional officers available to accompany you to the Sociologist's Office for our interview. Therefore, I am unable to help you at the present time. If your problem is not resolved, I will be returning from my vacation on March 12. If you wish my assistance at that time, please let me know.

The irony of the Bensinger-Twomey triumph at Stateville is that the rehabilitative ideal—which was supposed to redefine the inmate's status—resulted in more violence, worse general living conditions, and fewer programmatic opportunities. The food was worse. There was more fear, more violence, and more sexual assault. After the brief flirtation with night yard was ended (following a melee on the ball diamond in July 1971—to be described below, p. 163), inmates did more cell time under the liberal regime than under the conservative regime. The deterioration of the organization led to a weakening of security and ultimately to the lengthy lockups that upset any possibility of programming within the institution. The school completely ceased to function. In 1969, under Pate, the school had had approximately 125 students. Even with all the new civilian teachers available, between 1970 and 1974 Stateville processed no more than forty enrolled students at any one time. Insufficient manpower and poor administration resulted in the school's frequently being shut down completely.

The human relations model was not working. Twomey and his custodial staff were locked in a continuous struggle. The civilian counselors identified with the inmates. Inmates increasingly exploited the split between custody and treatment in their communications with the press and other outside interest groups.

By the summer of 1972, violence was becoming more frequent and the gang situation had never seemed more menacing. Fearing a riot, Bensinger replaced the "liberal" superintendent George Stampar with Vern Revis and charged Revis with responsibility for the day-to-day management of Stateville. Twomey remained the top administrator of the Stateville/Joliet prisons, but the change in personnel ratified his increasing commitment to the bureaucratic duties of his office and to managing relationships with the outside. A clear crisis for the organization's administration was posed: the Ragenites could not manage relationships with the media, the courts, and outside interest groups, to whom they appeared to be caricatures from a James Dean movie. But the rehabilitation-oriented reformers had not been able to find a strategy to control the prison organization firmly enough to maintain safety and security and basic organizational necessities.

Bensinger had expected to continue his tenure as director of corrections under Ogilvie's second term as governor of Illinois, but Daniel Walker's upset victory over the incumbent in the 1972 elections precipitated Bensinger's resignation in December. There followed a period of almost six months of drift in the Department of Corrections while the governor strived to have a director approved by the legislature. Walker first nominated

David Fogel, then director of the Minnesota Department of Corrections. Young, bearded, liberal, with a Ph.D. in criminology,[10] Fogel appeared the epitome of a flaming radical to the Stateville staff. Unlike Bensinger, he was also a professional commentator and administrator in the criminal justice system. It was with some degree of satisfaction that the staff followed the rejection of his nomination by the Illinois legislature, only ostensibly because of his controversial liberal record in corrections (but more probably because of a struggle between Walkerites and Daleyites over the Regional Transit Authority). Walker's second nomination—this time accepted—for director was Alyn Sielaff, Pennsylvania's commissioner of corrections, who also represented the new generation of professional correctional administrators.[11]

Sielaff brought to Illinois a "corporate management model" in an attempt to apply private-sector administration theory to prisons. Great emphasis was placed upon modern management techniques and tables of organization which were actually meaningful. He dismissed the medical model (which regards inmates as "sick" and in need of "treatment") as naive. Whereas Bensinger was ill trained to interfere with administrative decisions concerning day-to-day operations of the prison, Sielaff and his talented assistant director, David Brierton, were experienced prison administrators not hesitant about questioning the judgment of the local administrators.

The corporate model is highly centralized. Both authority and responsibility are concentrated in Springfield. Where the Bensinger administration had been content to formulate and issue directives, the Sielaff administration required that administrative responsibility be focused, and demanded feedback and quantitative evaluations. Assistants to the director were placed in charge of security programs and clinical services for all the institutions. The administration emerged as a very highly centralized line organization, thereby continuing the accelerated trend toward centralization and bureaucratization.

At the time Sielaff assumed office, Stateville was on lockup. The lockup had begun on 30 April 1973 (after a rumble between two gangs, the Disciples and the Stones—see p. 165 below), and had still not been dissolved by the fall. Twomey was weary of his clashes with the union and frustrated by the continuous cycle of violence and lockup. Neither he nor Superintendent Revis had any strategy to end the lockup. They had come to see the situation as impossible.[12]

Twomey resigned in the early fall 1973 to become chief federal marshal for the Northern District of Illinois and was replaced at Stateville[13] by Joseph Cannon, a former assistant to David Fogel in Minnesota. Cannon's background was in social work.[14] Previous to the Minnesota position he had been the director of corrections in Kentucky and Maryland. In both states it is said that he was fired when he advocated policies more liberal than the political situation would tolerate.

With Stateville still on lockup Cannon approached his job as warden cautiously, spending the first six months getting acquainted with the entire staff.[15] He consistently deferred to the custodial elite, accepting their definition of the situation: that Stateville was tense and potentially explosive, that there was a critical shortage of manpower, that security be given primacy, that there was a dangerous gang problem, that central office demands for change were naive and could be "waited out," and that any concessions to treatment would exacerbate the already grave morale problem among the staff.

The demands being made by Springfield were for positive action. The central office reiterated that Stateville must become "program-oriented." It must develop tables of organization, lines of authority and accountability. It must meet deadlines of all sorts imposed by Brierton. Most important, it must adhere to the Administrative Regulations.

Springfield abolished the Stateville isolation unit entirely and made several personnel changes. At one point, Brierton shifted around the entire administrative staff. The most important change left the warden with only two assistant wardens—one in charge of operations and the other in charge of custody.[16] Revis was relieved of all authority and was given a staff position as security adviser, and George Stampar was made an administrative assistant to the warden. Increasingly the prison was being run from Springfield. Each Springfield action increased resentment and lowered morale. More than ever, the Stateville administration was characterized by reaction—"What crisis should we deal with today?"

While a table of organization was developed in response to the incessant demands from Assistant Director Brierton, the table was not followed. Revis continued to be regarded as a warden, was called "warden" around the institution, and acted as he had always done. The same was true for Stampar and for the chief guard. It was the liberal Cannon who unwittingly emerged as the key impediment to change.

Cannon, like his predecessor, had little interest in administration per se. Trained as a social worker, his orientation, like Twomey's, was toward solving personal problems. He had little understanding or interest in budgets. His greatest strength as an administrator was his warm, personable style. Within a few months he was very well liked. He was open with staff and with outsiders.

Staff meetings were held almost daily. Twice a week the captains attended, and on the other days there was a fluid group of participants. It was common for outsiders like myself to be invited to sit in and participate at staff meetings. Typically those meetings had no agenda. Anyone could raise whatever topic was on his mind. Discussion would drift from what to do about the used tractor on the farm, to a particularly notorious troublemaker who was trying to manipulate his way out of segregation, to the week's grievances. Talk shifted aimlessly. So informal were the staff meetings that I was invariably asked my opinion on most issues.

At almost every meeting there was time reserved for an attack upon the Springfield office. The problem, according to the participants, was that Springfield just didn't understand what was involved in running a maximum security joint. None of the Springfield people had had experience in a place like Stateville. The demands being placed upon Stateville were said to be "unrealistic" and "naive."

Like Twomey, Cannon possessed no "program" for Stateville. He had no *strategy* for reducing the violence or for improving morale. He saw his main task as "holding the place together" and "building morale" in the face of pressures from inmates, courts, and central office. He spoke of "setting a tone." At one session Cannon explained to Brierton that he would wait before making many of the changes desired by Springfield until he had more than 50 percent of the staff with him. Brierton dryly responded by asking whether he would take a survey.

On 6 December 1974, Warden Cannon was abruptly reassigned to a position in the Department of Corrections Field

Services. Brierton, still assistant director of the Department of Corrections, assumed direction of Stateville and told the staff that he expected to remain several months until the situation was stabilized. Within a month, however, he decided that the problems at Stateville were so great that they required his full-time attention, and he gave up his position as assistant director.

The thirty-seven-year-old Brierton had for several years been the "rising star" of the Illinois correctional system,[17] having worked his way up from guard at the Cook County jail to become one of the most powerful and respected prison people in Illinois. Brierton's first assignment in the state system was to oversee the construction and opening of the juvenile institution at Valley View, which soon emerged without question as the best youth institution in the state. From there, Bensinger tapped Brierton to rescue the juvenile penal facility at Sheridan, where a scandal had erupted over the use of thorazine in behavior control.[18] In the course of the next year Brierton cleaned up Sheridan both by reducing the population and by instituting numerous concrete reforms. Thereafter, he discussed with Director Bensinger the possibility of managing Stateville or Pontiac. Before assigning Brierton that responsibility, the director arranged for him a six-month leave of absence at the Center for Criminal Studies at Harvard University Law School. There Brierton attended Lloyd Ohlin's classes and furthered the education (B.A.) which he had received as a part-time student at Chicago State University.

It was difficult to assess the impact of the Brierton regime at the time I completed my fieldwork (February 1975), since he had only been at the institution three months. In that brief time six out of nine department heads resigned or were fired.[19] Many more personnel shakeups appeared likely.[20] Brierton immediately introduced sophisticated management techniques and demanded that his assistant wardens study and implement them. He moved, of course, with considerable support from Director Sielaff.

Brierton sought to develop a task-oriented administration, keyed to identifying problems and finding solutions. In a manner reminiscent of Ragen he began his administration with a complete physical rehabilitation of the prison. The cell houses and tunnels were painted, here and there with graphic designs. The long central table in the visiting room was replaced by individual tables. The employees' dining room was remodeled.

No action is more indicative of his task and problem-solving orientation than the abolition of isolation in the fall of 1974, while he was assistant director of corrections. This decision stunned the Stateville custody force. They were convinced that discipline could not be maintained without isolation. By contrast, Brierton argued that throwing six inmates into a cramped cell, where it was likely that one or more would be beaten and raped, was not sound prison management. The changed rules provided that if an inmate broke a minor rule he would lose a privilege (telephone, yard, commissary). If an inmate made himself a serious threat to others and was found guilty at a disciplinary hearing, he would be placed in segregation for at least thirty days. All segregated inmates would be in single cells no different from normal cells. Television would be allowed. The effort was not to punish in order to preserve the moral order but to maintain control through restraint and social defense.

Brierton's main emphasis was upon building a modern organization. The numerous meetings were discontinued. Instead of meeting with captains, Brierton met with department heads (food, medical, recreation, security, etc.), leaving the responsibility for meeting with the captains to the assistant warden in charge of operations.

There can be no doubt that Brierton's taking over as warden of Stateville marked the end of the old-guard Ragenite power structure. The Ragenites are unlikely to have future input into policy making. The emphasis now is on staying ahead of the courts, on creating an organization which focuses responsibility and meets the due process demands imposed by law. The "fuck the courts" attitude expressed regularly at warden's meetings in the Cannon administration has disappeared.

Brierton's administrative and political skills have drawn praise from inmates, union leaders, Ragenites, reformers, and many of the treatment staff (although the abandonment of the medical model has soured some). Whether Brierton can reassert staff control while consolidating the legal and symbolic reforms of the past five years is a crucial issue that will require further research in the years to come.

Civilianization of the Prison

There have been three significant influxes of civilians into the

Stateville organization since 1969: administrators, teachers and counselors, and clerical workers. Noncustodial roles at the Joliet prisons never exceeded 15 percent of the total employees until 1970, when the percentage doubled to 30 percent. By 1975, the figure was almost 40 percent. The introduction of so many civilians into Stateville helped make the organization more differentiated, more divided, and more segmented. The civilian teachers, counselors, and administrators brought values and attitudes from liberal colleges and universities and contributed to a far less parochial attitude than existed a half dozen years before.

Until the time Bensinger took over as director of the Department of Corrections, there had never been a school system at Stateville where the instructors were civilians. The school system had been financed out of the inmate benefit fund, which was the repository for interest earned on inmates' savings and for profits from the inmate commissary. Bensinger ended the school system's reliance on that source by funding it out of general revenue. Under Sielaff, all the schools within Illinois prisons were organized into a school district under the authority of a governor-appointed school board and administered like any other school district in the state.

Ironically, the grade school and high school, even with civilian teachers, has never achieved the number of students it had before the civilian teachers were hired. In part this can be explained by the frequent lockups and the general rise in disruptiveness. Furthermore, the comparative value of being assigned as a student to the school (a nonpaying job) has diminished since the onerous assignments have either been eliminated (like the coal pile) or made less unpleasant.

The arrival of some half-dozen civilian schoolteachers (and in 1975 of an ex-convict administrator of the high school) was not greeted with pleasure by the custody force. Early in the Twomey administration a young teacher entered into a shoving contest with the assignment captain when the latter refused to accept his recommendation to transfer an inmate to the school. The incident resulted in the filing of a battery charge (later dropped) against the captain and a month's suspension (later reduced to two days). As the number of young civilian teachers has grown, so has the criticism that they are responsible for carrying drugs and other contraband into the prison. To some degree the school has come to be seen as a subversive enclave inside the walls.

Nor has the arrival of the civilian teachers met the wholehearted approval of the inmates. The reform movement was accompanied by an emphasis upon delivery of services to inmates (redefined as clients or residents) by professionals. This has served to eliminate inmates from some of the most self-respecting work in the prison—teaching for example. While the ideology of reform has promoted the moral status of the inmate, the operationalization of reform has narrowed the legitimate opportunities built into the role of the inmate.

The Sielaff administration, soon after it took office, eliminated all inmate clerical positions in the administration building. The reform ideology held that inmates should be clients, not servants.[21] According to this ideology, only "professionals" should have access to records. The removal of all inmate clerks required the hiring of a great number of civilian secretaries.

One key consequence of this development has been the breakdown of informal communications between inmates and staff. Until 1973, inmate clerks and "runners" served as intermediaries between staff and the general inmate population, articulating the concerns of the inmate population to the administrators and vice versa. The distance between the administration and the inmates has greatly expanded. Revis recalls that when he was assistant warden under Frank Pate, he and the warden knew the *majority* of the inmates by name. The reputation of an inmate followed him for years within the institution. Today none of the top administrators comes into contact with any particular inmates or even with inmates' names, except as a result of a grievance or a lawsuit. The warden's role has reverted to a bureaucratic office.

Counselors[22] were introduced at Stateville and other Illinois prisons in 1970 by Bensinger, who was publicly committed to reforming a prison system that had changed only marginally in decades. The establishment of the counseling program is best understood for its symbolic impact. The introduction of college-educated civilian counselors into the intensely criticized prison had the advantage of constituting a highly visible change that could be effected immediately. Indeed, the John Howard

Association had consistently decried the absence of a counseling program as a major weakness in the Illinois prisons. In a September 1968 report the association said:

> As far as it is known, Illinois is the only major state in the country where formal counselling services are relatively non-existent.... Without citing specific states, it can be conservatively stated that the prisons and reformatories in the larger states have a minimum of ten counsellors (excluding psychologists and psychiatrists). The Illinois Penitentiary System has only *several* where *several dozen* are needed.

Like the director of corrections himself, the counselors were outsiders to the prison, having been chosen on the basis of academic achievement rather than practical experience. Assistant Warden Revis argued vigorously that the counselors should be recruited from the ranks of the correctional officers and that further career opportunities for counselors should exist back in the custody ranks. His suggestion was not followed.

Counselors were not recruited from custodial ranks, nor were any of the original group either social workers or psychologists. They were drawn from diverse backgrounds. Several had recently graduated from college with a liberal arts education. Two were college professors between jobs. Only a few had had any experience in any kind of counseling. The state personnel office offered a general examination (used in filling more than one hundred different civil service positions) to qualify applicants for the job. The speed with which the program was formulated and the counselors hired left specific definition of job responsibilities to be formulated at the local level.

While the counselors' role was never specifically defined at the local level either, the original counselors assumed that their task was "to rehabilitate" or, at least, to help inmates by a mixture of good counsel, humane respect, psychoanalytic insight, and general friendship. In a December 1970 in-house newsletter, the special counselor assigned to the warden's staff wrote:

> Nevertheless, there is a distinction between counseling with one "1" which is Webster's definition of counsel or guidance, and between counselling with two "1's" which is therapeutic counselling and communication between a psychotherapist and counsellee. The latter term refers to in-depth consideration of a man's personal, emotional problems that frequently led to his criminal

offense and could easily prevent him from readjustment in the free community after parole or discharge. Professionally speaking, we are trained by education and experience to assist a man with advice or more importantly and lastingly, with therapy.

The Stateville counselors made claim to a professional role similar to that of the prison psychiatrist and to those psychologists and social workers who come into the institution on a contractual basis to provide group therapy. In the first two years of their experience, several of the counselors ran therapy groups, and several of the others picked out particular inmates with whom to work closely on a one-to-one level.

But the diffuseness of the role made it inevitable that counselors would become involved in a struggle over administrative policies. The counselors did not sit back and wait for voluntary requests for counseling sessions. Nor did they refuse to carry out inmate requests for assistance that did not involve therapy. Unlike the prison psychiatrist and contractual psychologists, they became involved in the day-to-day problems, requests, and demands of prisoners.

Anxious to establish and maintain their credibility with the prisoners, the counselors intervened to support inmates in whatever problems they were having with the guards and administration. Why was a certain inmate turned down for the minimum security unit? Why had inmate Smith been denied a cell transfer? Why couldn't inmate Jones receive a publication or a special visit? This ombudsman-like role was complicated by the fact that Stateville in 1970 was a prebureaucratic organization which relied upon traditional authority. Written rules were often hard to find or ambiguous. Tradition compelled decisions that could not be rationalized to counselors or inmates.

Inmates were interested in the counselors only insofar as the counselors could be of use to them. They were skeptical about therapeutic counseling, both because of the stigma attached to "seeing the bug doctor" and because of their belief that the counselors were not qualified to give any real therapeutic assistance. In any case, the inmates were more interested in enlisting the counselors as advocates than as therapists. Would the counselors stand up against the abuses that were occurring with the prison or would they be coopted by the "po-lice" like the other freemen within the prison regime? This kind of question placed the counselors under great pressure to support the inmates if their credibility was to be maintained.

For the custodial force, the counselors symbolized the crumbling of the old order. Up to 1970 almost no outsiders had penetrated Stateville's walls. The administrative positions were dominated by former guards who had worked their way up the ranks. Before he left Stateville, Ragen had predicted to his protégés that soon the sociologists were going to run the prisons. The intrusion of the counselors into Stateville's closed world was, therefore, traumatic because of the perceived threat they posed to the ultimate control of the organization.

The Department of Corrections' new administrative regulations called for the participation of counselors on both the disciplinary and assignment committees, which meant they entered into decisions that formerly had been carried out solely by the senior captain. The new committee structure sometimes degenerated into bitter feuding between the two custodial members on the one hand and the counselor on the other. In the spring of 1972, one of the younger counselors wrote a letter to the warden alleging brutality on the part of the senior captain in subduing a belligerent inmate at the disciplinary hearing. For the old guards, the counselors were like a fifth column given license to operate inside the walls. This view of the counselors is indicated in many of the complaints and demands made by the union in the tumultuous years between 1970 and 1975. The following is item 10 of the minutes of a union meeting held in June 1971 in the wake of the ball diamond melee in which several guards were injured:

> counsellors: not taking care of inmate requests, interfering in officers duties, abusing special letter privilege etc.

The counselors introduced a moral division of labor. The fact that they were hired to carry out "clean work" while the guards continued to be responsible for a great deal of "dirty work" generated further tension and conflict. Before the counselors' arrival, guards, particularly lieutenants, had carried out many favors for inmates, thereby giving moral balance to their role. While the guard might "write up" an inmate for a rule infraction, he could also act the "good Joe" by later "forgiving the inmate," checking on his parole date, "putting him in" for the minimum security unit, or conveying a message to his family. These were all tasks that the counselors took over, thereby narrowing the guard's role to that of a disciplinarian. Consequently, the guard's ability to manipulate a "reward system" in exchange for inmate conformity to rules and regulations was sharply attenuated. It became a common complaint of guards that "the counselors don't do anything that we didn't do." The Catholic chaplain was so concerned over the potential scope of the counselors' role that he submitted a proposal for the chaplaincy's abolition and the contractual hire of chaplains only for religious services.

The counselors opposed custody generally and supported inmates in whatever problems they encountered with the prison bureaucracy. Inmates deluged counselors with requests for information on their time served and time of release, transfer to minimum security, permission for special letters and visits, etc. Where one counselor was unsuccessful, inmates went to another with the same request.

The counselors could not possibly satisfy the inmate requests, both because of lack of manpower and lack of line authority. Yet inmates were quick to interpret failure as lack of sincerity. As the inmates began to complain that "the counselors can't do nothing for you," the counselors became more committed to an advocate role, all the more intensely supporting inmate definitions of the situation, sometimes in the vocabulary of political, social, and economic protest.

The lack of concrete line authority did not surface as an issue for the counselors. Instead, they tended to view their weakness, as did the inmates, in the context of an ideological and moral struggle. Their frustration intensified. From the outset, their participation on the prison disciplinary committee, which adjudicated innocence and guilt on rule infractions and determined how much time was to be spent in the "hole," was a focal issue for the counselors. This assignment epitomized what they saw as a fundamental contradiction in their role. How could they earn the trust of an inmate necessary to counsel him if they were linked to the despised disciplinary process? Repeated requests to be relieved from their rotating participation on the committee were denied. Warden Twomey argued that security was the first responsibility of all personnel and that the counselor's relationship with the inmate should be like a stern father with his son.

In May of 1972 the situation came to a head when the counselors revolted over what they felt was an illegal and unconscionable absence of due process afforded inmates at disciplinary proceedings. Basing their argument both on the Department of Corrections' own administrative regulations and on constitutional doctrine, the counselors addressed a petition first to the assistant warden, and then to the warden and the director, indicating their intention to "dissent on principle" from all future disciplinary hearings. The conflict did not focus on the issue of whether a therapeutic role should include participation in what was arguably an essentially custodial matter, but broadened to question the very legitimacy of the disciplinary process itself.

Director Bensinger responded to the revolt by coming to Stateville and, in the presence of Warden Twomey, asked each counselor if he intended to dissent at all disciplinary proceedings. Fearful of losing their jobs and demoralized by lack of support from any quarter, the counselors retracted their petition. Subsequently, the administration fired two young probationary counselors (one of whom was the only black), who were leaders in the counselors' revolt.

Convinced that the administration had sold out to custody, the counselors retreated into psychological alienation and physical isolation in their common office within the administration building. What ensued was a passive revolt against the organization. Some of the counselors now prided themselves on being able to pass an entire day at work without moving from their desks and without engaging in a single work task. The most cynical and sarcastic of them became the group's informal leaders. Counselors who continued to see their "caseloads" and who attempted to carry out therapy were ridiculed by their colleagues. Work slowdowns were sometimes carried out by functioning with exaggerated conformity to regulations.

The organization responded with more regulations and greater supervision. Counselors were now required to submit records originally intended as counseling instruments to their supervisor as a check on the amount of work being done. One counselor noted to me at the time, "What we do barely passes for work."

The work which was prescribed was identical to the "go for" tasks originally requested of the counselors by the inmates. The administration now told the counselors that they were responsible for checking on an inmate's time and for reviewing requests for transfers to minimum security or to another institutional assignment. They were given authority to approve special letters, special visits, and, later, emergency telephone calls. Such tasks were performed with resignation, counselors believing this work to be beneath what should be required of "professionals."

In addition to performing the "go for" tasks, the counselors over the course of the Bensinger administration gradually became more integrated into the administrative structure. The new regulations called for counselor participation on numerous committees, e.g., literary, grievance, furlough, and orientation. Furthermore, the counselors began to be called in to take over other bureaucratic jobs when manpower was needed. If the counselors "weren't doing anything" as was believed by many of the administrators, at least they could help with the paper work. The transfer of one counselor in the fall of 1974 to full-time assistance on gathering statistics for the affirmative action officer was indicative of the low administration regard for the counselors' role.

When David Brierton became warden in December 1974, the counselors—as part of the move to abandon the medical model—were redesignated "caseworkers." Their shifts were staggered, their offices moved to individual cells in each cell house. Their subculture was broken up. The new warden admitted that, while it was not precisely clear what duties the counselors would have, their role would evolve out of face-to-face interaction in the cell house. What had begun as a symbolic statement to the outside society about commitment to prison reform was thereby transformed into a symbolic statement to the inside community about administration commitment to reform. The individual counselor still remained outside of the central chain of command and without "professional" duties and responsibilities. Cynicism remained high as did constant talk about finding better jobs.

The greatest impact which the counselors have had at Stateville has been indirect and diffuse. The presence of college-educated civilians who have continuous contact with inmates has contributed to the amelioration of some flagrant abuses of the past. With the counselors sitting on committees and freely roaming about the prison, top custody officials had to be prepared to justify decisions for which five years ago they could not have been held accountable.

Additionally, the counselors' academic skills have slowly brought them a certain degree of both informal and formal respect and influence. As the courts have escalated counselors' demands for written justification for decisions and greater accountability at all levels, guards have placed more reliance on them. One counselor has seen his influence on the grievance review board grow as he has been relied upon by custodial members who worry that their decisions might be reversed higher up if properly articulated rationales for their decisions are not given.

Formalization Prisoner-Staff Relationships

The civilianization of the prison has been gaining momentum since 1970. The old inmate positions of clerks and runners in the administration building have been eliminated. The fluid communication channels that for decades linked the higher staff to the prisoners no longer exist. Increasingly the communication which does take place between the administrative elite and the general population is formalistic and bureaucratic. The relationship between staff and inmates has become more contractual, impersonal, and abstract.[23] The grievance procedure, begun by Bensinger and expanded under Sielaff, is the best evidence of this new relationship.

A grievance procedure is prescribed by the Unified Code of Corrections and implemented by the Administrative Regulations. Inmates under this procedure may lodge formal complaint about any aspect of prison life. The complaint must be investigated and answered in writing within ten days. This does not mean that an inmate will necessarily be satisfied. I found only 10 percent of a sample (of 100) of 1974 first-line grievances that could be considered as having resulted in even partial relief for the inmate. The point is not that inmates get what they ask for but that the procedure recognizes that the staff can be held accountable. The grievance procedure assumes legitimate grievances by inmates and weighs their complaints against formal and impersonal rules. In place of an informal, arbitrary, particularistic, discretionary system, the grievance mechanism supplies formalized and universalistic standards against which the legality of decisions can be measured.

As inmates have become familiar with the mechanism, they have filed more grievances; 48.7 per month in 1972 and approximately 61.5 per month in 1973 and 1974. It is well worth noting that the extension of more substantive and procedural rights to inmates has not reduced grievances or lawsuits. Indeed, just the opposite has occurred. Each inmate victory has stimulated new demands. Where an inmate was previously satisfied to bring his request to the attention of the warden, today inmates routinely appeal as far as they can and send "complimentary copies" to the director, the governor, and special interest groups.[24]

Until early 1975, the first stage of the grievance procedure was handled by a "special counselor." The second stage of the procedure called for a hearing *de novo* before a three-man Inquiry Board. Neither the grievance counselor nor the Inquiry Board had the authority to dismiss or throw out a meritless complaint. Any action by anyone in the prison was grievable. Every grievance had to be answered and every appeal had to be heard. This, of course, placed a large strain on administrative resources. While such a procedure may have been unwieldy, it served to create a dialogue between staff and inmates at a very formal level. The inmate no longer had to rely upon the whim of some guard to communicate his problem to the relevant administrative actor.[25]

If the inmate is not satisfied with the decision of the Inquiry Board, he can appeal to the Administrative Review Board in Springfield. This three-man board is chaired by one of the assistant directors. One of the other members is a Department of Corrections "prisoner's advocate" while the third member is an outside interested party, considered a reformer by the inmates.[26] The Administrative Review Board, which meets monthly at each institution often affords the appellant another hearing *de novo.*[27]

The setting up of the Administrative Review Board was the central office's attempt to establish credibility with the inmates. It also inspired considerable antagonism from the local administrators who felt that "they are trying to run it from Springfield." More than any other mechanism, the board made it clear that local autonomy was a thing of the past.

The first chairman of the Administrative Review Board saw in the mechanism a device to enforce institutional conformity to departmental regulations. Much as the exclusionary rule "punishes" the police by releasing criminals they "know" to be guilty, the board has released "known troublemakers" from segregation (and other disguised punitive assignments) where the institution did not comply with the rules in affording the "known troublemaker" a hearing or in basing their decision on solid factual evidence.

Conclusion: Bureaucratization and Mass Society

The erosion of local autonomy, the professionalization of administration, and the proliferation of administrative tasks and organizational roles contributed to Stateville's transformation to a rational-legal bureaucracy. All three of these developments are related to the prison's changing place in mass society. A politicized environment of the late 1960s, public opinion, court decisions, and media attention created pressures which required a professionalized administration and centralized authority. The old-time Ragen holdovers at Stateville could not manage the demands made by intellectuals, media, politicians, militant groups, and inmates themselves. Nor did they have the bureaucratic skills required to bring the prison into line with certain judicial decisions.

Under the first reform administration of Peter Bensinger, bureaucratization increased dramatically. The tremendous growth of the central office accelerated the trend toward greater and greater accountability of local administrators to the director of the Department of Corrections and his staff. The wardens were reduced in authority and power to middle managers. The central office was responsible for the drafting of the Unified Code of Corrections and the Administrative Regulations. These bodies of law applied equally to all the Illinois prisons and provided definitive standards against which administrative action at the local level could be evaluated.

The bureaucratization of the Illinois prison system did not in itself lead directly to the bureaucratization of each prison administration. Warden Twomey, at Stateville, faced the problem of trying to institute vague reforms in the absence of clear administrative strategies. There seemed to be no way other than moral persuasion to change the behavior of the staff so that they would treat the inmates with dignity and respect. Since the reforms took on ideological overtones and threatened the moral order of the old Ragenite world, it could only be expected that both the spirit and letter of reform would be resisted with intransigence.

But while Warden Twomey held a different ideology from that of the Ragenites, he did not necessarily hold a different view of administration. Like his predecessor Frank Pate, he was unable to make the change from patriarchal to bureaucratic administration. Twomey had been trained as a treatment specialist and not as a modern public administrator. When he did attempt to organize his own office bureaucratically (by withdrawing from the traditional duties of the warden of the yard), he met resistance and suffered loss of prestige.

The crisis in control that enveloped Stateville between 1970 and 1975 (to be discussed more fully in chapter 6) threatened to overwhelm the prison because the advocates of the rehabilitative ideology, first John Twomey and then Joseph Cannon, were unable to build an administration which defined duties and obligations, focused responsibility, and rationalized its procedures. The administrations of these two wardens were characterized by defensiveness and drift. Time and again the situation became explosive. What became increasingly clear was that, under current conditions, a maximum security prison could not meet the demands of prisoners, interest groups, and courts and maintain control at the same time without a fundamentally different type of administration—a rational-legal bureaucracy.

The Sielaff administration stressed bureaucratization rather than rehabilitation as the primary organization goal, at least in the short run. The size of the central office and its attraction of administrative professionals went well beyond the administration of Director Bensinger. From the outset, Sielaff and Brierton stressed management by objectives, zero-based budgeting, and tables of organization. Brierton went from prison to prison, as did other of the top departmental administrators, in order to conduct seminars on these management techniques for the staff.

When Brierton finally decided to take over the management of Stateville himself, he brought to the prison a commitment to scientific management rather than to any correctional ideology. This enabled him initially to maintain good relations with all of the prison's segments. Brierton is neither in favor of nor opposed to rehabilitation programs. His primary commitment is to running a safe, clean, program-oriented institution which functions smoothly on a day-to-day basis and that is not in violation of code provisions, Administrative Regulations, or court orders.

Brierton's whole management technique contributes to the demystification of the prison. He has deemphasized the need to punish prisoners for violation of rules, while focusing on the need to restrain those who can be shown to be a threat to institutional security. He is not committed to a particular standard of living that prisoners "deserve." That is a matter for the courts and the legislature.

To be sure, the bureaucratization and professionalization of the prison has not reached its limits. While a few college graduates are present among the guard force, the great majority of employees are poorly educated and weakly integrated into the bureaucratic structure. The greatest obstacle to the emergence of a period of restoration under Brierton is the traditional task orientation and lack of specialized expertise of the staff. There has in the past been a strong tendency toward cooptation of the new professionals on the staff by the old Ragenites. Some new staff members, anxious to earn acceptance, have been led to accept the long-term employees' definition of the situation. There is sharp collegial pressure to be seen as realistic, tough, and pragmatic.

The professional administrators identify with the inmates far less than do the counselors and teachers, whose roles are constructed around providing services to their inmate-clients. The professionalization of the administration has *not* resulted in a monolithic group of "reformers" committed to "treatment" on the one hand, and a monolithic group committed to "punishment" on the other.

Brierton has brought a new definition of administration to the prison. He stresses efficient and emotionally detached management. He has attempted to remove the affect attached to handling inmates. Whether this type of detached bureaucratic administration will ultimately be successful in a people-processing institution may be the crucial question facing corrections in the years ahead.

5 Intrusion of the Legal System and Interest Groups

[T]he view once held that an inmate is a mere slave is now totally rejected.... Liberty and custody are not wholly exclusive concepts.

Miller v. *Twomey*, Seventh U.S. Circuit Court of Appeals.

From 1970 to 1975 the prison's boundaries became increasingly permeable to juridical norms, government agents, private interest groups, and the press. The warden no longer dominated relationships with the outside. After 1970, relationships developed between outside forces and each segment of the prison organization—administrators, guards, and inmates—greatly complicating administration and adding substantially to potential conflict.

The broad legal reforms of the sixties undermined traditional authority in mental hospitals, schools, and the military, as well as prisons. The extension of constitutional rights to the heretofore marginal inhabitants of these institutions evidenced the "greater sensitivity of society's elite for the masses." Fuller participation of all segments of society in such an important central institutional system as the courts is a specific instance of the unfolding of mass society as analyzed by Edward Shils.

The decline of the "hands off" doctrine[1] and the intrusion of the federal courts required a rational decison-making process based upon uniform rules, formal decision mechanisms, and ascertainable criteria. The courts brought to bear outside pressure to bureaucratize the prison[2] in the same way that the money economy had provided the impetus for the rationalization of private enterprise in Max Weber's Germany. Liberalized court procedures[3] and the extension of the rule of law into the prison also served to raise inmate expectations as to the status and standard of living to which they are entitled. Such expectations have contributed to the proliferation of lawsuits at the same time that an increasing number of prisoners' rights have been validated.

The establishment of the federal government's Law Enforcement Assistance Administration, the concomitant growth in federal grants to state criminal justice agencies, and the great increase in state government itself have drawn the prison into a much more complicated organizational environment. Federal and state agencies issue guidelines that increase paper work and contribute to bureaucratization. In addition, they offer disgruntled employees a forum in which to air their grievances against the administrative elite.

Chicago's minority community had an important indirect effect upon prison decision makers after 1970. A greater concern for the rights and sensibilities of minorities is apparent in the administration of the prisons as in other areas of local, state, and federal government. While no prisoner or prison interest groups played a crucial role in lobbying for or drafting correctional policy, some of these groups served a watchdog function and were not hesitant to communicate to the press and to the public decisions and events within the prison system which they regarded as abuses.

The press itself has become increasingly professionalized and more detached in its coverage of the prison. None of the recent wardens enjoys the kind of particularistic relationships with key reporters that Warden Ragen shared with Finstone, Erickson, and others. A new variable has entered the prison equation in the form of a radical press, which has been given access to prisoner audiences by the courts and which explicitly aims to politicize the prisoners.

Intrusion of Juridical Norms

While the impact of the federal courts on the prison has been profound, the means by which this impact has been made are subtle and indirect. It has been the threat of lawsuits, the dislike for court appearances, the fear of personal liability, and the requirement of rational rules rather than revolutionary judicial decisions that have led to the greatest change in the Stateville organization. While the precise holdings of the court decisions have often been quite modest and even conservative, the indirect ramifications of judicial intervention into the prison have been far-reaching.

The Seventh Circuit Court of Appeals ruling in the *Cooper* case held that Muslim inmates could not be denied access to their religious literature, more precisely to their Bible, the Holy Quran. The court also held that, where security made it feasible, the Muslims, like other inmates, should be allowed to attend religious services. There would seem to be nothing in this rather cautious decision that might increase the probability of escape or of injury to inmates or staff. But the staff believed that by "giving" Muslims these rights, the courts were only encouraging broader expressions of protest.

Since the *Cooper* case, and extending at least up to the Brierton administration, the Stateville elite defined the courts as the single greatest obstacle to "running the institution." Almost any discussion with administrators or top guards elicits the same invectives against the courts, which are said to be "for the criminal," "naive," "unsympathetic," and "ignorant" of the unique problems of administration in a maximum security prison. The *Cooper* decision was resisted because it was perceived as an intrusion into what had been the absolute prerogatives of the organizational elite. The administration implemented the decision in its very narrowest form, thereby necessitating years more litigation on related issues of the right of Muslims to *Muhammad Speaks,* religious medallions, and pork-free diets.

In 1969 the U.S. Supreme Court held in *Johnson* v. *Avery*[4] that inmates in prison had a right of access to jailhouse lawyers if they did not have adequate legal representation. The Stateville administration characteristically did not move to implement the spirit of the decision but sought to walk the fine line of minimum compliance. The administration did not, for example, assign the most skilled jailhouse lawyers full time to the library in order to be available on a regular basis to assist fellow prisoners, but only interpreted the decision to mean that if a jailhouse lawyer did (somehow) legitimately obtain possession of another inmate's legal papers he would not be punished. Sometimes counselors were able to move legal papers from one inmate to another. At other times the inmates themselves exchanged them on an assignment, on the yard, or at the library. But the process of passing legal materials from inmate-client to jailhouse lawyers was never formalized; papers continued to be seized in shakedowns or "lost" or "misplaced."

In 1971 the Seventh Circuit delivered its historic decision in *Adams* v. *Pate,*[5] which considered several inmates' complaints against the Pate and Twomey administrations. Adams alleged that he was beaten by inmate nurses in the detention hospital (a frequent allegation over the years) on the orders of guards, and that he had not been afforded constitutionally required due process in being disciplined and placed in segregation.

As for the alleged beating, the court held that the warden would not be responsible unless he could be shown to have directly ordered the beating. The court then reviewed the Stateville disciplinary procedure, whereby (at the time) the inmate was summoned to the captains' office, informed by the disciplinary captain of the alleged rule violation, and given a chance to explain. The court, for the first time, recognized that some type of due process was applicable in disciplinary hearings, and then proceeded to find the existing procedure constitutionally adequate to meet all the process that was due. At a time when prison administrators were decrying judicial meddling, this decision reflected the great hesitancy of the federal courts (at least in the Seventh Circuit) to interfere.

Inmate Miller alleged in his complaint, consolidated with Adams's on appeal, that the deplorable conditions in the Stateville isolation cells amounted to cruel and unusual punishment. The Seventh Circuit court did not agree.

> With respect to the claim that the disciplinary confinements constituted cruel and unusual punishment in violation of the 8th Amendment Miller makes a general conclusory allegation that the cells were in an "inhuman, filthy and foul condition. . . ." While these alleged cell conditions undoubtedly would make confinement in such quarters unpleasant, they do not constitute conditions "so foul, so inhumane and so violative of basic concepts of decency" to fall within the proscriptions of the 8th Amendment.[6]

The punishment cells which the Seventh Circuit held not to be violative of the Eighth Amendment sometimes held six or eight prisoners lying head to foot in a stifling closed cell containing a single sink and commode. Even to a passing outsider the stench from the sweating bodies was sickening. For a prisoner unlucky enough to be placed in such conditions of confinement with members of an opposing street gang, the punishment was multiplied. It was in the very cells used to maintain discipline at Stateville that some of the worst sexual assaults and other aggressive acts of violence were perpetrated. The *Adams* decision could certainly not be seen as an indication of strong judicial concern for the rights and dignity of the prisoners.

No decision made by Bensinger was more fateful than the construction of the Special Program Unit (SPU) in one of the remodeled cell houses at the old Joliet prison. As early as 1969, Frank Pate was arguing that something had to be done to meet the expanding threat to security posed by the Chicago street gangs. Listed first among "top priorities" in John Twomey's 1970 five-year plan for the Department of Corrections was a "maximum treatment-maximum security" unit to accommodate "a relatively small but highly visible and significant element which is extremely disruptive, difficult to control, and seriously threatening to the welfare of our institutions."[7]

In the summer of 1971, Bensinger was sharply criticized by the black and liberal communities because of the dragnet which was carried out at Stateville following the July 1971 ball diamond "riot." More than one hundred alleged troublemakers were placed indefinitely on lockup in B house. SPU appeared to be a simultaneous answer to liberal criticism and conservative fear. In principle, SPU was supported by both Karl Menninger and Norval Morris, who believed that hard-core prison troublemakers could be humanely dealt with in a small treatment-intensive unit. Menninger was hired as a special consultant to the unit.

SPU had something for everyone; for the advocates of the individual treatment model and for liberal critics of the Department of Corrections, there was the three-tiered rudimentary behavior-modification plan and the promise of "treatment."

> The general purpose of the Unit will be to attempt through intensive therapeutic application, to assist the individuals assigned to acquire the necessary motivation and desire essential for integration into the general prison population. Personnel assigned to the

Special Program Unit will have the responsibility to create a therapeutic climate conducive to innovational diagnostic-treatment-program concepts.[8]

SPU also promised an answer to the breakdown of order at Stateville and the old prison. It boasted intensified security measures like mesh grating over the bars, strip cells, a mobile iron cage which permitted guards to enter tiers without being vulnerable to attack, and even specially produced ballpoint pens. All this indicated a high level of anticipation of extreme violence. In the same manual from which the previous idealistic statement of purpose was taken, it was said:

Such [a therapeutic] objective is not intended to imply that the Department of Corrections and its administrators are so naive as to assume that the program, no matter how well conceived or carried out, will be successful in changing behavior patterns of all or even a majority of the recalcitrant inmates assigned; however, it does clearly establish that creating the climate for positive behavioral change is our goal—not punitive practices and a pure "lock-up" philosophy—and this accountability for negative behavior becomes clearly the responsibility of the inmates assigned, as it must if we are to be able to defend correctional practices in this decade.[9]

The therapeutic potential of the unit was never realized. Inmates were determined to resist the institution from the beginning. Assignment to SPU itself became a status symbol among some gang members. They tore down the wire mesh and the heavier bars which replaced it, broke up their cells, and used porcelain fragments from the sink and commode for missiles and fluorescent light tubes as spears. They threw feces and urine on guards and on Dr. Menninger himself. After several months, a great deal of solidarity among the gangs was achieved. Guards and those few inmates helping to run the unit were constantly harassed. In their massive resistance to SPU, the inmates were encouraged by a class action, *Armstrong* v. *Bensinger,* brought by the American Civil Liberties Union challenging the constitutionality of the unit.[10]

The federal district court in *Armstrong* v. *Bensinger* held on 13 June 1972 that placement in SPU could not be justified on therapeutic grounds. Since SPU was a punitive disposition, assignment there required due process safeguards.[11] But Judge William

Bauer refused to declare that SPU itself constituted cruel and unusual punishment and further refused to accept the plaintiffs' contention that they should be extended broader due process rights than were found satisfactory in *Adams* v. *Pate.* Specifically the plaintiffs had asked for (a) prior notice of the charges against the prisoner, (b) a recorded hearing before an impartial arbiter with an opportunity to cross-examine adverse witnesses, (c) the right to retain counsel or counsel substitute, (d) a decision rendered in writing, and (e) an opportunity to appeal.[12] In citing the dicta in *Adams,* the court reiterated the judicial reluctance to question substantive judgments of prison administrators: "It is well established in this circuit and in others, that but for exceptional circumstances, internal matters of a correctional system, such as administration and discipline are the sole concern of the states."

The high-water mark in the success of prisoner suits in the Seventh Circuit was reached the next year. In *Miller* v. *Twomey*[13] the Seventh Circuit considered the impact of the U.S. Supreme Court's holding in *Morrissey* v. *Brewer*[14] on the extent to which "prison officials are vested with wide discretion in controlling persons committed to their custody." Here for the first time in the Seventh Circuit there was a lofty judicial pronouncement on a new relationship between prisoners and their captors.

> In view of the fact that physical confinement is merely one species of legal custody we are persuaded that *Morrissey* actually portends a more basic conceptual holding: Liberty protected by the due process clause may indeed, must to some extent—coexist with legal custody pursuant to conviction. The deprivation of liberty following an adjudication of guilt is partial, not total. A residuum of constitutionally protected rights remained. As we noted in *Morales* v. *Schmidt* the view once held that an inmate is a mere slave is now totally rejected. . . . Liberty and custody are not mutually exclusive concepts.[15]

Even the *Miller* court was careful to point out, however, that "*Morrissey* reminds us that due process is a flexible concept which takes into account the importance of the interests of state." It went on to hold that when charged with a rule violation that might lead to a "grievous loss," an inmate was entitled to some due process but not as much as the parolee facing revocation.

The prisoner must receive adequate advance written notice of the charges against him, he must be afforded a fair opportunity to explain his version of the incident, and, to insure a degree of impartiality the factual determination must be made by a person or persons other than the officer who reported the infraction.[16]

This prescription of a limited and circumscribed due process in prison discipline cases was later held by a cautious U.S. Supreme Court to be all that is required by the United States Constitution. In *Wolff* v. *McDonell*[17] the Court ruled that at prison disciplinary hearings there must be: (a) written notice of the charges no less than twenty-four hours before appearance before the disciplinary tribunal, (b) a written statement by the fact finders as to the evidence relied on and the reasons for the disciplinary action, (c) the opportunity to call witnesses and to present documentary evidence "when permitting him [the prisoner] to do so will not be unduly hazardous to institutional safety or correctional goals," and (d) some assistance from an inmate or staff member where the inmate is illiterate. The U.S. Supreme Court, like the Seventh Circuit Court of Appeals, refused to apply the full *Morrissey* safeguards.

Definition of due process in issues of prison discipline has been further sharpened in the latest Seventh Circuit decision arising out of a Stateville case, *Labatt* v. *Twomey*.[18] In *Labatt* the court held that the civil rights of the inmates were not violated by the two-month lockup following the ball diamond incident. The court said, "In situations such as the present, where prison authorities are allegedly reacting to emergency situations in an effort to preserve the safety and integrity of the institution, the state's interest in decisive action clearly outweighs the inmates' interest in prior procedural safeguards." However, the court seemed to suggest that had the lockup been more prolonged some sort of disciplinary hearing would need to be afforded.[19]

A similar decision emerged out of the lockup of some 300 inmates following the September 1973 takeover of B house. In *Murphy* v. *Wheaton*[20] it was held that the actions of the Stateville authorities in keeping petitioner Murphy in segregation without any hearing whatever for eighty-seven days did not violate the due process clause, at least in the aftermath of such an extraordinary event as a riot. Judge Herbert Will refused, however, summarily to reject the prisoner's contention that when he finally did receive his hearing before the disciplinary committee he should have been allowed to call witnesses to attest to his innocence. The case did not go so far as to say that the prisoner has an absolute right to call witnesses on his behalf, but there is a presumption in favor of such a practice, and it cannot be denied for arbitrary and capricious reasons. Finally, the court held that the prisoner should be given the opportunity to offer proof as to whether the conditions in B house segregation following the riot degenerated to the point where they offended the Eighth Amendment.

This brief review of the major prisoners' rights cases in the Seventh Circuit provides little support for the proposition that revolutionary court decisions have made it impossible to administer the prisons. On the contrary, the court decisions in the Seventh Circuit have consistently shown great deference to prison administrators, typically requiring no more than the demonstration of a rational decision-making process.

Where the federal courts have rebuked administrative practices and established new standards, there has sometimes been little change in the old ways. Court decisions do not enforce themselves. Orders must be framed, and an attorney of one of the parties of record must go back to court to ask for enforcement of decisions which have not been correctly implemented. This cannot be done when the original plaintiff has already been paroled or where no continuing relationship with counsel exists. Even when orders have been obtained, they have been difficult to frame so as to cover the multiplicity of contingencies that can and do arise.

There are limits to the capacity of the courts to police decision making inside the prison. *Wright* v. *Twomey*[21] suggests what is certain to be the most effective remedy devised by the courts for supervising administrative action-personal damages under section 1983 of the Civil Rights Act. Inmate Wright first sued the prison for providing improper medical services when he was in isolation. Judge Will dismissed the case as not amounting to a constitutional deprivation of right on the assurance of Warden Twomey that Wright could and would be provided adequate medical attention if a similar situation arose again. Two weeks later Wright was alleged to have been in a fight and was again disciplined and again placed in disciplinary lockup, and again he was *not* provided with the special diet required by his medical condition. Consequently he alleged severe medical and physical ramifications of this (mis)treatment.

The district court found that the denial of proper medical treatment amounted to deprivation of a constitutional right and assessed $500 damages against Twomey, one counselor, and two guards. The Seventh Circuit affirmed the district court's award. The U.S. Supreme Court declined to hear the case by dismissing the state of Illinois's motion for a writ of *certiorari.* It was the first time money damages had been successfully won against Stateville staff members, and the decision contributed significantly to a feeling among the top custodial officers that they would be financially ruined for trying to do their jobs.

Where decisions have been implemented, their impact has often been blunted. For example, contrary to the opinion of prison administrators that the courts have destroyed discipline, there is strong evidence at Stateville[22] and elsewhere[23] that the court decisions affecting prison discipline have had little effect on the number of inmates serving isolation and segregation time. The average daily number of prisoners in isolation jumped from thirty to fifty-two between 1967 and 1969 (see table 10).[24] From 1970 to 1975 the average number of inmates in isolation was forty as compared with thirty-five for the years 1944–69. On the average, no more than 1.29 percent of the inmate population had ever been in isolation before 1969, when the percentage increased to 2.06 percent. In 1973 it rose to 2.69 percent. (In 1975 isolation was abolished. Serious disciplinary cases are now all handled in segregation in B house.)

A similar pattern is shown for segregation, the designation given to those cells in the isolation building that are assigned to the most severe disciplinary problems, individuals who allegedly cannot be allowed in the general population without jeopardizing the safety and security of the institution. The highest average number of inmates ever assigned to segregation was forty in 1960 until a record high of forty-eight was reached in 1969. The number has declined since 1969, but this does not necessarily mean that there are fewer inmates in conditions of special confinement. The segregation unit that served to confine Stateville's troublemakers for four decades was found to be inadequate by the 1970s. First B house and then SPU were used for segregation. Beginning in 1969 there has been a greater percentage of the inmate population in segregation than in any previous year, even *without taking into account the special segregation in B house and SPU* which have consistently contained well over one hundred inmates between them.

The Stateville detention hospital has always served a dual purpose. It is a bona fide placement for inmates who suffer mental breakdowns. But it has also served as a residual segregation unit when the other cells were full or when, for one reason or another, it was thought necessary to give special treatment to a particular case. Both inmates and guards concur that the detention hospital has witnessed many confrontations between guards and violent inmates over the years, especially between 1969 and 1973 (see table 10).

Considering the average number of days served by inmates in isolation between 1946 and 1972, we also find that time so served in 1970 and 1972 is slightly higher than in other years (see table 11). Taken together, the statistics for twenty-four-hour confinement support the proposition that the court decisions have not prevented the administration from exercising control through traditional punishment mechanisms.

It might be hypothesized that while there were fewer inmates in special conditions for confinement from 1970 to 1974, they were being punished for more serious offenses. If this were true, it might indicate that the court decisions had the effect of forcing the prison staff to bring disciplinary charges only in cases of serious infractions. This does not, however, appear to have happened. Surveying isolation records to find the offenses for which inmates are serving time in isolation we find that the proportion of serious offenses ("Direct Challenges to Authority" and "Crimes against Prison Inmates") has remained constant over time, at least between 1946 and 1970 (see table 12).[25] Unfortunately, comparative data were not available for years after 1970.

A greater number and percentage of inmates are in special disciplinary confinement today than ever before. This can be explained by the fact that the same individuals continued to make the substantive disciplinary decisions. That the guard who writes the ticket is now barred from the decision-making function is hardly a decisive turn of events when his superior is the decision-maker. The old disciplinary captain at Stateville became chairman of the new disciplinary committee in 1970, and one of his subordinates, a guard officer, was a second member of the committee. While the counselors had the third seat on the committee and were, at least until 1973, a somewhat dissenting voice, the crushing of their revolt and the pressure on their minority position brought them reluctantly into line.

The prison administrators found ways to "get around" the clear meaning, if not the letter, of the court decisions. Instead of being brought to a hearing within seventy-two hours of the alleged infraction, an inmate might be brought before the committee and "continued," while being placed in "investigation" or "the reclamation gallery" or in some other form of sequestration not *called* segregation but equivalent to it.

Often inmates were not given written notice of the alleged infraction within the twenty-four-hour period. They were placed in isolation or segregation anyway. By the time the case was brought to court, it would be stale, and the factual dispute as to whether the inmate had actually received notice would be essentially unresolvable. The manner in which the Cannon administration "broke" the commissary boycott (discussed in chapter 6) by throwing the gang leaders in segregation without any hearings is a perfect case in point.[26]

While the courts might be able to impose a *form* of decision making on the prison, they are not in a position to overturn substantive decisions. The federal courts are totally unable to sort out who was lying in an old factual dispute or to question whether the substantive judgment of the prison officials, in instituting a lockup, was correct. By necessity the courts must assume the good faith of the administration. Therefore, unless the administration itself acts in good faith and assumes a responsibility to supervise the fairness of the process, inmates are essentially little better off than before, and without a remedy unless, of course, the administration completely fails to follow the required procedures.

The few reported federal court decisions discussed above give little indication of the degree to which the prison has become a legal battleground. We saw in chapter 2 that Ragen was called upon to defend approximately one lawsuit a year against him.[27] In 1969 alone, sixty-six lawsuits were brought against Stateville administrators. The figure had doubled by 1971 and has held constant since that year.[28] The head of the Prisoner Litigation Bureau of the Attorney General's Office estimates that between 50 and 60 percent of the prisoner cases are thrown out on summary judgment, 15–20 percent are disposed of by settlement or by mootness, and 20 percent proceed to trial or hearing.[29] Thus, not only has there been an explosion in the number of prisoner lawsuits, but more stringent rules on granting summary judgment and more liberalized rules on the consideration to be afforded *pro se* complaints have greatly increased the number of lawsuits reaching the discovery and trial stages. Each lawsuit that survives summary judgment may lead to broad requests for discovery, including searches of prison records, interrogatories, depositions, and affidavits. This has placed a tremendous strain on Stateville's administrative resources.

Under the administrations of Pate, Twomey, and Cannon the organization did not meet the demands of the courts for formal rationality. This was partly due to, and partly reflected by, the absence of structural adaptations to the necessity of managing new challenges at the organization's boundaries. Stateville has never had a lawyer on the staff, despite the fact that the prison has become a legal battleground. The chief clerk in the record office continues to prepare all interrogatories and affidavits. No file exists containing all the court decisions, much less consent decrees and court orders. The court decisions are poorly and inaccurately disseminated to the staff, even at the top levels. The litigation itself is handled by various assistant attorneys general, mostly inexperienced lawyers with little feeling for prison organization. The Prison Litigation Bureau (of the Illinois Attorney General's office), with eight part-time staff attorneys, has been in existence only since the summer of 1974.

The prevailing Stateville administrative belief that prison administration cannot be rationalized may have cost Warden Cannon his job. Failure to deliver to inmate subscribers the September 1973 issue of *On Ice,* published by the politically radical Chicago Connections, resulted in a $90 fine against Sielaff, Cannon, and the Stateville librarian. At issue was the failure of the Cannon administration to follow a court procedure regarding the censorship of incoming periodicals. An earlier case in federal court had been decided in favor of the admissibility of this same radical newspaper into the prison. Yet Cannon and other administrators (claiming that they were unaware of the court decision) summarily refused to allow distribution of the September issue, and neither informed the addressees and publishers nor submitted the issue to the literary committee responsible for censorship decisions. The Chicago Connections' lawyers proceeded to bring the officials to court on a show cause order to determine why the Department of Corrections' officials should not be held in contempt. The judge ordered the defendants to reimburse the plaintiffs for mailing costs.

The greatest impact of the court decisions on Stateville has come from the legal process itself. The decision makers don't like to be sued, hate going to court, and fear personal liability.[30] They feel that attorneys and inmates harass them with lawsuits and incessant demands for depositions and interrogatories.

The indirect consequences of the intrusion of juridical norms into the prison have been more significant than the few substantive holdings which have resulted from the many years of litigation. Seemingly unimportant court decisions pertaining to medallions, Qurans, and radical newspapers have given legitimacy to inmate protest against authoritarian rule. The Ragen system ultimately depended upon total suppression and total submission. The expression of inmate frustrations in terms of classic constitutional issues provided the ideological basis for a frontal attack upon the entire regime.

Adams, Miller, and *Wolff* (discussed earlier in this chapter) struck at the very heart of the authoritarian system, not because it was impossible to go through the form of a hearing and then throw inmates into segregation, but because they called into question the basis of authority itself. More than this, the battles before the courts exposed the deficiencies and limitations of the prison's leaders and undermined the charismatic quality of their leadership.

Wardens Ragen and Pate had great difficulty articulating the bases for their decisions. Many of their actions were grounded in the tradition of overwhelming the inmate with their power and authority. An important source of Ragen's political autonomy was his definition of the prison as a unique institution. The indirect consequence of the prisoner litigation was to further demystify the prison through the intrusion of the everyday rule of law.

The administrations of wardens Twomey and Cannon were no better able to respond to the demands of the courts for rationalization of the decision-making process. In this chapter it should become more clear that the halting attempts to implement the rehabilitative ideal at Stateville was not an explicit move toward greater bureaucratization. What bureaucratization there was during this period came from written rules emanating from the central office. Twomey and Cannon believed in "changing the tone," "improving communication," and "increasing respect." Their regimes and the rehabilitative ideal which they embodied were no more rationalized than the Ragen-Pate organization. Both Twomey and Cannon became as disenchanted with the courts as the old Ragenites.

Lacking a strategy for simultaneously liberalizing the rules, maintaining control and following universalistic standards, the Twomey and Cannon administrations went from lawsuit to lawsuit and from crisis to crisis.[31] The question for the future is whether Warden Brierton's corporate model of management will enable him to consolidate reforms and maintain control under the rule of law. Brierton has moved swiftly toward creating a rational-legal bureaucracy. There will no longer be a question, for example, as to the validity of an inmate's claim that he has not had a shower in two weeks or seen a counselor in two months. Showers are documented in writing. Counselors must keep a log of every contact with inmates and the actions they took with respect to their requests.

The limits to bureaucratization are obvious. Already there are daily hearings on discipline, literature, good time forfeiture, grievances, and appeals. On the horizon is the possibility of hearings and appeals on institutional and cell transfer and job assignment. The hearings themselves become more time-consuming and complex as due process safeguards (cross-examination, witnesses, transcripts) are added one by one. Each new decision for which a hearing is required generates more lawsuits, interrogatories, depositions, court testimony, and appeals. The limit to this process is marked by complete organizational paralysis.

Prison Legal Services

The proliferation of prisoners' rights litigation has generated a continuous flow of attorneys into the prison. The sign-in records from the gatehouse through which visitors must pass show that average visits of attorneys between 1968 and 1974 have risen from 1.3 to 2.4 per day.[32] Where the inmates are represented by counsel we can expect that demands for discovery are likely to be more frequent and more extensive, further burdening administrative resources.

Representation in prisoners' suits has come from individual lawyers and legal groups representing different segments of the legal community. The establishment law firm of Jenner and Block, for example, has had a long tradition of accepting assignment of prison cases by the courts. It was the counsel for the plaintiff in *Adams* v. *Pate, Thomas* v. *Pate* and several of the other major cases over the years. The firm reportedly receives several hundred direct requests for assistance per year from state prisoners.[33] Radical or "movement" lawyers like Jeffrey Haas and Mark Kadish, working out of the People's Law Office and the Lawyers Guild, have participated in several important prisoners' rights cases (*Armstrong* v. *Bensinger* and *Miller* v. *Twomey*). But, limited as they are by lack of resources and burdened by the tremendous demand for legal services among many segments of the poor, the impact of the radical lawyers upon the prison has been sporadic.

By far the most important outside legal group touching Stateville is Prison Legal Services (PLS).[34] The history and development of this project illuminates the articulation of the public-interest legal community, government funding agencies, and the prison.

Prison Legal Services was begun in 1971 by three public-interest lawyers who were involved in both consumer law and prisoners' civil litigation. Unable to support their activities from their fee-generating cases, they incorporated a not-for-profit corporation, Foundation for the New Business Ethic, and solicited contributions from the mainstream business community and the Department of Corrections, which first granted the foundation $17,000 in July 1972.

The three lawyers were only able to visit Stateville once or twice a month. In July 1972 they counseled only fourteen inmate clients. In August they hired Keith Davis, a Lutheran minister and former community organizer, to administer and develop the program. Between August 1972 and June 1973, Prison Legal Services had no full-time staff attorneys, although it operated closely with the three public-interest lawyers and several volunteers. Funding came from ninety-day grants from the Illinois Law Enforcement Commission, on which Bensinger sat as a director. The director of ILEC, David Fogel, who had sponsored a similar group of prison advocates when he was director of corrections in Minnesota, continued the grants, maintaining that it was healthy for prison administrators to be sued.

While Prison Legal Services had seen fourteen inmates in July 1972, by September 1972 it was seeing 130–140 inmates per month. Part of this increase is explained by a calculated strategy to become indispensable. "If you cease funding us, what would you like us to do with the 800 open cases we have?" In June 1973 the first full-time staff attorney was hired. By the fall of 1974, PLS was the largest prison law project in the United States, with seven full-time attorneys and a staff of forty-seven paid employees (some part-time).

Originally PLS sold itself to Bensinger and the prison authorities as a civil legal-aid group which would handle divorces, debts, estates, and other noncriminal and non-prison-related problems. It soon became apparent that a substantial part of the civil legal aid would be civil rights class actions, filed under section 1983 of the Civil Rights Act against the prison authorities.[35] Regular contacts were established with jailhouse lawyers and the omnipresent gang leaders.

The first PLS lawyers who came to Stateville in the fall of 1972 were contacted by the same inmates who contacted me when I entered Stateville that summer (see Appendix 1). The gang leaders approached one of the PLS attorneys with the request that he help Project ABLE (Adult Basic Learning Enterprise—see chapter 6), the nascent inmate council which they controlled, to incorporate as a not-for-profit corporation. The attorney carried out this favor, and ABLE obtained its long-desired charter in September 1972. During the next two and one-half years a continuous relationship was maintained between the gang leaders, in their capacity as ABLE representatives, and the PLS lawyers. They carried out such favors as making contacts for the leaders with legislators and community groups on the outside and running down former prison colleagues. The inmates continued to demand that PLS bring a federal suit to force the administration to recognize ABLE as a viable inmate council within the prison.[36] In the fall of 1974, PLS took on remand (after the case was won by Jenner and Block at the appellate level) *Falconer* v. *Bensinger,* a suit on behalf of a member of the Black P Stone Nation wherein the inmate claimed that the prison unconstitutionally disciplined him because of his membership in the Black P Stone Nation, infringing his First Amendment rights to association and religion.[37]

The prison staff vigorously resisted the intrusion of Prison Legal Services. Throughout the fall of 1975 every staff meeting included some account of a run-in with Keith Davis or one of the staff attorneys. Cannon for several months struggled to prevent Davis from bringing into Stateville an ex-convict staff assistant because "it would be bad for morale." Ultimately the warden was overruled by his Springfield superiors.

Despite the success of many day-to-day confrontations with staff over institutional rules and policies,[38] few major judicial law reforms have been won after several years of strenuous advocacy. So slow is the legal process that, during the first couple of years of their existence, only a handful of their lawsuits reached final decision. Some have been mooted because the inmates have been paroled.

The glacial progress of the cases through the courts reflects the massive workload that is said to plague the federal courts. The tremendous drain of prisoner suits on judicial resources has brought comment time and again from the chief justice[39] and other federal judges[40] concerned that the federal courts are becoming the forum for every dispute between inmates and prison staffs. In addition, the discovery process itself tends to generate time-consuming conflicts over what data the prison should be responsible for compiling and providing. Finally, the tremendous pressure on the attorney general's staff has, according to the statements of AG staff attorneys, led them to seek delays and continuances whenever and wherever possible.

Equally important is the tremendous pressure upon PLS resources. PLS was funded first by the Department of Corrections and then by the Illinois Law Enforcement Commission for short periods ranging between one and four months. Because of the real possibility that each short grant might be the last, PLS desired to entrench itself. Its main strategy for doing this was to take on as many inmate cases as possible. It collected hundreds of files, many more than could effectively be handled. This strategy involved costs, however, since it was impossible to give effective representation to so many inmates. Furthermore, many of the complaints were lacking in merit. And by emphasizing the civil representation that could be delivered to inmates in matters of individual but not systemic concern, PLS attenuated its capability for bringing test cases against the prison organization. Instead of achieving major law reform, PLS found itself increasingly becoming bogged down in "petty cases." Like the counselors, if the PLS attorneys were to maintain credibility they could not turn down cases, even those with little significance or probability of success.

It is not victory in great judicial decisions that constitutes PLS's greatest impact on Stateville. It is the PLS staff members' daily presence at the prison, their persistent questioning of the rules, their relentless demands to see files and records, and the fear they invoke in the hearts of many of the prison staff that has the most profound effect on the day-to-day administration of the prison. Somehow the prison authorities must find a way to accommodate these lawyers and law students who so doggedly camp on the doorstep. A cordial working relationship has evolved with the chief clerk in the record office and slowly with other top members of the Stateville staff. If PLS could not be locked out of the prison, as many of the administrators and custodial elite initially believed could be done, then the institution would have to adapt, at least to some extent, to the PLS presence. Some of the more egregious practices were halted; short phone calls and meetings with the warden increased; adherence to the rules and regulations necessarily became more observable and explicit.

Organizational Environment

We have seen in chapter 4 that Stateville's autonomy was severely undermined by the emergence of a centralized department of corrections with an active central office. Policy affecting the organization at all levels is today decided in Springfield. What role the counselors will have, what courses will be taught at the high school, whether a white applicant can be hired before a search has been made for a black, are examples of decisions which emanate from the central office and are imposed upon the institution.

The prison is directly affected by several other governmental organizations. The Illinois Law Enforcement Commission (ILEC) founded in 1968 pursuant to the establishment of the Law Enforcement Assistance Administration, channels federal and state funds into the various agencies comprising the criminal justice system. By granting or withholding funds, ILEC has an enormous influence on the prison organization. Before 1973 ILEC had no program of its own, no planning document, and no conceptual approach to the criminal justice system.

When David Fogel, a criminal justice planner with a special interest in corrections, took over ILEC (after the legislature had turned back his nomination as director of corrections), he pushed for planning and almost immediately implemented several important projects. The first was the Illinois Correctional Academy (on the campus of St. Xavier's College in southwest Chicago), which was established in order to centralize and professionalize pre-service and in-service staff training for correctional officers. While the full impact of the academy is still unclear, a few consequences are indicated.

The academy represents an alternative to the traditional process by which guard recruits were socialized into their occupation. The civilian instructors at the academy prepare recruits to meet certain resistances among the old guards, and provide them with a professional reference group that is, to an extent, an alternative to the peer reference group inside the prison. In his 1974 study of new guard recruits at Stateville, Liebentritt found a split developing between the academy guards and those old-timers who might be considered the tradition bearers of the institution.[41]

The academy itself is evolving an independent role within the Department of Corrections. Quite recently, after a guard carelessly fired a weapon from one of the towers, the Stateville administration ordered that the ammunition be removed from the towers. The academy (along with the union) lobbied successfully both to have the central office return the ammunition to the towers and to have no guard assigned to the towers unless he had been trained in the use of weapons. There are direct lines of contact between the academy and Stateville.

Another ILEC grant early in Fogel's administration went for the remodeling of the cell houses and for the transformation of the centralized dining room (which during Ragen's days fed 1,800 inmates at each of two sittings) into a new gymnasium. New tables and chairs were placed on the main floors of each cell house so that each cell house can feed individually. This 1973 architectural change not only provided a highly desirable new recreation facility but allowed the administration to break down the prison into smaller units and to dissolve the longest lockup in Stateville's history.

Third, Fogel committed himself to Prisoner Legal Services, which ILEC finances through the University of Illinois Circle Campus, and under a larger umbrella organization charged with coordinating all prison legal services throughout the state.

Fourth, ILEC introduced a "manpower project" at Stateville which reports the daily movement of prisoners and guards on computer printouts. For the first time a college-educated computer programmer attended staff meetings and was recognized as having some useful role to play at Stateville.[42] The assignment captain uses the printout to find available cell assignments and job openings. Warden Brierton plans to locate computer terminals in each cell house (under another ILEC grant) in order to facilitate cell house management.

Fogel has also had an important informal role in the management of the prison. Because he was Walker's first choice for director of the Department of Corrections there is a widespread (albeit unfounded) belief among staff people that he really runs the department from ILEC. Thus Fogel enjoys considerable prestige among employees. In the fall of 1974, the recreation supervisor of Stateville claimed that unless his expanded gym program was accepted by the recalcitrant custodial staff, he would appeal over Cannon's head to Fogel because the ILEC grant was not being properly implemented. On another occasion an argument in the guard hall between PLS director Keith Davis and an assistant warden led Davis to call Fogel and thereby successfully resolve the dispute. The assistant warden noted that "Davis must have some kind of clout"; the point is that Fogel and ILEC carry a great deal of weight at Stateville and have a somewhat independent correctional program which must be assimilated into the administration's own planning.

ILEC is not the only governmental agency which has an impact upon Stateville. The Department of Corrections' Affirmative Action office has been the crucial force behind increased minority hiring. Likewise the Civil Service Commission, the Equal Employment Opportunity Commission and the Fair Employment Opportunity Commission limit administrative actions with respect to hiring, promotion, and dismissal by posing a threat of reinstatement and other sanctions if the prison organization does not comply with guidelines contained in federal statutes.

The Affirmative Action Office was begun in 1971 when Director Bensinger appointed Jack Porche Affirmative Action officer and charged him with drawing up a plan to increase minorities throughout the department. At the same time, Bensinger called together representatives of the Urban League, NAACP, Operation Push, Malcolm X College, and other black community groups to discuss ways of increasing minority recruitment. Bensinger appointed twenty representatives of these groups to a special advisory committee on manpower development. Porche began a campaign to increase the numbers of black recruits by contacting community groups, placing advertisements on radio, and urging the Department of Labor to refer black job applicants to the prisons. For the first time large numbers of blacks began applying for work at Stateville. In 1972, 146 blacks were hired at Stateville compared with 49 in 1971. "Informal" quotas were imposed by Bensinger on the Stateville administration. This amounted to an ultimatum that there would be no hiring unless *x* percent of blacks were hired. Porche went to Roosevelt College to recruit Mel Hampton to be Stateville's first black counselor.[43] In addition, a Model Employer Program was begun with federal money under the Illinois Department of Personnel during the summer of 1974. Under this program a special recruitment and pre-training drive was initiated to recruit and pre-train black and Spanish-speaking guards from the central city. Recruitment trailers and sound trucks were sent into the inner city to interview and hire guards on the spot.

Porche has two sources of leverage to improve the position of minorities within the organization: (1) under the Sielaff administration he makes an input in the performance evaluations of all supervisory personnel according to how well they are fulfilling their affirmative action responsibilities, and (2) all grants applied for within the department cross his desk so that he can comment on what percentage of minorities should be hired if a grant is to be processed. The results of these efforts in bringing minorities into high-level decision-making positions are still unclear.[44] Many staff members at the local level view Affirmative Action, like the court decisions, as an intrusion to be passively resisted. "Perhaps this too will pass in time?" Affirmative Action not only challenges the autonomy of the organization through its effect on hirings, promotions, and firings, but the agency itself makes considerable demands on Stateville's administrative resources by its continued requests for reports on all personnel matters.

Colleges and Universities

Colleges and universities have had associations with Stateville since its inception, albeit sporadically. Ernest Burgess and Edwin Sutherland had contacts with Stateville in the twenties and thirties. Donald Cressey conducted the interviews with embezzlers at Stateville in 1949 which led to his doctoral dissertation and book *Other People's Money*.[45] A 1959 bulletin from Warden Ragen announced that a University of Illinois professor would be at Stateville to administer some tests to the inmates in connection with research. Daniel Glaser points out that "hundreds of studies in many disciplines" have been carried out over the years with the cooperation of the criminologist and sociologist-actuary.[46] But there were no routine relationships established with colleges and universities, or any direct links between professors, students, and administrators except for the TV college which began in the mid-1950s under the auspices of Wright Junior College.

The Bensinger task forces brought the academic community into much closer touch with the prison administration. For the first time academic penologists served on task forces and advisory commissions; they helped draft the Unified Code of Corrections and the Administrative Regulations. In addition, under Twomey's regime a handful of inmates at the minimum security unit were released during the day to take classes toward the B.A. degree at nearby Lewis University. The first Lewis B.A. was granted to an inmate in 1972. Beginning in 1973, a bilingual educational program for Spanish-speaking inmates, was brought into the prison (funded by a large federal grant) coordinated by Northern Illinois University and Northwestern University. At the outset, there were many clashes between the outside professors and the prison administration over scheduling. More recently, the full-time coordinator of the program has been accused of becoming a self-styled spokesman for all Latinos and of wandering around the prison (even into segregation) on matters unrelated to his program. It is precisely this "going beyond what they came in here for" that is the principal objection of staff members to outsiders.

The creation of the prison school district put academicians on the school board. The creation of the governor's advisory board and two departmental advisory boards constitutes another area of academic participation. In 1974, Cannon invited a criminal justice professor from Lewis University to head an ad hoc committee on prison discipline.

Probably the most important institutional affiliation has been with Joliet Junior College, which in 1970 brought several academic and vocational programs into Stateville. The college continues to see the provision of prison education as part of its community college mission. Several new vocational programs have been added although the relationship between JJC and Stateville has not been successful. Between 1970 and 1974, JJC staff complained that Stateville had never provided the space or the cooperation to make programs like culinary arts and auto mechanics viable, another example of administrative inability to implement the reform program. Indeed, it is claimed that no inmate has ever graduated from culinary arts and only a few from the auto mechanics course despite the fact that they have been at the prison for years. It has only been under express assurances from the new administration (as well as a favorable financial arrangement) that JJC has agreed to maintain and expand its program.

Aside from the relationship with Joliet Junior College, the prison has very few institutional or individual ties connecting it with the local Lockport/Joliet community. An association of businessmen (Will-Grundy Manufacturers Association) met several times with prison officials during the summer and fall of 1974 to discuss the possibility of bringing some skilled industrial apprenticeship programs into the prison, but negotiations fell apart when the manufacturers refused to bring a union into the plan.[47] Stateville has never been tied to its local environment the way the southern Illinois prisons have been.[48] The administrators at Stateville are, for the most part, unaffected by and even unaware of the local political scene. Department of Corrections administrators are, to this day, concerned about political interference in the hirings and promotions at Menard; but such interference has not occurred at Stateville since Ragen.

Prison Interest Groups

Despite the pervasive defensiveness among the Stateville staff (particularly the old guard but including many members of the administration), there have been few, if any, organized groups acting on behalf of inmates.[49] Where such groups have been active, they have, without exception, focused on traditional issues (e.g., lack of rehabilitation programs) rather than on such radical issues as a prisoners' union, minimum wage, conjugal visiting, and prison abolition.

Since 1970, there have been perhaps a half-dozen individuals from the black community at large who have worked seriously and with consistency to bring about change in the prisons. Several of these individuals have been discouraged by what they perceive to be an indifference in the black community to the plight of prisoners.[50]

Beginning in 1971, Dorothy Mason began to visit Stateville as a representative of Operation PUSH (People United to Save Humanity), a community organization headed by one of Chicago's most influential black leaders, Jesse Jackson. While prison reform was not one of PUSH's top priorities, Mason's personal interest coincided with a need of the community-based organization to address itself to black prisoners.[51] Peter Bensinger was approached by Operation PUSH with the request to allow a representative to enter Stateville in order to help the men maintain contact with the outside. Dorothy Mason was extremely popular during the years that she represented Operation PUSH. She met regularly with inmates who contacted her at PUSH and attempted to resolve personal problems within and without the organization. The first time I saw Mason was in June 1972 at the high school graduation at the Stateville chapel. Her arrival (a little late) was met by a standing ovation and a thunderous outbreak of applause.

Like others from the outside community who entered the prison to "work with the inmates," Mason was soon meeting with the gang leadership on each visit. According to a newspaper report of a speech she gave at the University of Illinois, she cited the problems encountered by Project ABLE, a Stateville prisoners' organization founded by former Chicago gang members. "The administration is up-tight because they are afraid the gang members will run the institution," she said. "Well, in effect, they run it anyway."

"If I'm taking a program down there, all I do is tell the inmate leaders that I don't want any trouble and there won't be any."[52]

After Dorothy Mason was barred from entering the prison (except to visit an inmate, whom she later married), Ma Houston became Operation PUSH's prison representative. Now in her seventies, Ma Houston, a religious fundamentalist,[53] has been tending to the needs of jail and prison inmates for decades. Over the years she has stubbornly and persistently made her way to the prisons around the state, taking gifts to the inmates, helping them with simple requests. She enjoys great respect and popularity among the inmates. Quite recently she was appointed to the three-member Administrative Review Board in Springfield (see chapter 4), which is the last-appeals stage of the disciplinary and grievance process. Houston, like Mason, is no revolutionary. Her main concern at Stateville seems to be that the men are being treated as fairly and humanely as possible under the circumstances. Her presence, like that of others from prisoner interest groups, is met with apprehension and hostility by the staff.

The second key figure from the black community to have an impact on Stateville is Peggy Smith Martin, a one-term legislator in the Illinois House from the Woodlawn district of Chicago. After her inauguration as a legislator in January 1973, Martin seemed to take over the role that Mason had played during the previous two years.

Dorothy Mason and Ma Houston had already told Martin about the prison (gang) leadership, and she proceeded to contact them immediately upon entering the prison. She saw her role as providing a communication conduit between the rival gangs. She claims also to have attempted to make them more politically aware. "I think that around me I brought a great deal of communication among the organizations, including the Muslims and Black Panthers. We all met in a single room—they realized they needed to cooperate rather than be destroyed."[54]

Martin was more difficult to neutralize since there was no danger of her being expelled and excluded from the prison. In addition she was appointed to the Governor's Visiting Committee, which strengthened the legitimacy of her presence. Antipathy toward Representative Martin reached a peak in the late fall 1974, when she brought news columnist Barbara Reynolds to the prison as her "assistant." The result was a *Chicago Today* article ("Fear Rules Stateville a Year after the Riot") which was bitterly critical of the administration and the lack of rehabilitative programs.[55] During this period, Martin was having difficulties with the Cook County Board of Elections (ultimately her name was kept off the November ballot). A circular urging prisoners to support her campaign by canvassing their families and friends was distributed by unknown means throughout the prison.

On 10 January 1975, after two years in office, Peggy Smith Martin released her findings on the state of the Illinois prisons. In an introduction she wrote: "Illinois' prisons fester with racism; resident development and rehabilitation in the true sense of the word are the exception; extreme disciplinary action was discovered; punishment was found to be more emphasized than return to the community."[56] The report was generally critical of the administration and the guard staff. Martin charged that the administration lacked "meaningful and realistic" goals and "that there are no departmental goals, written and mutually agreed upon; [instead there are] a hodge-podge of thousands of differing and often conflicting personal objectives operative in wardens, guards, staff and residents."

With respect to the guards, Peggy Smith Martin explained that she found great cooperation among some [of the young black] guards and absolute intransigence among others [the rural whites].[57]

> Illinois is lucky to have hundreds of fine guards and front-line staff. I hope these men and women read this report. . . .
>
> Unfortunately I have also met a large number of not-so-fine front-line personnel. I have dealt with people who are obviously unqualified and unfit to work with inmates. I have met discourteous and uncouth staff; I have been on the receiving end of hate stares, lies, and intentional inconveniences. I have been given the run around and ignored on numerous occasions.

After the newspaper article and the release of the report there was extreme emotional reaction toward Martin at Stateville. In the waning weeks of her term of office in January 1975, the warden and top staff refused her the favors (lunch, pitchers of juice, etc.) or the deference to which she had been accustomed at the prison as a legislator.

The only current group[58] with regular contact at the prison is the Citizens Visiting Committee, which was formed under the persistent efforts of the Illinois Prison and Jail Project, a committee of the Alliance to End Repression.[59]

The Citizens Visiting Committee was formed by nominations made by dozens of community groups. The composition of the visiting committee was chosen by the chairman of the Adult Advisory Board of the Illinois Department of Corrections (then Norval Morris) and representatives of the Urban League, the League of Women Voters, Casa Central, and the Illinois Congress of Ex-offenders. A full-time employee of the Illinois Prison and Jail Project was appointed chairman of the committee which was ultimately composed of prominent establishment figures like the Reverend Victor Obenhaus of the Chicago Theological Seminary as well as self-avowed radicals. The committee began visiting each of the "northern" prisons in May 1974 and issued monthly reports. Mostly they criticized cases of organizational mismanagement, such as improper handling of food, dirty cell houses, and improper handling of inmate medical problems, and asked why the administration had seemingly failed to implement its own rules and policy.

As with the other groups and individuals discussed here, the administration reacted defensively to the Citizens Visiting Committee. The following written report of the committee's 7 March 1975 visit to Stateville, and the bitter official response by the assistant warden, which once again indicates the strong tendency toward cynicism even among reformers on the staff, evidence the hostility.

> Counselors now have their offices in the cellhouse in cells converted for that purpose, providing inmates greater accessibility to counseling services. However, as one inmate remarked, "There are so many guys with serious problems the counselors just can't get around to them." Another man observed that some of the counselors are afraid of the inmates.
>
> The cellhouse appeared cleaner than on previous visits, but there was a heavy odor of perspiration in the air, and many men complained that they had not had a shower in two weeks. Regulations called for clean bed linen to be provided for each week,

but CVC noted many cells without any sheets and others with very dirty sheets. Some inmates claim that if they turn their sheets in to the prison laundry, they don't get them back, a situation the Warden said he would look into.

New disciplinary procedures calling for minor infractions to be handled in the cellhouse by a Program Team with more serious violations referred to the Institutional Adjustment Committee, have been operative in Stateville since the middle of January, 1975. The committee was somewhat disappointed to hear the same complaints from men in segregation charging that they were being continued in segregation status due to an accumulation of petty tickets, or had been placed in segregation for a non-violent infraction such as calling an officer a name. Warden Brierton stated that a constant review was being conducted to ensure that inmates were not receiving "harassment" tickets.

Mr. Brierton spoke with some enthusiasm about the decorating design and color scheme planned in the repainting of B House. Nothing can make B House a pleasant place to be, but Mr. Brierton feels that redoing the drab interior with bright colors provides a more livable environment for the residents housed there. The committee agrees, looks toward the time when official thinking and public consciousness will demand that such buildings be razed and more humane solutions be found to cope with anti-social behavior.

And the assistant warden's reply:

There is a special sort of tension that develops when one has to respond to a report that is essentially inane in its content. The Committee fails to provide a coherent and relevant perspective regarding administrative operation of the Stateville Correctional Center. They prefer to discuss procedure without providing a perspective as to where particular procedures fit into the overall operation of the institution. They prefer to rely on the statement of a few inmates who they apparently treat as spokesmen for all the residents at the Stateville Correctional Center. An example is that of counselling; they talk about greater accessibility, then relying on the statement of one inmate, they conclude that counsellors are afraid of inmates or they just don't get around. Such statements do not provide a total picture of the counselling activities and certainly can mislead readers of their reports.

We find pathos when they refer to the operation of the "B" House Segregation Unit. They fail to understand that behavior in segregation is a worthwhile indicator to be used in evaluating a man's return to general population. I take issue with the statement that there are harassment tickets. I don't agree with their pathos that nothing can be done to change "B" House. Such thinking is reminiscent of the late 60s and early 70s when people decried that large maximum security institutions would have to be razed. They fail to understand that construction of prisons is expensive and that we have no alternative but to improve the conditions of our present maximum securities. Is the CVC prepared to donate millions of dollars to build new institutions? Perhaps my pathos is showing, but I doubt it.

The Press

Stateville's current warden, unlike Ragen, does not regard the press as a potential ally. There is little attempt to draw the press's attention to positive achievements at Stateville. The basic feeling is that the more invisible the prison is, the better.[60] Most of the staff have defined the press as an adversary. This feeling has led to bitterness against the Springfield administrations of both Bensinger and Sielaff, which declared an open relationship with the press.[61]

The newspapers themselves have become more professionalized and bureaucratized. News stories are less colored by the views of the publisher. On the other hand, the media is still dependent upon the top administrative officials for most of their prison news.[62] Aside from a very few special features on the prison, there has been little media coverage of Stateville except for disturbances, the appointment of new wardens, and the termination of the United States Army's Malaria Project, which had been conducting research at Stateville since World War II.

The large Chicago dailies assign no regular reporters to cover the prisons and rarely report prison news. The *Chicago Defender,* a major black Chicago newspaper, gives greater and more critical attention to the prison. Lu Palmer, a black news commentator who wrote first for the *Daily News* and then for his own newspaper, the *Black Express,* as well as anchoring a radio program on WVON, has probably been the most significant media critic of the prison in recent years. During the summer of 1972, Palmer produced a column or radio program almost daily on the "inhumane and racist conditions at Stateville."

The radical press was, of course, barred from Stateville. To get subscriptions to the inmates numerous court battles had to be fought. The most popular radical papers are *Rising up Angry, Up against the Bench,* and *On Ice.*[63] Whether the inmates subscribe to them because the administration has tried to keep them out or because of a considerable radical sympathy—or both—is unclear.

Every time that censorship of the underground press has become a point of dispute, the administration has lost. The administrative staff cannot understand the rationale behind the courts' approval of militant literature (including white racist hate literature), since the literature is believed to heighten tensions in what they regard as an already volatile prison situation. The most important dispute to date over radical literature involves two issues of *On Ice* published by the Illinois Congress of Ex-offenders, an affiliate of Chicago Connections. The lead article in volume 3, number 2 (undated), issued shortly after inmates seized cell house B (fall 1973), was entitled "Stateville Penitentiary—Incubation of Disease." It began:

> To those of us on the outside who are familiar with the oppressive environment of Stateville Penitentiary and with the brutality which occurs within its walls, the uprising of September 6th was not a surprise. We were continuously amazed throughout the summer at the patience and endurance of the men inside. In this series of articles, we attempt to show the bases for our amazement and our perspective.

The issue went on to portray the various "inhumane conditions" at Stateville—no showers, dirty food, cold cell houses, etc. The Cannon administration decided to stop the issue from being distributed, but it did not follow the clear censorship procedure that had been prescribed by consent decree in Judge Frank McGarr's federal courtroom. When the issue was excluded summarily, without written notice to the inmates and without a written decision having been made by the literary committee, *On Ice* went back to court to ask for a citation of contempt. Almost a year later, a federal court ordered Stateville to distribute the paper to the prisoners and to reimburse Chicago Connections for its mailing costs, and withheld a decision on whether to hold Sielaff, Brierton, Cannon, and several lesser administrators in contempt and liable to jail sentences. Cannon was removed from office shortly after the hearing.

Conclusion

The transformation of the prison into a rational-legal bureaucracy has not proceeded without setbacks and even now is not complete. Such a transformation was incompatible with the tenets of the authoritarian regime. It was also incompatible with the human relations model of management that characterized the Twomey and Cannon administrations. Brierton has openly embraced the rational-legal bureaucratic model and has taken the initiative in its detailed articulation.

The reforms mandated by the courts can only be implemented by well-run organizations. Even for mature and efficient bureaucracies the costs of complying with court orders may be high. Due process procedures, hearings, and appeals place considerable strain on administrative resources and may impair efficient management.

We need to reemphasize that the courts have raised the expectations of the inmates about the standards of treatment to which they are entitled. The very proliferation of inmate lawsuits is to be explained in terms of higher expectations as well as by liberalized procedures. Whether rational administration and responsive grievance mechanisms will be sufficient to meet the press of inmate demands is a serious issue to be faced in the future.

The most significant outside organizations with respect to shaping the institution's goals are the panoply of public agencies intersecting with the prison. ILEC to some degree has its independent correctional program built around the "justice model" propounded by David Fogel.[64] The "justice model" calls for a far greater redefinition of authority relationships and organizational roles than does the "corporate model" adhered to by David Brierton. To date tension has been avoided by agreement on the need to sponsor programs for the physical reconstruction of Stateville and for the addition of much security technology. Whether in the future strains in the relationship will develop is a matter to watch closely.

There are already signs of strain between the affirmative action office and the prison. Much objected to are the special recruitment drives in the inner city. There is also disgruntlement among whites and blacks over race being considered an issue in promotions. The Affirmative Action office continues to raise questions about hiring decisions and especially about the high percentages of black guards who are discharged.

The outside private-interest groups are less significant in determining organizational goals and behavior than is apparent from the rhetoric of administrators. It is doubtful whether these private interest groups have had any direct impact at all on policy making. They do, however, affect staff morale, which is sensitive to what seems to be pervasive public sympathy for the prisoner. The importance of what is perceived to be the prevailing public opinion should not be discounted.

Nor does the press appear to have an important impact on policy formation. During the September 1974 B house takeover, the *Chicago Tribune* quoted a Stateville guard as blaming a television special on Stateville for triggering the riot. But the accusation hardly seems justified. The few TV news spots on Stateville have tended to be objective and dispassionate. Certainly the radical press has contributed to politicizing the population, but it is difficult to assess how deep or widely disseminated is its influence.

6 Penetration of the Gangs

> The gang leaders have absolute control. T. could just have told his men to tear it down and they would—a lot of these guys would die for their gang—dying doesn't mean anything to them. They'd rather die than let it be said that they wouldn't go all the way.
>
> Fifty-year-old black inmate (Stateville 1972)

The dominance of four Chicago street gangs at Stateville since 1969 must be related to the rise of professional administration and to the intrusion of the courts. The abandonment of the "hands off" doctrine exposed an authoritarian regime to outside accountability, limited the institution's recourse to coercive sanctions and provided the inmates with a legitimate means of expression with which to challenge the system of social control. The rise of professional administration, informed by the rehabilitative ideal and the human relations model of management, led to intrastaff conflict, a decline in the morale of the guard force, and ultimately to the deterioration of the organization's capacity to meet basic control and maintenance goals. It was only in the context of this organizational crisis that the gangs were able to organize, recruit, and achieve dominance.

The Politicization of Chicago Street Gangs

Three black gangs—the Blackstone Rangers (who later renamed themselves the Black P Stone Nation), the Devil's Disciples (sometimes referred to as the Black Gangster Disciple Nation) and the Conservative Vice Lords—have been given extensive attention by the media and by scholars.[1] The Latin

Kings, while less well known nationally, seem to have followed a somewhat similar pattern of growth and development. Each of the four gangs is territorially based in Chicago's slum districts, and, because of their great size, the relatively high age of their leaders, and their imperialistic annexation of smaller gangs they might aptly be termed "supergangs."[2]

Not only are the supergangs larger and more violent than their predecessors of the past several decades but their location at the intersection of the civil rights movement, the youth movement, and a reconstructed relationship between the federal government and grassroots society suggests a divergence from the traditional street gang.[3] Supporters of these gangs have interpreted their development as an evolution toward political and social consciousness.[4] The police and other critics have defined the gangs' flirtations with politics, community action, and minority movements as a thin facade, and have labeled those who have accepted the gangs as legitimate community organizations naive dogooders.[5]

Beginning with the Kennedy administration, large amounts of federal monies became available for programs aimed at fighting juvenile delinquency.[6] In 1965 Chicago received a $685,000 grant to coordinate all street work programs ("Streets") in the city *under the direction of City Hall.* But, according to Lawrence Sherman, Streets failed to maintain a working relationship between the police and the social agencies for two complementary reasons: "its expanded purpose of social change and the changing socio-political environment."[7] Sherman attributes the termination of Streets to the aldermanic candidacy of detached gang worker Fred Hubbard in 1966. "The great fear at city hall was that Streets would channel gang members into the civil rights movement."[8]

After 1966, relations between the police and the city government on the one hand, and the gangs and their supporters in various social agencies on the other, deteriorated completely. The aspirations of certain liberal and radical groups to politicize gangs, and the intense fears of the Daley administration that gangs would indeed become politicized, coincided to define these street gangs as proto-grassroots community organizations whose goal was to seize political and economic power in Chicago.

The emergence of the Black P Stone Nation, and to a lesser

extent the Devil's Disciples, as potentially powerful political forces on Chicago's South Side was the consequence of a combination of factors: talented charismatic leadership, support from local liberal and even radical groups, federal intervention, and violent police opposition.

After 1965, the First Presbyterian Church (in the Woodlawn area of Chicago), under the leadership of Reverend John Fry, became the central headquarters for the Blackstone Rangers and the catalyst for its organizational growth. Several of the Stones' leaders (including President Eugene Hairston and Vice-president Jeff Fort) were placed on the church payroll in order to carry out community work with their own gangs. From the beginning, Reverend Fry attempted to transform the Rangers from a traditional lower-class gang built around conflict with rival gangs (primarily the Disciples) into a political organization that would dominate Woodlawn and possibly the entire city of Chicago.[9]

The spring of 1968 brought a $50,000 grant from the Kettering Foundation (General Motors money) to the First Presbyterian Church to continue its work with the Blackstone Rangers. The money was primarily used to pay bail for the increasing number of Rangers who were arrested, as conflict with the police escalated. More significant than the Kettering grant was the almost one million dollar OEO Youth Manpower Project grant of June 1967.[10] Originally the Reverend Fry had attempted to obtain the grant for the Stones alone, but the Office of Economic Opportunity balked at the idea, requiring that the Disciples be brought in and that the grant be used to stimulate opportunities for a broader cross section of Woodlawn's youth. The grantee for the project was to be The Woodlawn Organization (TWO), a broad-based grassroots community organization begun by Saul Alinsky in 1961, and one often at odds with the mayor. OEO pushed through the program against apathy from the mayor's office and intense opposition from the Chicago Police Department, thereby defining a new relationship between the federal government and the grassroots minority community which had, heretofore, always looked to local government as the source of public benefits. The only concession to local government was OEO's last-minute announcement that the head of the Youth Manpower Project would be chosen with the consent of the mayor. None of the candidates proposed by TWO was approved by the mayor, and a full-time administrative director for the Youth Manpower Project was never chosen.

The goal of the Youth Manpower Project was to train ghetto youth in rudimentary academic skills and place them in private industry. The teaching was to be carried out by gang leaders acting as "subprofessionals" at four centers in Woodlawn, two manned by the Rangers and two by the Disciples. One of the Rangers' centers was the third floor of the First Presbyterian Church. Gang leaders were employed as assistant project directors, center chiefs, and instructors for annual salaries of $5,000–$6,500. Gang members attended the centers for instruction and received $45 per week plus traveling allowance. The program was novel, experimental, and highly controversial. School officials claimed that the gangs were forcing students to drop out of school in order to participate in the Youth Manpower Project and to pay kickbacks to the gang leaders. The police claimed that the centers were being used for narcotics, sex, gambling, and storing weapons.

Following the award of the OEO grant in the spring of 1967, the Gang Intelligence Unit (GIU) was reorganized, placed under the internal investigation division of the Chicago Police Department, and assigned a new "tough" commander. Participants in the project were regularly stopped on the street, searched, verbally abused, and arrested on disorderly conduct and curfew violation charges. The training centers and TWO headquarters itself were frequently intruded upon by the police without search warrants.[11]

The newspapers, especially the *Chicago Tribune,* continually criticized the Youth Manpower Project. In the spring of 1968, Senator John McClellan's Permanent Subcommittee on Investigations of the Committee on Government Operations held public hearings in Washington on the grant and project.[12] Senators McClellan, Karl Mundt, and Carl Curtis were clearly committed to exposing the deficiencies of the program, particularly in light of the large OEO grant to YOU (Youth Organizations United) pending at the time as well as the request by the Youth Manpower Project for another year's funding. The senators spent more time illuminating sordid details of the relationship of Fry and LaPaglia to the Stones than they did investigating TWO and the Youth Manpower Project. In fact, the senators often seemed confused about the organizational affiliations of the various witnesses and tended not to distinguish between TWO and the First Presbyterian Church.

The committee's star witness, George "Watusi" Rose, was a former leader of the Stones turned police informer who described the ways in which the Stones were colluding with Fry and LaPaglia to milk the project and deceive The Woodlawn Organization. He testified that the Rangers coerced children to pay tribute in order to be allowed to go to school, conducted shakedowns of Woodlawn merchants, and received kickbacks from the trainees. Jeff Fort was called to testify, but his attorney, Marshall Patner, led Fort out of the hearings when his request for the right to cross-examine all the witnesses who had leveled charges against the Blackstone Rangers was denied.

Once the hearings indiscriminately brought out even the thinnest rumors of scandals associated with the Youth Manpower Project, there was no chance that it would be funded anew as had been requested. The project terminated in the summer of 1968. (The YOU grant was subsequently vetoed by the White House.)

At the same time that the Blackstone Rangers and Disciples were receiving government money (and some private grant money as well) on the South Side, the older Vice Lords gang[13] was beginning to move in the same direction on Chicago's West Side. In the summer of 1967, a young white liberal graduate of Dartmouth, the University of Michigan School of Social Work, and the Peace Corps arrived in Lawndale to conduct research on the attitude of ghetto youth toward poverty programs for TransCentury. Over the course of the next two and one-half years David Dawley became deeply involved with the Conservative Vice Lords, lived in their neighborhood, and took part in their highest-level decision making.[14]

Whether the involvement of the Vice Lords in a host of social action programs would have occurred without Dawley is an open question. While he was associated with them, however, the Vice Lords moved further than any of the other Chicago gangs toward programs of community betterment. In the summer of 1967 the Vice Lord leaders attended meetings at Western Electric and Sears Roebuck; the result was "Operation Bootstrap," which formed committees for education, for recreation, and for law, order, and justice. But things did not really get off the ground for the Vice Lords until February 1968, when they received a $40,000 grant from the Rockefeller Foundation. In rapid succession the Vice Lords founded a host of economic and social ventures.[15]

Until 1968 the Vice Lords maintained good relations with the Regular Democratic organization and the police, but their movement toward political and social activism brought increasing strain to these arrangements. The Vice Lords worked with Jesse Jackson in Operation Breadbasket, and in the summer of 1969 joined with the Coalition for United Community Action to protest the lack of black employers on construction sites in black neighborhoods.[16]

In the 1968 political campaign the Stones and Vice Lords both worked against the Chicago Democratic machine. At least on the South Side, according to Sherman, the traditional Democratic majorities were deflated.[17] After the election the Gang Intelligence Unit was increased from thirty-eight to two hundred officers. In early 1969 the mayor announced a "crackdown on gang violence." State's attorney Edward Hanrahan announced that the gang situation was the most serious crime problem in Chicago.

It is difficult to say with certainty how many members of the Blackstone Rangers, Disciples, Vice Lords, and Latin Kings were committed to the state prisons between 1967 and 1975.[18] Membership lists for the street gangs are not available (even assuming that membership could be defined). The warden of the Cook County Jail told the McClellan committee in July 1968 that there were approximately 275–300 Blackstone Rangers and the same number of Disciples in the Cook County Jail. During the summer of 1968, the jail experienced the kind of gang violence that became commonplace in the state prisons during the next half-dozen years.[19]

The mayor's office's 1970 report "Organized Youth Crime in Chicago" gave no total number for gang members who were sent to the penitentiary.[20] The report dealt exclusively with three gangs—Vice Lords, Blackstone Rangers, and Disciples. The report stated "that of the approximately 300 total indictments [of members of these three groups] for 1969, there have been over 100 felony convictions, 20 for murder." Assuming that a substantial percentage of this group of 100 was sent to prison (and there is not the slightest reason to believe that they received any leniency) this suggests a sizable gang presence, which was swelled by vigorous recruitment, in the state prisons by 1970. Many of those named before the McClellan committee as leaders of the Stones and Disciples, and as employees of the Youth Manpower Project, have done time at Stateville.

How can one evaluate the experience with businesses, social agencies, politicians, and police shared by the Blackstone Rangers, Disciples, and Vice Lords during the late 1960s? What kind of world view did they carry with them to the state prisons as they were increasingly arrested and convicted after 1968?

Whether these supergangs had indeed become politicized has been the subject of considerable public and scholarly debate.[21] The most thoughtful comment on the question of the politicization of the late 1960 street gangs has been provided by Walter B. Miller, who recognizes that there are at least two views of what is meant by "politicized gang."

> The notion of "transforming gangs by diverting their energies from traditional forms of gang activities—particularly illegal forms—and channeling them into 'constructive' activities is probably as old, in the United States, as gangs themselves." Thus, in the 1960's when a series of social movements aimed at elevating the lot of the poor through ideologically oriented, citizen-executing political activism became widely current, it was perhaps inevitable that the idea be applied to gangs. Two major models of activism existed—a more "radical" militant model, which saw gangs as a spearhead in the attempt to undermine established sources of power (often white power), and a less radical "social betterment" model, which conceived gangs as the basis of a kind of indigenous community service enterprise.[22]

Miller counts the Blackstone Rangers and Devil's Disciples as having been politicized on the "social betterment" model but concludes that "even among the most affected, there is little evidence that activism replaced illegal and/or violent pursuits."

This is not to say, however, that the supergangs were not affected by the social movements of their day or by their intermittent contacts with liberals and radicals. As Miller argues:

> One product of the Civil Rights Movement was the addition of a new kind of justificatory vocabulary to the traditional modes for explaining gang activity. This new vocabulary incorporated basic ideological tenets of the Black Rights Movement and applied to customary forms of gang behavior concepts such as "exploita-

tion by the power structure," "restitution for past injustices," and "brutalization by the system." But verbal behavior must be distinguished from actual practice. By and large, black gang members continued to do the kinds of things they had always done.[23]

To state that the Chicago street gangs became politicized in the late 1960s thus means one of three things: (1) that the street gangs adopted a radical ideology from the militant civil rights movement, (2) that the street gangs became committed to social change for their community as a whole, or (3) that the street gangs became politically sophisticated, realizing that the political system could be used to further their own ends—money, power, organizational growth.

I believe that the third sense of the term is most applicable to the Rangers and Disciples. The effect of increased media and establishment attention was to make their gang leadership less parochial and more aware of the opportunities that might be realized from "milking the system." Insofar as the gangs had a model of development, it was the Daley model rather than those of Jesse Jackson or Eldridge Cleaver. Insofar as the supergangs became politicized, in the sense of linking their interests to the social and economic betterment of their communities, the Vice Lords went the furthest.

No doubt there are considerable differences with respect to the type and degree of politicization of different leaders even within the same gangs. While some leaders may have been affected by the radical rhetoric of the Panthers and Students for a Democratic Society, this never seemed a likely path of development for the supergangs. The request by 1968 demonstration leaders that the gangs join in protesting the Democratic convention was rejected by all the gangs.

To the extent that the gang structure provides a status system for its membership, there exists a highly vested interest in its perpetuation for its own sake. Radical politics requires commitment to transcendent values and leaves less opportunity for achieved status for the average youth. Gang leaders from these organizations think less of acting on behalf of their neighborhoods than acting on behalf of their membership.

While the gangs may have become politicized during the late 1960s, their very gang structures set the limits for the degree to which this politicization could progress. Unwilling to give up their primary loyalties to their own gangs on the streets or in prison in favor of more inclusive political symbols and ideologies, the gangs ultimately served as a counterforce to radical politicization.[24]

Transition of Stateville's Inmate Social System[25]

Whatever "truth" there is to the claim that the crackdown on street gangs was politically motivated, the gang leaders interpreted it this way. They brought with them to the prisons a sense of political prisonership as well as a set of high expectations about the kinds of deference they could demand of institutional authorities. They also maintained important ties with outside forces who continued to believe in their capacity to provide leadership to the minority community. To the prison administrators of the early seventies, the gangs posed the challenge of intact organizational structures, highly charismatic leaders, support from the streets, and a long history of inter-gang warfare.

By the summer of 1972 it was the consistent estimate of Stateville gang leaders, of "off brands" (non-gang members), and of guards and administrators that at least 50 percent of the inmate population was affiliated with one of the four gangs. The approximately 400 members of the Black P Stone Nation were governed at Stateville, as on the streets, by the gang's president and vice-president—Eugene "Bull" Hairston and Jeff Fort—and by a council of the "Main 21." Since at least several of the Main 21 have been consistently incarcerated at Stateville, daily decision making requires a consensus of the "Mains." Intermediate leaders are called "ambassadors" and "emirs." Hairston and Fort have been in relative isolation from the rest of their gang at the Diagnostic Depot in the Joliet branch; yet even in exile they make decisions for the Stones in all the Illinois penitentiaries. "The word" comes down from Hairston and Fort through transfers between the penitentiaries and through visitors who may be, for example, the sister of one leader and the wife of another. The recent introduction of telephone privileges also contributes to a fluid communication between street and various penitentiary chapters.

The Disciples claim a membership approximately as large as the Stones at Stateville. The Disciples are the least organized of the gangs, although their capacity for coordinated activity and collective action varies according to the particular leaders that are at Stateville at any point in time.[26] There has been considerable rivalry between leaders of the different branches and continual struggles for power. Ideally, decisions are made by a committee of chiefs and are implemented by cell house chiefs and by lower-ranking superintendents on the assignments. As is true for the Stones, complex, coordinated collective action rarely occurs, and formal decision making is often problematic. The following mimeographed document was turned up by the chief guard in the fall of 1974.

The eight names above are the names of the eight chiefs that will run the joint from here on out. All of them are capable of holding and handling their positions. They will pick another member of the organization to set on the committees with them making it nine. These men are not cell house chiefs. "They are chiefs of the entire joint" the reason this committee is set up is to assure that no Disciple no matter what branch he is from will be abused by a cell house chief. They will use their heads as well as their hands when necessary to keep things running smooth. As you can see from the names above they are from many different branches of the organization this so that as many branches of the organization as possible will be represented. I realize that there are many chiefs whose names are not mentioned above. This is not meant to be disrespectful. Common sense tells us that all of us can not be on the committee. There will be many things these men will have to do to get the joint in order after coming off lockup. The members with problems are to take them to these men. If you do not know all of these men on the list I advise you to seek them out and get to know them.[27]

Like the Stones, the Disciples at Stateville remain tied to their organization on the outside. In the fall of 1974, David Barksdale, king of the Disciples since its inception in 1961, died (of natural causes). This precipitated a struggle for power inside Stateville.

Dear. S. Everybody feels bad and think this is the end. Don't no nation crumble because it has lost its king. We have to get a successor and make this the beginning of something new and more powerful. King David got to live thru us all! We can't let his death be in vain. So everybody must ask themselves those questions that got to be answered here and now! What am "I" going to do?! Am "I" going to be a Disciple until the day "I" die? See I already know what I am going to do because I have made that

> individual decision that everybody else have to make, as thats I'm going to be a Disciple forever! And I know all of the most righteous ones feel the same way. They will stand tall and these are the only ones we want and need.

The struggle for power does not seem to be totally resolved as of February 1975, but a new king, who is an inmate at Stateville, has been chosen as Barksdale's successor.

Within the penitentiary there are estimated to be between 150 and 200 Vice Lords. Their administration is very well structured. Responsibility for decision making remains in the hands of BH,[28] who before being committed was one of the Vice Lords' top leaders. Because decision making is vested in one individual, the Vice Lords appear to make decisions with the least difficulty. They are far less involved in "humbug" at the prison than the Stones or Disciples.

The Latin Kings are the largest Latin gang in Chicago. They cannot be identified with any single neighborhood, as their chapters are sprawled across the city. Most of the Kings are Puerto Rican, but there are Mexicans as well. On Chicago's streets the Kings have also been involved in a number of economic enterprises. The Stateville Latin Kings constitute an autonomous and distinct chapter of the Latin King federation. Inside Stateville the Kings associate almost exclusively with Spanish inmates. Most of the staff members agree that "we never have any problems out of the Kings." Rarely does a King come before the disciplinary court for a serious rule infraction. Decisions for the Kings are made by a council of ranking chiefs.

Whether an individual has grown up in one of the gangs or has only recently "hooked up" in jail or prison has important consequences for the gang as well as for the individual. Even among those who have a long history of association with their organization there are various degrees of involvement.[29] One of the Disciple leaders at Stateville pointed out:

> Approximately 15–20 percent of the members are highly committed which means that they would knock down a screw [guard] if I asked them to do it. About 40 percent of the Disciples are least committed. They may have joined because they like the leaders. They cannot really be counted on—in case of trouble they'll run to lock themselves up in their cells. The others are somewhere in between.

The recruited members correspond for the most part to the least committed. From discussions with leaders and independents, I estimate that between 25 and 50 percent of the Disciples at Stateville have been recruited within the penal institutions.

In contrast with the intense pressures experienced by an unaffiliated convict, the gang member from the street has no difficulty at all adjusting to the new environment. The warden of the Pontiac prison told me: "When a new guy comes up here it's almost a homecoming—undoubtedly there are people from his neighborhood and people who know him." The chief of the Disciples claims to have known about seventy-five of the Disciples upon arrival at Stateville. A young leader in the Latin Kings noted that, because of his active participation in the superstructure of the Kings on the street, he knew all but two of the Kings upon arrival. His first afternoon at Stateville he received a letter from the ranking chief of the Latin Kings at Stateville welcoming him to the "family."

BH, chief of the Vice Lords, explains that when a young Vice Lord is spotted coming into the prison, the leaders will see to it that he is set up right away with coffee, tea, cigarettes, deodorant, and soap. Normally the gang member will have the situation run down for him by his cell-house chief. Consider the following written rules passed out by the Disciples.

There are certain allegations that a Disciple must govern himself by. We as a united coalition must dutily abide by these rules and regulations thus far provided by the omnipotent Prince, or your commandering chief of your designated cell house.

I. Degradation of another Disciple, will not be tolerated at any time.

II. Disrespect of any Governing body of said cell house, will not be permitted.

III. There will not at any time, be any unnecessary commotion while entering the cell house.

IV. Homosexual confrontation toward another Disciple, will definitely not be tolerated.

V. Dues will be paid up on time at any designated schedule.

VI. Fighting another Disciple, without consulting a Governing chief will result in strict disciplining.

VII. Upon greeting another Disciple, proper representation will be ascertained.

VIII. There will never be an act of cowardice displayed by any Disciple, for a Disciple is always strong and brave.

IX. There will not be any cigarettes upon entering the hole for those who relentlessly, obstruct the rules and regulations of the organization, or the institution.

X. Anyone caught perpetrating the above rules and regulations with disorder and dishonesty, will be brought before the committee and dealt with accordingly.

DISCIPLE LOVE:

Govern yourself and walk like a true Disciple, the eyes of the nation are upon you.

The gang in prison serves important economic and psychological functions. To some degree the gang functions as a buffer against poverty. Each organization has a poor box. Each of the six cell-house chiefs in each gang collects cigarettes from his members and stores them for those who are needy. When a member makes a particularly good "score," he is expected to share some of the bounty with the leaders and donate to the poor box. The following notice was circulated to members of the Black P Stone Nation.

CITIZENS OF THE ALMIGHTY B.P.S.N. ATTENTION: F-House
For the past month, no Stone has placed anything into the Nation's box (which is for every Stone in need). At present the Box contains twenty-five (25) packs, and none of this comes from any Stone in the Cell House. There have been many Stone's receiving but None have given. "THE EMIR" plainly stated that the Stone's Box was necessary (Mandatory). So therefore it must be kept up, at all time's. As of the above date, all Stone's must pay two packs weekly. There is no reason for any Committee Member to come to you, when you know it's due. "Eusi Outlaw," and JM, are in charge of the box so you can give them to either. Records will be kept of everything coming in, or going out, and everyone shall be kept informed on the progress of all thing's coming in.

This observer has often seen the leaders giving away cigarettes and other items. When a gang member is placed in isolation, he can expect to have food and cigarettes passed to him. While this welfare system may be more recognizable in its breach, at least some degree of material security is provided for those members who are without resources. This is especially true for members of the Vice Lords and Latin Kings. The Vice Lords sometimes provide correspondents and visitors for those gang members deserted by their families.

The gangs function as a communication network,[30] serving

to keep "their people" informed and placing a coherent definition of the situation on new policies and events. Inmate leaders often knew I was in the institution with a visitor upon our arrival. By means of "soldiers" assigned to jobs up front and as runners, yard gang workers, and cell house helpers, information and messages flow from front to back with great precision.[31]

There are several other functions which the gangs perform for their members. They provide a convenient distributional network for contraband goods. One Latin King informant explained that where an independent might be hesitant to make a large score because he might be caught with too much stuff, an organization member knows that within a number of minutes he can divest himself of the major share of the contraband.

The role of the gangs in organizing illicit activities is unclear. They have not in the past had a unified plan for organizing illicit enterprises, but individual members were active singly and in groups in supplying liquor, marijuana, nutmeg, and heroin, as well as in shaking down (robbing) independents. One reliable informant estimates that 75 percent of the "off brands" pay off to gang members. Recently the gangs have become more sophisticated in organizing the narcotics trade inside Stateville, and rivalry between Stones and Disciples for control is intense. The following Disciple memorandum was recently confiscated by guards.

STRUGGLE FOR ACHIEVEMENT

In order to be what we profess to be we must begin to utilize some of the same principles here (Penitentiary) that we will use in the fields (streets).

We must produce revenue in order to fuse our people together. We need revenue, and most important, activities in which to school and keep our people busy. Using the Concept that what we do today will help to strengthen us tomorrow.

(1) *Playing for Position:* This principle consist of putting our people into different positions, so we can begin to control some of the activities (Kitchen, General Store, Commissary, Voc. School, Tailor Shop, etc.).

If we have some of our people in these different shops, their prime objective should be to move into position so they can be of some use to the organization. In each of the shops there are goods that can be sold or exchanged, our job is to set-up the correct technique.

(2) Another Principle is the establishment of revenue making projects (Parlay Tickets, Pornography, Alcohol, Gambling, Marijuana/Pills, Numbers Game, etc.).

ANALYZATION

In any activity in which we choose to get involved with, we will need the necessary revenue:

(1) In establishing ourselves in the Alcohol/Marijuana/Pill trade we need—money, connection, buyers/sellers.

MONEY

Money is no problem if we have a pay job, or receive money from home on a regular basis; these monies are good for some of the activities in which we want to get involved in. What we need besides these monies is some people in the fields (streets) who would be willing to invest either the necessary monies or materials, until we can become self-supporting. On second thought, even the money that we have here can be mailed to an individual in the field so we can get the necessary materials.

CONNECTION

We will have to make arrangements with those people in the fields who are willing to buy, and transport the materials in which we need to conduct business. This should not be as hard as it may seem, we can utilize a guard working here or establish someone (our people) as a guard, or we will have to get help from the people in the fields.

BUYERS/SELLERS

Buyers and sellers is not a problem, we have plenty of both. Our problem will come in at the selling of the merchandise such as Marijuana/Pills, Pornography, and Alcohol, we have to receive as much cash as possible, in order to keep our business activities going. The cash do not necessarily have to be paid to us, but to some certain individual in the field. There are a couple of ways that this can be done. The buyer can mail the money from the institution, or he can have one of his people pay the debt.

By far the most important function the gangs provide their members at Stateville is psychological support.[32] GL, prison leader of the Disciples, explained, "These guys in my branch [of the Disciples] are closer to me than my own family. Anything I do around them is accepted—for stuff that my parents would put me down for, these guys elevate me to a pedestal." Every inmate informant expressed this opinion—that the organizations give to the members a sense of identification, a feeling of belonging, an air of importance. According to the chief of the Vice Lords, "It's just like a religion. Once a Lord always a Lord. People would die for it. Perhaps this comes from lack of a father figure or lack of guidance or from having seen your father beaten up or cowering from police. We never had anything to identify with. Even the old cons like me—they are looking for me to give them something they have been looking for for a long time."

Time and again gang members explained that, whether on the street or in the prison, the gang "allows you to feel like a man"; it is a family with which you can identify. Many times young members have soberly stated that the organization is something, the only thing, they would die for.

Members "represent" to each other by esoteric salutes and verbal greetings. The Disciples, for example, cross their arms hitting their fists against the chest, while the Stones offer a black power salute accompanied by "Stone love" or "Stone thing." Each organization has its own colors and insignias, often boldly flaunted on prison T-shirts and sweat shirts. The Latin King's insignia is a crown; the Stones' is an inverted pyramid.

All of the gangs are confluent with the justificatory vocabulary of protest. Leaders regularly maintain that they are "political prisoners," under the slogans of racial oppression, black nationalism, and revolution. The gangs demonstrate a rudimentary solidarity opposed to white society, white administration and white inmates. The explanation for this solidarity is not explained by formal organizational goals or by prison deprivations but by the political climate on the streets of the ghetto. Writing from his segregation cell at the Special Program Unit, a Stones' leader announced to the administration a new relationship between "gang bangers" and prison authorities.

I, Prince Namore, speaking as a representative of the Black P Stone Nation, would like to clarify important facets that have been overlooked in regards to the way citizens of the Nation have been classified as potential security risks and confined within S.P.U. First I would like to acquaint you with the philosophy of our nation. We have been branded with the stigma of being a "Chicago street gang." This allegation stems from the days when we were not fully aware of our potential of being a meaningful structure in our community. Our realization of this brought about a vast reconstruction of our views and aims, and we began to strive for the uplifting and refinement of our community.

Similar politicized vocabulary runs throughout recent underground Disciple literature circulated throughout Stateville.

The Oppressor (The power elite—the few people that rule most of the world) wants the oppressed (the minorities and poor whites who haven't and want to be given the opportunity to join their ranks) to remain ignorant, to prey on each other for monetary gain and for other obsolete reasons. They know that it is less easy to manipulate a mature man—a thinking man.

Since we have been incarcerated, we have been forced to think and as on the street (in the so-called civilized world) a large number of penal colony inhabitants have regressed. They had rather remain in childhood stage but as I have stated, it is against nature and therefore impossible.

We gradually become aware of various things quicker than a great number of people on the other side of these walls, mainly because we are not subjected to various forms of pacification, as they are. There is very little within the Penal Colony to divert our oppressors and their agents. We are compelled to see them as they are—our enemies—enemies of the people!!!

I am a very sad man. . . . I cannot begin to be happy until we, the oppressed—unite! I will be extremely pleased only when our oppressors heads are attached to their "flagpoles"! It wouldn't gratify me to take from someone who had little more than I. People who do that are agents whether they realize it or not. Just as anyone who deals or peddles dope to the oppressed. I couldn't get any pleasure wearing expensive clothes, etc., etc., and at the same time be fully aware that I acquired all those things as a result of helping the oppressor make my people sleeping giants!!!!!!!

Black consciousness and the political ramifications of incarceration have become salient issues. In contributing to the transformation of a group of inmates in itself to a group for itself, the gangs can be said to have contributed to the politicization of the prison. One articulate white inmate has summed up the situation as follows:

It is quite understandable that the polarity between the administration and the major force of inmates is increasing daily, despite the fact that the administration is attempting to allow the maximum amount of individuality and human expression by the inmates within the limits of their confinement. Although the benefits to the inmate are increasing daily, they are becoming increasingly more resistent and unresponsive to the enticement of the administration. Clear and simply, emerges the fact that the new inmates, especially the militant blacks, are no longer interested in the reform policies of the administration, because they symbolize the White Society that is oppressing them on the streets of Chicago. Prison reform is no different than ADC or Urban

Renewal, to the cynical blacks who have been bombarded with promises since the moment they became aware of their environment as children.[33]

While gang leaders have on the one hand adopted a "justificatory vocabulary," they have not abandoned their primary commitment to the organizational success of their own gangs. The few Black Panthers at Stateville have remained very much aloof from the gangs. They view gangs as counterrevolutionary and are viewed by the gangs as johnny-come-latelies to the problems of the black communities in which the gangs have grown up. An administrator once told me, "Fred Hampton was very out of place here; he used to talk to me for hours; he just couldn't identify with the gangs."

Even independent inmate observers have found it remarkable that gangs which have been killing each other for years on the street are able to communicate and cooperate smoothly behind Stateville's walls. GL, leader of the Disciples, for example, has told me that the man who stabbed his mother to death is reportedly at Stateville but that he does not want to learn his identity or he would be required to take action, which would be disastrous for him and the organization under the present circumstance of total confinement. During the summer of 1972, when I was carrying out my fieldwork with inmates, there was an absolute consensus among the leadership that inter-gang war must be avoided at all costs because the winner in such an event would only be the security staff, who were said to be anxiously awaiting an opportunity "to drag out their heavy artillery."

Any fight between members of rival gangs can have explosive consequences. Consequently, the leaders have developed a list of "international" rules to which all gangs have pledged to abide. The rules include the following:

1) There will be no rip-offs between organization members.
2) Each organization must stay out of the other organizations' affairs.
   a) In a dispute between members of two organizations, members of the third are to stand clear.
3) No organization will muscle in on a dealer already paying off to another organization.
4) Organizations will discipline their own members in the offended party's presence.
5) The organizations cannot claim to protect non-members as friends.

The Disciples, during the summer of 1972, did not feel that the international rules had been equally upheld. In two cases, the Disciple chiefs claimed to have disciplined members who were wrongfully involved in disputes with members of another organization. But when the situation was reversed, the Stones did not discipline their man and, as a consequence, the rules now seem to have ambiguous authority.

Most of the disputes within the prison occur between the Stones and the Disciples. The Latin Kings almost never become embroiled in any conflicts. When there is a fight between a Disciple and a Stone, the leadership is usually able to work out a solution, often by giving up their member for a head-to-head fight. During such negotiations the chief of the Vice Lords (recently described to me as Stateville's Henry Kissinger) is often placed in a mediating role. He may go to both sides and discuss the situation, stressing the importance of cooling things down and discouraging the indians from "jumping off." Many informants have described incidents which they were sure had ignited tensions to the breaking point, which were later quelled by negotiation among the leaders.

That a major riot, despite all predictions to the contrary, did not occur at Stateville during the summer of 1972 cannot be explained in terms of an accommodation between the formal and the informal organizations. It was the near universal opinion of "off brand" informants and some administrators as well that the absence of a riot was due to Project ABLE (to be discussed later in this chapter) and to the gang leaders. Time and again examples were cited of leaders stepping in to break up a fight or to cool imminent conflict.

The gang leaders explained their restraining activities by noting their fear that an Attica-type situation or an even worse slaughtering of "their people" would occur at Stateville if something "jumped off." They constantly reiterated the futility of any direct hostile confrontation with staff. Thus, the status quo has been guaranteed not by interests vested in an elaborate accommodation system but by a more calculated, strategic, and utilitarian analysis of the benefits and losses anticipated in a full-scale conflict.

The emergence of the four supergangs as the predominant inmate force at Stateville has had a profound impact on the inmate social system. First, the norms which once held the allegiance of a large majority of inmates have become less compelling. Prisoners at Stateville no longer identify themselves primarily in terms of their inmate status but according to their organizational allegiance. This has severely undermined whatever unifying effect the inmate code may once have had and balkanized the inmate social system. Inmate interests are often at odds with fractional interests. In many cases, the fractional interests prevail, as evidenced by the fact that the concept of serving group time now enjoys wider acceptance than doing one's own time.[34]

Many informants have pointed out that up to 1968 it was rare for inmates to steal from one another at Stateville. While a member of the Italian clique from Taylor Street in the 1950s might order another inmate to do his work for him or even order him to give him something, there was no widespread thieving or strong-arming like that which now pervades the prison.

Gang members simply see nothing wrong with "ripping off" independents. The fact that they occupy adjoining cells does not seem to offer a basis for solidarity. While the leaders are more likely to urge definitions of inmate solidarity on the indians, they are differentially committed to this definition of the situation among themselves and ineffective in operationalizing the commitment when it does exist.

While at one time inmates may have endorsed the principle of "doing your own time," the gangs endorse the morality of "doing gang time." Both chiefs and indians assert the leaders' responsibility to intercede on behalf of their people. Leaders want to inquire why an indian is being disciplined or why some off brand is giving a gang member a hard time.

Status and power within the prison prior to 1968 depended upon status within the formal organization. Inmates competed for good jobs. Those inmates who held the clerk jobs were in key positions to "lose" disciplinary tickets, arrange cell transfers, and collect daily parlay (gambling) slips. Runners had mobility to arrange homosexual liaisons and to relay parlay slips. Certain inmates under the Ragen and Pate regimes accumulated great influence and power.

When the gangs emerged at Stateville in 1969, they placed the old con power structure in physical and financial jeopardy. For the first time those convicts with good jobs were not necessarily protected in their dealings, legitimate or illegitimate. Seeing strength in numbers, the gang members attempted to take what they wanted by force. They seemed unconcerned about doing fifteen days in the hole (the limit imposed by the courts). When they went to the hole they were thrown in a cell with five or six fellow gang members. For the first time in history the old cons who "knew how to do time" found their lives disrupted and in danger. Gang members moved in to take over the "rackets." One informant described an instance where a half dozen "gang bangers" simultaneously put knives to his throat. Rather than cut the gangs in, many of the dealers went out of business.

The importance of the gangs on the prison community was not lost on some old cons. In one way or another, after 1969 they had to adjust to the new situation. Certain cons became "spokesmen" or "front men" for the gangs. BT of the Disciples and LB of the Stones both served as advisers to the leadership. LG helped Stone members with legal problems and was in turn granted a degree of respect by the organization leaders. However, these "old con" advisers have no standing or authority over the younger inmate gang members. Nor would they be able to claim a position of rank in the organization on the street.

It is true that no off brand remains unaffected by the gangs' presence. Those blacks, usually "old cons," who are not in the nations are victims of assault, theft, and extortion. Much depends upon the old con's ability to stand up for himself and to manipulate his environment. In numerous cases old cons have joined the gangs in "advisory capacities" rather than attempting to carve out a precarious independent role. A tough, young, and aggressive black inmate who is unaffiliated explained that "you must respect what the hierarchy says. If they ask for a work stoppage, for example, you'd have to stop work or be badly beaten."

Off brands generally remain unorganized, but there have been several attempts to create independent organizations as a counterforce. There are at least three cases where off brand black inmates were able to form not-for-profit inmate betterment corporations dedicated to helping inmates and achieving prison reforms. At its peak, the most successful of these organizations, the Kings New Breed, claimed two hundred members and was given recognition by the administration which allowed them a time and place to meet. The organization has far fewer members today because its founders have left Stateville.

The situation at Stateville is by far the most precarious for white inmates, who bear the brunt of the minority inmates' racial animosities. Among the white inmates no organizational structures existed in 1972, but one could distinguish secure and vulnerable cliques. Members of the former were secure because of fighting ability, gangland ties, legal skills, or alliance with staff members. Whites within vulnerable cliques were exposed to physical assault, rape, extortion, and constant harassment. By the fall of 1974, there were indications of the beginning of formal white organizations. The Ku Klux Klan and the House of the Golden Dragon began to develop at Menard, which has an approximately 50 percent white population. These racist organizations soon spread to the "northern" institutions, but the much smaller number of whites (10–15 percent) attenuates their effectiveness in providing protection. It is only the Spanish inmates, whether gang members or not, who seem not to be directly threatened by the gangs in the prison. Perhaps their security can be accounted for by the widely shared belief that "the Spanish stick together, if you fight one you fight them all," and by the often repeated phase, "the Spanish don't cut, they kill."

Thus, the old inmate social system characterized by its stratification system according to offense has been replaced by a balkanized social system where inmates relate to one another in blocks. To be unaligned in such a situation is to place oneself in a highly vulnerable position. Despite such organizations as the (black) Kings New Breed and the (white) House of the Golden Dragon, between 30 and 50 percent of the Stateville population remains independent. Where an inmate's influence was once rooted in his ability to manipulate the system through his position in the formal organization, today influence is based on organizational rank carried over from the street. The changing basis of power in the inmate social system means that there are fewer grounds for accommodation between inmates and staff.

A Crisis in Control

According to nearly all Illinois prison officials, the "new inmates" of the 1970s are impossible to control and are responsible for the crisis in control that has prevailed at Stateville and at the other Illinois prisons since 1970. But one has to exercise care in speaking of the "new inmates." There is reason to believe that each generation of prison officials looks back nostalgically to the "good old inmates" of previous decades. In fact, according to age, type of offense, and county of residence (but not race), the inmate population that swelled the penitentiaries after 1969 was little different from its predecessor generations (see tables 13–16).

Despite the strongly held belief of prison officials that today's inmates are younger and more aggressive, there is little indication that this is the case. In 1950, 40.9 percent of the inmates admitted to the Joliet Diagnostic Depot were under the age of twenty-five, compared with 25 percent in the early 1970s. (Some of this reduction of the younger age groups is perhaps accounted for by the expansion of the juvenile division.) Likewise, 31.7 percent of the inmates admitted to the penitentiary in 1953 had been convicted of robbery; of these 65.7 percent had committed armed robbery. In 1973, 26.4 percent were admitted for robbery, of which almost the same percentage, 65.5 percent, were in for armed robbery. It should also be pointed out that the percentage of Stateville/Joliet inmates from Cook County in 1955 was 81, and in 1973 almost the same—86.6.

All this is not to say that the inmate population of the 1970s is no different than the inmate population of previous decades. Quite to the contrary, we have seen that the percentage of black inmates increased from 47 percent in 1953 to 75 percent in 1974 and that the turnover of the inmate population has been greatly accelerated by a reduction in time served. We have also seen in the first section of this chapter that the cultural and political milieu of the inner city, which produces so great a percentage of the Cook County inmates, experienced a profound transition during the 1960s. While previous generations of inner city felons may have belonged to gangs, the forces of the late 1960s served to politicize the gangs of that period and raise their expectations about the type of demands that could be made upon institutions of authority.

My thesis is that while the minority members of the Chicago supergangs in the late 1960s did pose some difficult and unique problems of control for prison administrators, these problems merely exposed weaknesses in the prison's effort to establish a new system of authority consistent with the rehabilitative ideal, the human relations model of management and the demands of the courts.

One indication of the crisis in control is the high percentage of inmates held in special conditions of confinement. It was noted in chapter 5 that the percentage of inmates in special conditions of confinement increased dramatically after 1969. But the challenges to authority overwhelmed the capacity of the punishment mechanisms available to the staff. In part, the amelioration of conditions in isolation and segregation and the limitations placed upon the amount of time that an inmate could serve may have weakened the efficiency of coercive sanctions. More significantly, the absence of a strategy to maintain control, a general demoralization of the guard force, and a breakdown of any system of expectations about what rules would be enforced led to intensified challenges to authority.

After 1969 (the year the gangs first became prominent), maintaining order became increasingly problematic. Having lived through a period of intense harassment by the Gang Intelligence Unit, the minority gang members entered prison belligerent toward all institutions of authority. Nor were they motivated by the prison reward structure which had ceased to keep pace with the material expectations of the new inmates. While old cons may have continued to be satisfied by sneaking extra coffee and scoring for prison hooch, the young gang members were preoccupied with issues of status and gang rivalry. Inmates simply refused to follow orders, refused to work and refused to follow the rules. When a lieutenant was called to "walk" an inmate, he was often confronted with ten or twelve of the inmate's fellow gang members surrounding him, challenging his authority. One Stateville guard explained: "The inmate will say, 'Fuck you Jack, I'm not going.' Then a group of his gang will gather around him. I'll have to call a lieutenant. Sometimes one of the leaders will just come over and tell the member to go ahead." The chief guard on one occasion was confronted by a line of inmates in the F house tunnel while he was escorting a gang leader to isolation. The inmates shouted threats. There were calls to "tear it down." The chief guard backed off while his captive returned to the cell house and barricaded himself in his cell. One lieutenant explained, "The gangs have made our job a helluva lot tougher. The things that I could do when I was an officer now take a lieutenant because the officers and sergeants don't get the respect. There is no regard for discipline; no respect for officers; most of them hate us."

If a gang leader was reported for a disciplinary infraction, the case was handled delicately. GL explained that the last time he had a ticket for "refusal to work," he was able to discuss it with two captains before he went to the disciplinary court. My own field notes for 11 July 1972 include the following:

> Today CE was brought before the disciplinary court. He is probably the highest ranking member to come before the committee when I've been there and I was anxious to see what would happen. There were 5 lieutenants in the room. After CE was questioned as to his presence in the vicinity of the disturbance last Sunday he left the room and a discussion about his character ensued. The lieutenants told the disciplinary captain that CE doesn't lie to them and that in the past he has been helpful in keeping his people in line. Perhaps lieutenant W [who wrote the report] was mistaken? The case was continued.
>
> After the hearing I spoke at length with lieutenant S. He showed me CE's disciplinary card (one of the longest I've ever seen) and explained there was nothing serious here except having beaten one guy and he deserved it.

Accident reports filed by Stateville/Joliet guards between 1966 and 1974 show a substantial increase in inmate attacks upon guards beginning in 1971, indicating deterioration in control and rising violence (see table 17).

While most confrontations between gang members and guards occurred spontaneously, there were many instances of calculated attack and collective action. In 1968, the gang leaders decided to "come up from underground" and "represent." Insignias, bandanas, posters, and tattoos appeared overnight. Gang members began recognizing one another by esoteric greetings and salutes. In January 1969, the gang leaders, along with several old con "advisers," coordinated a food strike. Administrators estimated that 75 percent of the inmates, either voluntarily or because of fear of reprisals, went along with the strike. A food strike at the Joliet prison was coordinated at the same time. In neither institution were written demands presented. The strike was generally interpreted as a protest over food and as a show of force by the gangs. The administration responded to the strike by calling a general lockup, which lasted for ten days. About five hundred inmates, including most of the identifiable gang leaders, were segregated in B house. In response to the administration's action, inmates in F house, led by a Disciple leader, began to burn up the cell house. Carts of clothing were set on fire, and metal springs and other missiles were shot and thrown at the guards who attempted to put out the fire and restore order.

In June 1971, at a baseball game between a visiting Southern Illinois University team and the Stateville team, two black inmates began a fight on the ball diamond. When the officers came in to break it up, inmates poured out of the stands. They knocked seven guards to the ground, kicked and beat them, and then dispersed. No reason for the violence was ever articulated. The administration attributed the incident to a gang conspiracy, but gang leaders denied any planning and pointed out that the inmates involved in the fight were not gang members. Whatever the cause of the melee, there is no doubt that, once it had begun, gang members actively participated. Again, the institution responded with a general lockup and transferred approximately one hundred troublemakers, including many gang leaders, to segregation in B house.

The ball diamond incident broke out at Stateville after Assistant Warden Revis had been transferred to the Joliet prison to deal with the deteriorating situation there. The gangs had completely intimidated the staff of the Old Prison. Independent inmates could not trade at the commissary or exercise on the recreation yards without paying off to the gangs. In a manner reminiscent of Stateville during the 1930s, when a gang member was brought before the disciplinary court, fellow gang members would leave their assignments, gather at the disciplinary unit and chant gang slogans while the hearing was in process. In several instances, the guards let the defendants go without punishment rather than precipitate a riot. Revis's transfer stimulated an immediate confrontation. One evening in June, an entire cell house refused to lock up their cells. As was often the case during the seventies, demands were made for Revis's resignation. When the inmates finally returned to their cells in preparation for being released from the cell house for night yard, Revis deadlocked the entire cell house, initiating a lengthy general lockup at the Joliet Prison.

The crisis in control convinced the liberal Bensinger administration that drastic security measures needed to be instituted. SPU was constructed during the summer and early fall of 1971 to provide a super-maximum security situation for the most disruptive inmates. Between September and December 1971, over a hundred Stateville inmates were transferred from B house to SPU. Each inmate had to be forcibly taken from his cell. Tear gas, shields, and mace were used on a daily basis. Part of the solidarity of the resistance can be explained by the decision to transfer the gang leaders last. Each indian felt compelled to make a strong show of resistance before he was dragged out of his cell and off the tiers in order not to lose face with the leaders. The violence continued at SPU, where for the first six months guards could not walk on the tiers without being pummeled with porcelain, steel, and feces. The prisoners completely destroyed the cells. The entire unit was then rebuilt with the inclusion of the most sophisticated security technology.

Even with the removal of Bull Hairston of the Stones and Hy Smith of the Disciples and scores of other leaders, gang violence at Stateville escalated, while employee morale continued to decline. Director Bensinger responded to the deteriorating situation by removing Warden Twomey's Stateville superintendent, George Stampar, and once more calling upon Revis, who was in poor health, in July 1972. Shortly after Revis's return to Stateville as superintendent, two Stones attacked and seriously injured several lieutenants with baseball bats in E house. During the incident, leaders of both the Disciples and the Stones led groups of gang members from the chapel and from several recreation yards to the scene of the assault. Finally, Assistant Warden Meyer persuaded the gang leaders to give up the two assailants, but he allowed one of the leaders to accompany them to isolation to make sure that there were no reprisals. The prison was placed on lockup for a month.

On 11 January 1973, a guard was fatally stabbed and thrown off the gallery in B house. On 24 January about three hundred inmates reported to sick call as a demonstration of gang strength and solidarity. On 13 March a guard was attacked by an inmate with a knife. The assault was widely attributed to a "hit" ordered by the gangs. On 18 March the inmates assigned to the dining room staged a strike. On 18 April a known gang member killed an inmate and wounded another in the officer's dining room apparently in retaliation for their interference with a homosexual prostitute "belonging" to the Stones. On 29 April, a full-scale rumble broke out between the Disciples and the Stones on D yard (apparently because of a gang killing at Pontiac some weeks before), quickly drawing in the inmates from C yard as well. As the captains and lieutenants moved in to break it up, the inmates turned on them. A shot fired from one of the towers ricocheted off the ground, hitting one of the leaders in the back, thereby dispersing the crowd. There were dozens of injuries to both Stones and Disciples. Six inmates were taken to outside hospitals; fourteen were placed in the Stateville hospital, and approximately fifty were treated and released. Some hundred inmates proceeded to the hospital gate and demanded the right to monitor the medical attention that their fellows were receiving. They refused to disperse for several hours. This incident was followed by the longest lockup in Stateville history, almost six months' duration.

All but two of the cell houses had been released from the lockup by 6 September 1973, the date of the B house takeover. In an action initially instigated by Disciples, Stateville's largest cell house was seized and ten hostages were held. Once all the cells were unlocked, the leaders of the Stones joined the leaders of the Disciples in drawing up demands.

1. No prisoners will be singled out as leaders of the uprising.
2. Amnesty for those participating in the uprising, including immunity from prosecution.
3. Removal of Supt. Vernon Revis, Supt. George Stampar and five other Stateville officers.
4. Review of Stateville conditions by members of the news media.
5. Improved medical facilities.
6. Improved educational system.
7. A grievance committee to meet with prison officials at least once a week.
8. An end to experimental medical programs at the prison.
9. Modified disciplinary procedures.
10. End of censorship of prisoners' mail and selection of newspapers.
11. Psychological evaluation of all present prison officers and officer candidates.

Director Sielaff negotiated the end of the rebellion by outlining his reform program and promising to take up several of the inmate demands. The inmates thought that they had been promised amnesty but this later proved not to be the case. At the trial of the ten inmates accused of leading the insurrection it became clear that several of the guard hostages had been raped, a fact overlooked in media praise for the dispatch with which Governor Walker and Director Sielaff "peacefully" negotiated an end to the riot.

Violence continued. In the summer of 1974 the gangs organized a coordinated "boycott" of the inmate commissary, claiming that prices were exorbitant. Inmates who intended to trade at the commissary were threatened with violence. In several instances those who tried to defy the gangs were severely beaten. The administration finally responded by summarily removing thirty-five gang leaders to segregation. Almost overnight the boycott dissolved. The gang leaders immediately appealed to the courts (see the discussion of *Arsberry* v. *Sielaff* in chapter 5, n. 26).

Finally inmates took over a cell house and seized hostages at the Old Prison in April 1975, protesting the transfer of three leading members of the Black P Stone Nation to Menard. One inmate, said to have been an informant, was stabbed to death during the day-long insurrection. In a subsequent press conference, Director Sielaff disputed charges that "the gangs ran the prisons" but publicly admitted their presence and strength throughout the system.

At the same time that the gang-oriented inmates were challenging authority, the prison guards were becoming increasingly demoralized. The new reform administration seemed to them "pro-inmate" and unsympathetic to the problems of keeping order. The lowest point in guard morale coincided with Revis's year-long absence from the prison. With Revis gone and George Stampar serving as superintendent, and with John Twomey the incumbent warden, the old Ragenites felt that they had lost all influence in the administration of the prison. The number of disciplinary reports (tickets), the number of inmates sent to isolation, and the number of privilege denials was lower between June 1971 and June 1972 than during any other period between January 1970 and December 1974. During Revis's absence, guards tended to retreat from actively disciplining inmates.

For the first time in Stateville's history, guards were afraid to come to work. At SPU the guards were demanding hazardous duty pay, and, throughout the system, the growing guard union (discussed at length in chapter 7) was demanding a return to tighter discipline and control.

Not only did the emergence of the gangs place a strain on the roles of correctional officers, it also placed a severe strain on civilian roles within the prison. It became harder and harder for those individuals charged with running rehabilitation programs to carry out their goals without bargaining with the gangs. In exchange for their commitment to keeping order in the programs, the gang leaders were informally shown deference and allowed a voice in decision making. The school and TV college, for example, have been largely controlled by the gangs for several years. Inmates could not remain in school unless they were members of the Stones. The following letter was seized by the guards.

> Comrade T. and B.H.,
> Found out yesterday that they're definitely moving the college and high school to B house on the 11th of September. That's a bunch of bullshit. . . . You know what time that is. S. has [the director] under control and there won't be any static from him about your getting into college. Simba and I both got back without any trouble. There may be a problem with these honkies if you try to transfer before they move us to B house because they are going to claim that they don't have any cells. . . .

When an instructor from a local community college brought an automotive course to Stateville, the gang leaders came around to ask whom he worked for, whether the course would be worth anything, and how long he would be there. The instructor has told me, "The gangs are highly disciplined. It's remarkable the way they are able to keep the class in order—there are no disruptions. It would be a much more serious challenge to carry out the program without them. I don't know if I could do it."

Gang leaders also attracted the most attention from outsiders. Just as on the street, some of these outsiders saw in the gangs the potential for a powerful constructive force if their energies could be redirected. The part-time Episcopalian chaplain has probably been closer to the gangs over the past several years than any other full or part-time employee. He encouraged the gang leaders to enter Right Angle, a group therapy program based upon "reality therapy." The gang leaders saw in the program an opportunity for mobility and contact. They were further encouraged to attend by the fact that at the end of the meetings they were given an opportunity to transact "nation business." While their motives were transparent, the chaplain hoped to bring them to a better understanding of their personal situations once they began participating. As the gang leaders entered Right Angle, the independents left it until most of the therapy groups became homogeneous.

Prison reformers, like Dorothy Mason of Operation Push and Peggy Smith Martin, the Illinois legislator, regularly met with the gang leadership on their trips to Stateville (see chapter 5). The gang leaders have been, and continue to be, the spokesmen for the inmate population in articulating concerns to the outside. There is, in fact, no other way for outsiders to become accepted by the inmate population. Being seen with the gang leadership gives them credibility with a large majority of the inmates. In addition, it reinforces the status of the extant leadership.

Throughout these years of challenge, the administration has maintained the public position that it "refuses to recognize the gangs."[35] It is an article of faith among administrators today that gang leaders are not to be dealt with and that the prison contains only inmates, no leaders nor organized groups. While this policy has enjoyed widespread verbal support, in actuality the policy toward the gangs has been a divisive issue for the staff.

The top custodial staff and those individuals trained under Ragen have been the most resistant to any concessions to the gang presence. Administrators who entered the system laterally from a college background have tended to be more flexible. Stampar noted, "I tried to deal with the gangs when I was superintendent. The gangs are here and they must be recognized—the leaders have tremendous power—no doubt they could inflict terrible damage on the place if they wanted to. They have not done it so far because there is nothing to get out of that kind of thing."

While affording them no formal recognition, security and administrative personnel have nevertheless had to accommodate to the gangs and their leaders. The chief guard, while adamantly maintaining that he doesn't deal with gangs, told me that in several cases he has called upon gang leaders to discuss problems he has had with various gang members. In one case, he brought to his office one of the Latin King chiefs to discuss the pressure being placed on a Spanish-speaking inmate (not a King) at the commissary. The chief was able to resolve the situation in a couple of days. In another situation, a Disciple refused to move from his cell to isolation; the situation could have been explosive. The chief guard called the Disciple chief to his office and discussed the matter with him. The gang chief then went to the cell of the irate inmate and talked to him about the pros and cons of provoking a violent confrontation. The next morning the inmate went peacefully to the hole.

The closest the administration came to formally recognizing the gangs as a legitimate force in institutional life was the formation of Project ABLE (Adult Basic Learning Enterprise). This project was the creation of several old cons, one of whom had become an important leader in the Latin Kings. ABLE was an attempt to develop a dialogue between inmates and staff over issues of inmate concern. As originally conceived it would have been a formal council containing representatives of the administration, guard force, clinical services, and inmates. Even before it was accepted by the administration, the counselors and other civilians were meeting with ABLE organizers in order to discuss strategies for getting the project off the ground. While ABLE has always sought to bring inmates into formal organizational decision making, the following document illuminates some of the ambiguity of ABLE's goals:

The real purposes of Project ABLE are:

1. To establish rapport between everyone concerned with Penal Reform and Rehabilitation of those incarcerated in prisons: the Department of Corrections, the Parole and Pardon Board, Institution Officials, the Resident population, and the Communities from which our residents came, and must eventually return;
2. To open up an avenue for the Resident population to have a voice in the decisions, policies, and programs which affect their daily lives;
3. To coordinate the efforts of all concerned people that want to work toward these ends, and to assist them in every way possible.

In retrospect it seems incredible that an administration as traditional as Stateville's would ever have accepted the legitimacy of an inmate council. What was at stake in ABLE's recognition was the relationship of inmates to staff within the Stateville organization. Never had inmates been given a formal role in questioning, debating, or deciding policy or in setting institutional priorities.

Like everything else at Stateville, the legitimization of ABLE partly depended upon particularistic relationships. Lowell Fentress, the prime moving force behind ABLE, had been a prisoner at Stateville for more than twenty years. Having literally grown up within the prison, he maintained excellent relations with various administrators. Most important, he was Superintendent Stampar's clerk. In the course of daily interactions he was able to convince his boss that much could be gained by attempting to turn the destructive energies of the inmates to constructive pursuits.

This argument was particularly persuasive in the aftermath of Attica. Indeed, ABLE's motto, as if to remind the administration of the dire consequences that might result from refusal to cooperate, was "Let's do it different from Attica!" The chief guard recalls that discipline had so thoroughly broken down by late 1971 that he was willing to accept ABLE in order to forestall a riot. The idea of "inmate involvement in their own corrections" (as ABLE put it) was also palatable to Director Bensinger, who was looking for changes that would indicate the sincerity of his commitment to reform.

From the outset the gangs dominated ABLE. The preamble to the charter implicitly spoke of the factional organization of the inmate populations: "Project ABLE at the present time represents the efforts of a small group of those incarcerated, who are really concerned with the welfare of *their people*" (my emphasis). ABLE was not intended to be a democratically elected council but a kind of confederation representing the interests of various constituencies. In the provisions for membership it was provided that "Membership in Project ABLE is open to any organization, group or individual." A group could ask for representation only if it had at least fifty members. An executive committee was designed that would conduct most of the actual business of ABLE. In addition the members of the executive committee were to be given a "special detail" which allowed them almost absolute freedom to move around the institution in order to keep the inmate council in touch with the grassroots. There was one provision inserted in order to provide a check on any single gang's gaining too much power: "*Equal Representation.* There is to be equal membership accorded all Organizations and Groups which shall operate solely for a check and balance of power so that no one Organization or Group can seize control of the Project."

The special details were approved in January 1972 by Superintendent Stampar. Eight inmates were given the most coveted privilege in a maximum security prison—complete freedom of movement. The eight inmates were drawn as follows: one each from the Black Panthers, Disciples, Vice Lords, and Latin Kings; one from the independent white and one from the independent black populations; and two from the Stones.

There was immediate consternation among the top custodial staff. Frequent conflicts occurred when guards tried to stop the leaders or interrupt their activities. Custody people complained that the administration had "given (the prison) away." The open pipeline to Stampar helped to keep the ABLE members functioning in light of this widespread hostility. Meetings were carried on by the executive committee and by the entire membership without supervision. (I attended several of these meetings in my capacity as researcher when it seemed to the leaders that I might be useful to them.)

Little headway was made by the inmate leaders in winning any concrete concessions from the administration, although ABLE members constantly complained to administrators that they needed some tangible successes to maintain their credibility with their memberships. As long as the administration was at least willing to recognize these leaders and, by the special details, give them certain deference, including the right to intervene for their people, the leaders strove to develop a reform agenda and to prevent a riot. Almost all informants, both staff and inmates, attribute to the activities of the gang leaders the absence of a riot at Stateville during 1972.

Superintendent Revis disbanded ABLE after meeting with them once in July. During the meeting (at which I was present) he asked the leaders whom they represented, and each gave his gang affiliations. Revis further demanded to know what they had accomplished. The ABLE members responded that their dearth of accomplishments merely reflected the administration's bad faith. The baseball bat incident (see p. 164) which occurred soon thereafter enabled Revis to call a general lockup. ABLE never again was formally recognized, although it has been kept alive by the sporadic and informal activity of the gang leadership and outsiders.

The gangs at Stateville have not grown weaker since 1972. Indeed, the yard incident of 29 April 1973, the B house takeover of 6 September 1974, and the coordinated commissary boycott of July 1974 indicate that the gangs remain a powerful force. What has changed, however, is the relationship between the formal organization and the gangs.

There is far less interaction between the administration and the gang leaders. This is due partly to the fact that the staff has more control of the prison now than it did in 1972. Also, there is a profound cynicism about the advisability of working with the gangs, particularly in light of the collapse of that policy at Pontiac.[36] In addition, the parole or transfer of several of the old cons who began ABLE has disrupted the gang leaders' conduit to the administration. A lessening of reform pressure from the outside has taken away much of the public relations value of an inmate council. To be sure, civilian program heads still have to share their power with the gang leaders, and outside reformers continue to articulate with them, but one senses that this too will change as the Brierton administration becomes stronger yet and the gangs turn their attention away from political and reform issues to developing the rackets within the prison.

Conclusion

Between 1970 and 1975 a crisis in control at Stateville was manifested by the numbers of staff and inmates who were attacked and by numerous instances of collective rebellion. The first guard in thirty years was killed; the first hostages were taken since the 1920s; the first escapes occurred since the 1940s.

The crisis was precipitated by the presence of four supergangs behind the walls, but the underlying cause was the failure of the reform regime to find a new equilibrium to replace the authoritarian regime of personal dominance. The human relations model of management had no effective strategy for attenuating the stresses of maximum security incarceration. When the stresses threatened to overwhelm the organization Warden Twomey,

Superintendent Stampar, Assistant Warden Meyer, and Director Bensinger fell back upon the old solutions; general lockup and the Special Program Unit.

The gangs entered Stateville after 1969 having experienced a remarkable period of development on the streets of Chicago. What distinguished these gangs from their predecessors was the way in which they had been redefined as legitimate grassroots community structures by representatives of the larger society's institutional center. Having been so defined, the gangs came to see themselves as alternatives to religious, political, economic, and social structures.

But the accommodation between the gangs and central political institutions was strained and short-lived. Ultimately, the gangs were repressed through a shift in law enforcement resources and priorities. They were sent to prison en masse after 1969. They brought to the state prisons heightened expectations about the types of demands that could be made on central institutions, the kinds of deference that their leaders could expect to receive as community spokesmen, and a sense of defiance toward institutions of social control.

Inside Stateville the gangs found that the lack of staff control made easier their recruitment of new membership. As on the street they moved to take over the rackets as well as to achieve a voice in the decision-making process. They saw nothing inconsistent about exploiting both legitimate and illegitimate opportunities.

At the lower and intermediate staff levels accommodations had to be reached with the gang leaders. In exchange for their cooperation in keeping things cool, they were shown deference and given some informal voice in lower-level decision-making. For a time this formed the basis for maintaining order at the prison. Project ABLE represented a serious, if vacillating, attempt to establish a new equilibrium by sharing authority with the charismatic gang leaders. But cooperation with the gangs was an unstable strategy. First, it was anathema to the old Ragenites and intensified their alienation. Second, the more established the gangs became, the more precarious became the life of non-gang members, especially whites. Third, there was no assurance that the gangs would not turn against one another.

By 1975 Stateville seemed to have weathered the worst of the crisis in control. Many of the top gang leaders had been paroled. More important, the formal organization was reasserting its authority through the guard union and through the security-conscious administration of Warden Brierton.

7 Transition of the Guard Force

> I was back there on the job when it broke out. I was frightened. I think every officer out there was frightened because we had no weapons. The tower officers—they didn't know exactly what to do. They were firing warning shots. You couldn't see clearly what they were doing, so you didn't know whether to duck, run or stand still—and then you look at the inmates and they are coming with sticks, baseball bats, iron bars and all this stuff. Any man who says he wasn't afraid, I've have to call him a liar.
>
> Middle-aged white guard,
> Stateville Penitentiary, 1974

Despite serious strains in the organization, the Stateville staff until 1970 was characterized by racial and ethnic homogeneity, intense personal loyalty to the institution and to the warden, complete submission of the rank and file to the authority of the captains, and a pervasive belief in Stateville's mission to control the toughest prison population in the state. After 1970 three developments had the effect of transforming the social organization of the staff: the introduction of the reform administration and the new "professional" roles, the advent of public employee unionism, and the much increased racial integration of the staff.

The Reform Movement and Social Organization

Even before Twomey took office, the tenor of the new Bensinger administration's program appeared to the guards to be "inmate-oriented." Among other changes, the first six months of 1970 brought two outgoing letters a week for each inmate, Sunday visiting, and $50.00 gate money. On 14 July 1970, Warden Pate attempted to soften a departmental bulletin on corporal punishment with the following remark: "The attached directive was received from Springfield today. I wish to point out that this is not something new to us.... Rule 75 of the Employees' Rules and Regulations has been in effect for a long period of time." But the thrust and tone of the directive were clear.

> *Corporal Punishment*—Corporal punishment or mistreatment of individuals, under the custody and control of the Adult Division of the Department of Corrections, in any of its institutions or facilities or those on parole is strictly prohibited.
>
> Corporal punishment or mistreatment is defined as ... the striking, pushing, or the shoving of an individual for the purpose of causing physical pain or discomfort; improper use of chemicals in any of its forms; violence of any nature; use of profane or abusive language, or any other measures which may be injurious or which may tend to degrade the individual.

Among themselves, guards spoke sarcastically about now having to be careful "not to verbally abuse the inmate."

Almost universally, the guards felt that the new warden and director were "permissive" and "for the inmate." For the next five years it was a constant complaint that guards had "no support" and "no backing." The captains' meetings were discontinued entirely. Communication between the guards and the new civilian administration became intermittent and strained. That the warden was infrequently in the yard was interpreted as further proof of his lack of concern. Stateville guards had come to expect the prison to be directed by a leader with whom they could personally identify. This was central to the military model according to which the staff had been trained.

Rumors that Twomey was a long-haired radical from Berkeley who was going to fire many of the staff were scarcely allayed when the new warden delivered to the inmates his notorious "I am here to serve you" address, and when he gave out information to inmates over his prison radio program (before the guards were informed) about new liberalized commissary policies. Criticism mounted when he walked through the prison chatting with inmates and failed to acknowledge the officers. Guards today recall a dramatic episode in the inmate dining room in Twomey's first months: the new warden dumped on the ground several trays of melons that were on the line to be served to the inmates, proclaiming them "unfit for human consumption."

The reform movement which catapulted "treatment-oriented,"

"correctional" people like John Twomey and Joe Cannon into wardenships carried an injunction to morally uplift the inmate and to provide him with services. There was a theme of concern about "treating inmates like men" and eliminating the "dehumanizing" conditions of penal confinement. One of Twomey's earliest orders (never fully implemented) was that inmates be called to their visits by name rather than by their institutional number.

On 28 October 1970, only seven weeks after becoming warden, Twomey announced his new policy eliminating the line officer's authority to have an inmate "walked" from his assignment. This reversal of a deeply rooted, traditional, and emotionally laden Stateville procedure would have met resistance under any conditions, but the change came at a time when the line officers' authority had become highly problematic. The gangs had recently surfaced, sporting insignias, emblems, tattoos, and stylized salutes. Gang members were defying orders, refusing to give officers their names and numbers, and grouping together in collective defiance. Inmates no longer traveled in orderly lines; nor would they go to their own cells upon entering the cell house. For the first time in Stateville's history, a "safekeeping" tier was designated for those inmates who were afraid to go out on the yard and who preferred to serve their sentences without ever leaving their cells.

Under the new warden, guards flocked to join the union. A job action (partial strike) was called when Twomey refused to rescind his order on the "walks." Guards refused to unlock the cell houses and capitulated only when one of the cell house keepers gave in. But soon thereafter, Twomey did rescind the order and replaced it with a compromise whereby lieutenants were required to remove an inmate from an assignment at an officer's request but did not necessarily have to take him to isolation (see chapter 4).

As the gangs grew stronger and the administration became more yielding, guards experienced pervasive fear on the job. More guards were injured in 1972 than in any other year in the history of the prison. Nor has fear abated. It was on 10 January 1973 that James Zeiger was fatally stabbed and then thrown off the highest tier in B house to the cement floor forty feet below. On 6 September 1973 ten hostages were taken in cell house B. A survey of former guards who resigned from Stateville between 1 July 1973 and 30 June 1974 found that more than 50 percent cited "lack of safety" as their reason for quitting.[1]

While Bensinger and Twomey continued to articulate a philosophy of reform and rehabilitation in the face of escalating violence and loss of control, the guards became more and more demoralized and alienated. One consequence was that the guards themselves came to be seen by the administration and by the "outside" as the crucial impediment to the implementation of reform. A John Howard report issued early in Twomey's administration, and given wide publicity by the media, concluded that "some prison guards at Stateville Penitentiary near Joliet have provoked incidents with prisoners to discredit relaxation of prison regulations."[2]

This "fifth column theory" was popularly held throughout the Twomey years and was brought up time and again in press interviews with Warden Cannon. Twomey's own critical perception of guards was illuminated in his Five Year Plan for the Adult Division, written shortly before he became warden: "Yet an honest appraisal of the nation's "war on crime" priorities makes it clear that our essential response has been to pour virtually all available resources into prevention and enforcement activities, while virtually ignoring the gross deficiencies in our correctional institutions, the most glaring of which is the *substandard quality* and inferior training of the correctional officer" (my emphasis). Having been socialized into a custody versus treatment definition of the situation at Menard, Twomey continued to reinforce that definition, while at the same time verbally repudiating it. Staff was quick to point out that Twomey even had separate parties for treatment and custody.

Warden Twomey, and Warden Cannon after him, seemed to endorse the 1967 President's Commission's recommendation for a "collaborative model" of prison. According to that model, the role of the guard had to be transformed from turnkey and disciplinarian to counselor and agent of rehabilitation.[3]

To the primary goal of preventing escapes, riots, and predatory behavior, rehabilitation was added. That these primary and secondary goals are fundamentally incompatible has been the subject of considerable scholarly comment.[4] It is not surprising that contradictory organizational goals have caused conflict in such organizational micro-units as the guard role. Under the role prescriptions dictated by the rehabilitative ideal, the guard is to relax and to act spontaneously. Inmates are to be "understood," not blamed, and formal disciplinary mechanisms should be triggered as infrequently as possible. These are vague directives, but no more precise rules concerning the "how" of rehabilitation can be formulated since the essence of rehabilitation work, as practiced by "professionals," lies in treating each individual as unique according to professional judgment, which belies adherence to hard and fast rules.[5] What is allowed one prisoner may be denied another depending on evaluation of individual needs.

Where guards have attempted to follow these vague role prescriptions, they have often met with frustration. Inmates themselves believe that differential treatment based on individual needs requires professional competence. While competency and proficiency may be imputed to psychologists and social workers based on academic credentials, inmates are quick to point out that they will grant no such discretionary authority to "screws." The very essence of the professional's authority lies in his claim to charisma while the guard's only basis for authority is his rank within the caste system.

The rehabilitative ideal has no clear directives for the administration of a large-scale people-processing institution. In order to carry out primary tasks and to manage large numbers of men and materials, bureaucratic organization and impersonal treatment are necessary. Furthermore, to distinguish between inmates on the basis of psychological needs leaves the nonprofessional open to charges of gross bias, discrimination, and injustice.[6]

Treatment personnel in their administrative capacities are likely to hold guards responsible for preventing escapes and riots, ensuring order, and maintaining the prison as a smoothly functioning institution. The consequence of these contradictory demands on the guard is evidenced by the extremely high rates of staff turnover.

The old-timers look back nostalgically to the "old days" when they knew what their job entailed and how they would be evaluated.[7] One told me that "during Ragen's days you knew every day what you were supposed to do and now you are in a position where there are too many supervisors and too many changing rules. First one will come and tell you it's got to be done this way and then somebody else comes along and says to do something different. In the old days we knew what our job was."

Guards are more likely to fall back on their security and maintenance role because it is the only one on which they can be objectively evaluated. No guard will be reprimanded or dismissed for failure to communicate meaningfully with inmates. On the other hand, the guard whose carelessness smooths the way for an escape or whose lack of vigilance contributes to opportunity for a stabbing or rape will most likely find himself out of a job.

When Twomey and the other college-educated civilians took over many of the elite positions within the organization, the captains became a shadow government resisting any changes from the traditional routine. "They can do whatever they want to in the courts or in Springfield, but we run it" was an attitude frequently spoken and even more frequently implied. The captains were never in open rebellion; their response to change was more like passive resistance; they simply ignored new rules, directives, and orders.

There had been a strong feeling at Stateville for years that eventually the reformers would lose interest and go away, and the feeling was even stronger under Twomey and Cannon. The captains were rarely held accountable for the failure of policies to be implemented or for failure of the organization to carry out basic tasks. Often they were able to sustain their definition of the situation as "impossible." Using confiscated inmate letters, informants, and other esoteric omens, the captains were always detecting signs of trouble; gang flare-ups, escapes, and massive rebellion. Typical is the following excerpt from my field notes of 17 September 1974:

> Last night at the movie, the residents from E House walked out after 15 minutes of an 80 minute film on soccer. They damaged some of the projection equipment, but moved back peacefully to the cell house. The major says he is deeply disturbed by this incident and thinks it portends something much more serious in light of the weapons found in E House last week.

And with respect to the central office in Springfield (field notes, 30 September 1974):

> ——— [an administrator] said, "Sometimes I think that Springfield doesn't want any of us here. Maybe they want to clean us out and replace us with their own people. ——— [another admin-

istrator] agreed. "Maybe when they were sending us 30 trouble-makers from Pontiac in exchange for 30 of our more stable population, they were precipitating a situation where this place would blow up and they could use us as scapegoats in order to replace us. They would also be taking heat off their golden haired boy at Menard who has lost 17 inmates in the last two months on escapes.

The captains believe that they should be left alone to run the prison the way they knew how. Neither Springfield, nor counselors, nor do-gooders, nor John Howard, nor legal aid, nor the courts, in their opinion, know the slightest thing about how to run a maximum security prison.

Captain ——— says that the Administration of Corrections has not become professionalized, but is pseudo-professionalized because they don't know anything about corrections; they don't know anything about institutions.

The old tradition bearers are quite smug in the belief that they are the only ones who really know how to "run" an institution. One needs to hear the oft-repeated phrase, "the old boss, he *ran* it," fully to understand the commitment to a system of management where every inmate move was scrutinized for its ulterior (antiorganizational) motive, and where the elite was preoccupied with the task of always being one step ahead of the inmates.

The captains still define the prison in terms of the old ground rules. The assignment captain, for example, continues to operate according to the old strategy of trying to keep the "no good" inmates off balance, despite attempts to bureaucratize his office. For example, he tears up tickets of "troublemakers" who *he thinks* are merely going to the gym or to the library to "contact" a fellow conspirator, despite the fact that this could bring him and the Stateville administration into conflict with Springfield and the courts.

In the one year that he was warden, Joe Cannon reached a friendly accommodation with the captains and the old guard. In contrast with Twomey, who rarely ventured onto the prison yard, Cannon spent his first several months at Stateville "trying to get accepted." Having been fired from two previous positions in corrections, Cannon was determined "to win the guards over to his side." In his first few months of becoming acquainted with Stateville, Cannon lived at the prison, ate his meals with the guards in the employees' dining room, and left the day-to-day running of the prison to Assistant Warden Revis.

Cannon worked every shift and every assignment. He did achieve a great deal of acceptance among the custody staff, particularly among the captains. If they had to live with an "outsider" in control of the institution, at least they preferred one humble about his abilities and ready to admit that he "had a lot to learn about running a joint." Unlike Twomey, Cannon met several times weekly with his captains and allowed them the same kind of collegial and consultant role which they had enjoyed under Frank Pate. (The key difference was that the captains and the warden, in exercising their authority, were now more limited by the central office and the Administrative Regulations.)

While the warden may have been popular with his staff, to the Sielaff/Brierton administration it appeared that Cannon had been "co-opted" by the Ragenite subculture which they were determined to dissolve. Cannon's removal from his position and his replacement by David Brierton sounded the death knell for both "the medical model" and for the power of the old Ragenites. Brierton was not concerned with popularity or acceptance because of his own sense of personal security and because of the security of his position with Springfield. He made it clear from the outset that *he would do the accepting and rejecting.* After his first day on the job, several old-time employees were comparing him with Warden Ragen. At the end of the first several months, more than half the department heads had resigned or retired. The chief guard took a transfer to Menard.

While the problem with John Twomey, in the eyes of the guard force, was lack of support, the problem with Brierton (although he is extremely popular among all ranks) is lack of empathy. While a Peter Bensinger or a Joe Cannon could be convinced, for example, that it was "impossible" to get the B house inmates out for showers or out on the yard because the cell house was short handed, Brierton (with eleven years of institutional experience) demanded to know the rationale for the scheduling of the shift and the justification for the assignment of officers. He has placed tremendous demands upon supervisory personnel, requiring that they exercise their authority in a situation that for so long had run by consensus and drift.

The bureaucratization of the prison has necessarily changed

the captain's role. The disciplinary captain, once invested with absolute authority to discipline an inmate, now is merely a voting member of a committee. Whereas once the captains could summarily suspend a guard for any reason, they now can only send a report to the Employee Review Board. The chief guard, once the eyes and ears of the warden, is now tied to his desk much of the day carrying out "bureaucratic bullshit." The captains talk repeatedly of how their time and that of the lieutenants is being wasted on paper work, when they should be out in the back doing their "real job"—shaking down lines (searching inmates), and supervising cell houses and assignments.

But employee evaluations must be filled out quarterly. Line officers must be counseled before being disciplined. Captains and lieutenants have to sit on promotion committees, grievance hearings, inquiry boards, etc. Whereas they were once evaluated according to their ability to get information and "bust" (discipline) an inmate or for some heroic act demonstrating their fighting ability, the Brierton administration evaluates captains according to how well they handle their supervisory responsibilities, much of which involves expediting paper work.

The lieutenants became especially hostile toward the Twomey administration. The warden's rescinding of their right to demand that inmates be taken to isolation struck at the heart of their fighting tradition. Within a two-year period, a half-dozen lieutenants resigned their jobs outright; all of the rest joined the union. In desperation over the deteriorating security situation, they accepted and even encouraged the appointment of several black lieutenants. The lieutenants felt, at the time, that they had "no support—no backing." Repeatedly they urged the warden "to lock it up." Their decisions were questioned and overruled by committees and by the warden himself.

Today there is a general feeling that the lieutenants are not what they once were. Several of the black lieutenants and a few of the white are seen by the others as permissive and weak. Quite recently a fight broke out in the guard hall between a white and a black lieutenant over the former's handling of a black inmate. Like that of the captains, the lieutenants' role has also been transformed. While they are still "policemen," they are far more tied down to cell house duties than they were five years ago, when sergeants ran the cell houses.

There are limitations to the degree to which the guards can become bureaucratized. Although weakened, the old institutional ideology is still significant. Lieutenants and captains are still promoted out of the ranks of those closely conforming to the old military fighting tradition.

A riot or change in the political and juridical environments could once again promote some of the old guards into top administrative positions, thereby restoring the traditional type of organization. Furthermore, there is some question whether the limited training and education of captains, lieutenants, and other supervisors and middle managers will prevent them from mastering "management by objectives" and "zero-based budgeting." To date, there remain many snags in the organization. Some orders are still not carried out despite Brierton's deadlines and follow-ups.

Racial Integration

According to the captains, not only have the inmates completely "gotten out of hand" but the employees have also "gone to hell." They are disheartened at the policy of paying guards for "excused" absences and at the failure rigorously to enforce the employee dress code. It is a common complaint that "the guards look worse than the inmates." In the minds of the top guards, the deterioration of the guard force is linked to the massive infusion of minority guards into the system. It is felt that an increase in narcotics trafficking and in absenteeism is attributable to this group of new recruits. In one captain's opinion, "the new officers from Chicago aren't worth a damn. Some are just in a daze, others don't show up for work and others don't want to work. If they're criticized, they cop an attitude. They don't want to take orders."

Until 1963, only thirty blacks had ever been appointed to positions at Stateville-Joliet. The first black lieutenant (who subsequently became the first black captain) was not appointed until Twomey became warden. However, under pressure from inmates, civil rights groups, and government agents, 195 minority guards were hired in 1974. By 1975 approximately 44 percent of the Stateville guard force was black.[8]

Of the thirty-four black guards appointed in 1963, twenty terminated their employment that same year; six more left before the end of 1964, and only seven lasted two years or more (see table 18). Since 1963, the tenure of black guards on the job has, indeed, been very brief. While there are no comparable statistics on the turnover among white guards, it is the judgment of white and black guards alike that tenure for whites is much longer. Of a cohort of eighty-eight guards followed by Liebentritt in 1974, 66 percent of the blacks and 58 percent of the whites were gone by the end of six months. While recent Affirmative Action pressures may have slowed the turnover of black guards, there is strong support for the proposition that blacks and whites continue to be differentially assimilated into the organization.

In an attempt to understand the way minority guards are assimilated, we surveyed a sample of all guards who terminated their employment at Stateville between 1 July 1973 and 30 June 1974.[9] The most obvious difference in the experience of black and white guard recruits is the significantly higher percentage of blacks who leave Stateville by discharge—61 percent as compared with 18 percent of the whites. This might suggest a differential recruiting process, with higher standards being applied to white applicants from the beginning and lower standards being applied to minority candidates. Although the Department of Corrections has sent recruitment trucks into minority areas of Chicago to recruit applicants for guard positions,[10] none of the individuals in our sample was hired in this manner.

Within the six-month probationary period, the guard recruit can be terminated for any reason. The most common reasons for dismissal are: failure to come to work, failure to carry out orders, and "trafficking" with inmates. The first reason is perceived by administrators and top guards to be by far the most common. Of those men in our sample who were discharged, 60 percent of the whites and 47 percent of the blacks indicated that they, too, believed poor attendance to have been a factor contributing to their discharge.

Contrary to the opinion of the administrators and top guards, overall absenteeism for blacks, both those who have terminated their employment and those who are still employed, is lower than for whites (see table 19). On the other hand, blacks are more often docked (not paid) for their absences. This might be explained on the assumption that blacks less often call the prison to explain their absences or fail to cover themselves in some other way, or that superior officers are stricter in evaluating the validity of the minority guard's excuse for his absence.

Of guards who have been discharged, absenteeism among whites seems to have been worse than among nonwhites (see table 19). Perhaps superior officers are more reluctant to discharge whites? Another explanation might be that a greater percentage of black guards are discharged for reasons other than absenteeism. Stateville lieutenants and captains in private are not sanguine about the performance of recent black guard recruits. They suspect that the higher rate of trafficking in contraband with inmates is attributable to the influx of minority employees hired out of the same Chicago neighborhoods from which inmates are drawn. They also object to what they describe as the "shuckin" and "jivin" that sometimes goes on between black guards and black inmates. There have also been several reports (to date unproven) that a few black guards are members of the same Chicago street gangs as the inmates.

The legacy of the Ragen tradition was primarily carried on by the eight captains and one major, the elite among the guards. Seven of the captains and the major are white; one captain is black. Their average length of employment is 12.4 years. Six were born and raised in southern Illinois, two in Central Illinois, and one (the black captain) in the Joliet area. The eight whites among this guard elite share a cultural affinity, a common ideology, and a lengthy service together—having risen through the ranks. They "fought together as lieutenants," and often retell "war stories" about some particularly tough fight with a "no good son of a bitch."

The captains and the long-time guards are profoundly conservative men. They view change in the prison as well as on the outside with apprehension. Both on the outside and on the inside, they find conspiracies forged by radicals and dissidents aimed against the forces of order. One guard captain I talked to believed that "the whole thing" (prison reform) was a liberal movement from the East and West coasts. He pointed out that, after the election, Governor Walker's campaign manager went to the West coast to work for Bobby Seal. He then suggested that it was all related to the overthrow of the country.

While it would be incorrect to say that the captains are manifestly racist, they clearly are less comfortable with black employees than with whites. One of the captains remarked to me during a casual discussion, "These blacks will be the downfall of these United States." A lieutenant said there is no discipline at Stateville anymore. He pointed to a list of officers on the 7:00 A.M.-3:00 P.M. shift and told me that out of 140 or so officers, more than 37 had terribly unsatisfactory attendance records—either having unexcused absences or unexcused lateness—and that the morale of the rest of the officers was severely undermined by the fact that these men were subject to no disciplinary action whatsoever. Upon further questioning, the lieutenant admitted that these thirty-seven officers were almost all black—that the problem with the new officers corresponds to the recruitment of more urban blacks which began in the past several years.

Records of the Employee Review Board, the three-man committee that adjudicates infractions of the rules by guards, indicate a disproportionate number of black guards being disciplined and a disproportionate number being *severely* disciplined (by suspension). A survey of 127 cases that the board heard between 20 January 1975 and 14 April 1975 reveals that 83 of the guards involved were black and only 44 white. Of the 83 black guards processed by the board, 46 received suspensions, the most severe penalty. Of the 44 whites disciplined, only 12 were suspended. The only lieutenant to be suspended was black.

The kind of extreme racism that has been described in some other prisons has not been evident at Stateville. When we asked our respondents whether they had experienced "racial problems" on the job, 41 percent of the whites and 57 percent of the blacks answered affirmatively. For discharges, the percentages of affirmative responses were 60 and 59 percent respectively. Blacks who were discharged felt they had experienced racial discrimination no more frequently than blacks who resigned.

The striking difference between the white and black respondents is the group to which they attributed their racial problems. Of the sixteen blacks who reported experiencing racial problems, eleven named superior officers as a group responsible. Ten of the eleven whites experiencing racial problems named inmates as a group responsible, illuminating the familiar picture of racial and cultural conflict between a guard force dominated by whites and an 80 percent minority inmate population.

If we look at all the guard recruits who terminated their

employment (for whatever reason) before their six-month certification, we find that 57.1 percent of the blacks but only 15.3 percent of the whites attributed their greatest difficulties to their relationship with superior officers. Several black recruits expressed an awareness that they departed from the stereotype of a "good prison guard." Several blacks (as well as a few young white guards) reported consciously presenting themselves to the inmates in ways that would distinguish them from the traditional guard stereotype. They wore mod clothes, fancy shoes, and long hair, acted in an open and friendly way, chatted informally with inmates while on duty. This behavior brought guards into conflict with superiors, which, for several men, was "the real reason" why they were pressured to leave.

The picture which emerges is that of black guard recruits failing to meet the expectations of old-time and top-echelon guards or refusing to accept the definition of the situation prescribed by the elite. It is not surprising to find culture conflict in a situation where southern Illinois white guards dominate the higher ranks (8 of 9 captains and 17 of 23 lieutenants) and young Chicago blacks account for approximately 50 percent of the recruits.

In April 1976, shortly before this book went to press, a letter was sent to Governor Walker by an organization calling itself the Afro-American Correctional Officers Movement, complaining of racist oppression of minority employees as well as inmates at Stateville and other Illinois prisons and enclosing a list of seventeen demands. The demands called, among other things, for the resignation of the warden and several other senior white officials, for the removal of Ku Klux Klan organizers from Stateville, and for a review of all guard dismissals that had taken place within the last twelve months.

Unionization

Prior to the establishment in 1966 of American Federation of State, County and Municipal Employees (AFSCME) local 1866, there had been several attempts to organize employees in the Stateville-Joliet prison complex. In the mid-1950s an educational administrator tried to organize a union around the issues of low pay, a six-day week, and summary suspensions. This effort, like others that followed, failed to attract more than a dozen employees. At no time would Joe Ragen meet with organized *groups* of employees or inmates.

In 1962 Charles Vaught, a line officer at the Joliet Prison and a former member of the UAW, began distributing newsletters and leaflets at the trailer court arguing the need for employee organization. His efforts, however, were stymied by Ragen, who had the known organizers transferred to different shifts and to the towers and other remote assignments. According to one of the captains at the time, a sergeant's dues were paid by the administration so that he might infiltrate the underground union and report on its activities. That the union was ultimately extended recognition in late 1966 can be attributed to the continued energies of its organizers, the retirement of Ragen from the Department of Public Safety, and the assistance of outside professional union organizers from AFSCME.

As soon as Randolph assumed the directorship of Public Safety, several Stateville/Joliet guards traveled to Springfield for a meeting. They came back with Randolph's approval of an employee union. The approval letter, which was signed by Randolph, and tacked on prison bulletin boards, was almost immediately torn down, indicating the strong resistance of the old line staff, who felt (as they did later in the case of the reform administration) that if they held out long enough the union would fold as the previous ones had. Vaught and others returned to Springfield and extracted Randolph's pledge that he would recognize a prison employee union and that he would not allow retaliation against union members.[11] While union check-offs had been permitted under state law since 1962,[12] they were authorized in the prisons for the first time in 1967.

Coinciding with Randolph's accession to the directorship was the rapid statewide growth of AFSCME. Professional union organizers assisted the guards in drawing up by-laws and a union charter in 1966. Once the union was chartered, several guards were sent to a two-week school for union stewards in Ottawa, Illinois. In addition the union hired a hospital worker at Stateville to its staff, and he became a liaison between the union and the local.

Early in 1967, two of the union leaders entered Warden Pate's office for the first union/management meeting in Stateville's history. Pate is reported to have stared out of his office window and mused out loud, "You know, this is the first time any union people have ever set foot in this office." It was a further instance of the erosion of the prison's autonomy. Union minutes taken at the meeting indicate that three issues were raised: salaries, seniority, and compensation for the fifteen minutes daily during which guards were required to stand formation. Even though the "success" of the first meeting (nobody was fired) brought a score of new members, organizing was impeded by widespread skepticism as to the viability of a public employee union, fear of reprisal, and the strong sense of identification of the employees with the administration, particularly with Warden Pate.

In the following two years there were frequent conflicts over union organizing on state time on state property. On several occasions AFSCME representatives were denied entrance to the prison or were held up at the gate house and subjected to thorough searches. Organizing was stimulated, however, by the success of union lawyers in cases before the Workmen's Compensation Board. In addition, the union lawyers won reinstatement and back pay for several guards who had been discharged. In one of the cases, the union attorney successfully showed that so widespread were the "pink slips" (disciplinary reports) in the files of all cell house guards that no inference could be drawn from them regarding poor performance on the job.[13]

The advent of the Bensinger/Twomey regime was traumatic for Stateville/Joliet employees. Rumors circulated throughout the prison that prison jobs would once again become "political." There was a widespread feeling that the new young warden would "give it away to the inmates." The situation was further unsettled by increasing inmate defiance of authority. The local *doubled* its membership in 1970 (from 179 to 360). Of major significance was the fact that the lieutenants joined the union.[14]

Up to 1970 the union's main function was to provide guards with representation before the Workmen's Compensation Board, the Civil Service Commission, and at the ultimate stage of the grievance procedure in Springfield. Until Pate's departure the most salient issues were "bread and butter"—salary, overtime, insurance, job security. After Twomey took office, the union fulfilled a different function entirely; it primarily emphasized the need for more stringent security. At the local level, and in Springfield, the union argued that the prisons were unsafe, that the new programs were creating too much movement with too little supervision. The following minutes reflect the concerns of the guards following the June 1971 ball diamond incident at Stateville in which several guards were injured.

The items listed below were compiled from suggestions brought to the floor at the special meeting of local 1866, Stateville-Joliet Prison Employees Union, which was held on Thursday night, June 10, 1971. This entire agenda could be summed up in one statement—put the Prisons back to where they were two years ago in regard to security and discipline.

1. Take mattresses out of isolation and return isolation to one meal per day.
2. Walk inmates when line Officers or Supervisors deem it necessary.
3. Towers—replace old, worn-out and out-dated equipment, i.e.: tear gas grenades expired 1961, gas masks torn and useless, telescopes, rifles not accurate. Replace tower instructions with readable up-to-date documents which clearly state when a tower guard is to fire his weapons.
4. Make provisions to separate troublemakers and wrong doers by lock-up until proof is shown of their willingness to abide by the rules and to show proper respect for the employees.
5. Why was riot squad disbanded? We need one more now than ever.
6. Better communication system from front to back of cell house B.
7. A set of rules for dress and grooming for inmates and Officers alike (including counsellors).
8. Automatic isolation time for inmates not coming down from cells in all cell houses, for all details, on time.
9. Inmates to come around to the towers and clean refuse buckets with brushes, soap, and water. Not just dump them and leave them to stink.
10. Counsellors: Not taking care of inmate requests, interfering in Officers duties, abusing special letter privileges, etc.
11. Reinforce rules pertaining to clean cells, no pictures, clippings, etc. on walls, nothing to be hung on windows, beds, etc. which obstructs vision into cells in all cell houses.
12. Hire more guards so that all assignments may be safely and adequately manned at all times.[15]

The demands illuminate the lack of confidence in the administration's ability and willingness to protect the line employees. The situation was so volatile that Twomey felt that if he did not implement a lockup the guards might walk out.[16] He recalls that during the period it "was a struggle to keep the place open." There were constant union demands for lockups, shakedowns, and changes in administrative policies.

According to one long-time lieutenant, "at one point it seemed that there was a union meeting near every other day to talk about security." The union demanded that lieutenants be supplied blackjacks and mace, that tiers above the ground level be barred in, that blind spots on the yard be fenced off, that the sheet metal shop be closed entirely until some effective means of preventing the scrap from being fashioned into knives was found. Most important, the union demanded the creation of a special segregation facility for troublemakers. Ultimately they settled for SPU.

Tension between Twomey and the union did not abate. The union charged that Twomey was inaccessible and unresponsive to their problems. When Twomey discharged three guards for "allowing" three inmates to escape in early 1972, the union took their cases and won reinstatement for each.[17] Twomey concluded that it was "useless to fire anyone" and that the union had "undermined my authority."

The first captain to join the union did so in 1972. He had been given a thirty-day suspension by Warden Twomey for physically throwing a young schoolteacher out of his office when the latter came in to demand an assignment to the school for a particular inmate. Although the captain was not a member of the union, the union took the case, seeing in it an excellent opportunity to increase its strength. The suspension was taken to Springfield via the grievance procedure and reduced to two days. Subsequently all the captains, save one, joined up. The chief guard himself became a member in September 1973 "because a union member came to me and told me about an administrative change that was about to take place and about which I had been told nothing, despite the fact that I thought I was a part of the administration"—further evidence of the consequences of the split between administration and the guard elite.

After the baseball bat incident of 2 July 1972 (see p. 164), another walk out was threatened, and once again the prison administration responded by calling for a general lockup. This time union pressures on the warden were revealed in the press.

A shakedown of cells is now being held at Stateville and an employee told the *Daily News* that he saw the guards take either a radio or a phonograph out of the inmate's cell and throw it over a railing. "They are going through cells tearing pictures and other personal things off the walls," he said. "The men consider this unnecessary harassment and intimidation." It was learned that the Stateville guard lieutenants met Sunday night and threatened to go on strike if Twomey did not order the prison population locked up.[18]

Officer James Zeiger was the first officer killed in the line of duty since 1946. Not only was his death (10 January 1973) a highly emotional event, but it also provided an extremely opportune moment for union organizing. Following the incident, the union voted to lock up Stateville if demands for security were not met. On 27 January the 7 A.M.–3 P.M. shift reported to work but followed the union orders not to let any of the inmates out of their cells. One by one Warden Twomey called each of the keepers and then the other guards to his office and asked each one if he was going to open the cells; upon refusal, he suspended them.

Outside the prison a crowd of some one hundred guards gathered while professional AFSCME organizers from Chicago directed the job action. AFSCME representatives were in contact with the governor's office and were assured that nobody would lose their job and that the situation would be worked out. Director designate David Fogel was dispatched to Stateville, where he negotiated an end to the day-long walk out by promising to place all the demands upon an agenda to be addressed as soon as possible. Once again command of the local situation was taken over by Springfield.

By 1973 the union had become a potent force in the Illinois prisons.[19] Fogel contacted AFSCME representatives even before he came to Illinois and met with members of the union's executive board (with the governor in attendance) before his nomination was made public and before he introduced himself to his own central office staff. When Alyn Sielaff became director of corrections, he ordered monthly union/management meetings at each institution. He also maintained department level negotiating sessions with members of the union's executive council. The first collective bargaining agreement was ratified in the winter of 1975.

The demands which the union brought to the collective bargaining table were mostly bread and butter (pay, retirement, hours, etc.). However, issues involving the management of the institutions themselves hold the greatest potential for conflict in the future. Just how broadly the clause by which the department promises to ensure "safety and security at all times" will be construed is likely to raise the toughest problems.[20]

The trade union movement itself is basically incompatible with the prison's paramilitary organization. As professional organizers gradually build a spirit of trade unionism at Stateville, the prison is becoming demystified; the fighting spirit and sense of mission are waning. The union maintains that the guards are "working stiffs" laboring for a living in order to raise their children and support their families. They argue that, while on the job, prison employees are entitled to respect, dignity, and decency. As far as the union is concerned, "taking orders" is not consistent with dignity on the job. The union would prefer to remove the military ranks (and uniforms) and substitute simple job descriptions and job titles.

As the union argues that this is "just a job" and that "you're not being paid to be a hero," it can be expected that the guard will become less committed to an esprit de corps. In early May 1975, for example, hostages were seized at the Joliet prison. Tension was high at Stateville and the administration feared that a similar riot might be triggered. As the guards came off the 7 A.M.–3 P.M. shift, the captain asked for volunteers to work overtime (at time-and-a-half) in case of trouble. Only one man volunteered. Five years earlier it was reported that in similar circumstances guards *demanded* to stay on the job until the threat had passed.[21]

The expansion of prisoners' rights has been paralleled by the drive for both substantive and procedural rights of employees. Under Ragen and Pate, guards could be summarily suspended for "a dirty assignment," "making a negligent mistake," "being antagonistic to other employees," or "having a bad attitude." The Bensinger administration inaugurated the Employee Review Board, made up of administrators and captains, to hear cases of alleged rule infractions by employees. In addition, under Sielaff the union was finally given the right to represent any employee who demanded representation before the committee. The whole process is now infused with a proto due process, like the inmate disciplinary court; and, as with the inmate court, it is not clear that the substantive outcomes are any different. In 1969, for example, 171 guards were summarily suspended during the year for various reasons, and without hearings or written findings. This is an average of 14.3 suspensions per month. For the Employee Review Board cases from January to April 1975 there were fifty-eight suspensions or 14.5 per month.

Like the inmates, the guards now have a (five-step) grievance procedure which can be used to appeal disciplinary decisions or any other conflicts that arise on the job. Under Bensinger the last stage of the grievance procedure was heard by the assistant director in Springfield. A union representative recalls that the union never won a single grievance from Bensinger's assistant director. The same AFSCME representative estimates that during the Sielaff administration (1973–75) the union has won about 50 percent of the grievances at the level of the assistant director. From 1 July 1974 to 30 June 1975, of thirty-six union grievances to reach the assistant director, six were concluded totally favorably to the grievant, twenty-two totally unfavorably and eight ended with mixed results. And there is now a further appeal to an "outside" committee with no members from the Department of Corrections.

Whereas the union complained that Twomey was inaccessible, both Cannon and Brierton have been in constant contact with the union stewards at Stateville and with the state AFSCME representatives. It is not at all unusual for the warden to call in the union to discuss some policy or security change. In 1969 the union president was four times refused entrance through the gatehouse because it was alleged that he had been carrying out union business on the job. Today the relationship is far more normalized, particularly with Warden Brierton, in whom the union has confidence.

There are limitations to the development of a union movement inside the prison. The union's efforts on behalf of Assistant Warden Vern Revis, first in presenting him $500 for a kidney operation, and then in trying to mobilize support for a job action when he was relieved of his line responsibilities, demonstrates that at least some of the esprit de corps of the old regime still remains. Several of the lieutenants went to the union meeting ready to demand a strike if Revis was not reinstated in his old position. This gesture indicated a feeling of solidarity and loyalty between some of the guard staff and some of their superiors who came up through the ranks and are looked upon as heroic leaders. The AFSCME representative argued vigorously that a labor union does not strike merely because one of the bosses is laterally transferred. He told the membership that it would be impossible satisfactorily to explain to a guard's family that his job had been put in jeopardy because of a top-level administrative shake-up. At the end of his speech, nobody at the meeting was willing to make a motion on behalf of Revis.

It also remains to be seen how legally strong the public employee union in Illinois will become. The legislature has still not passed legislation providing for collective bargaining despite the fact that it has been proposed during several sessions. While it is unlikely that the legality of establishing collective bargaining by executive order will ever be tested in court (because of the issue of standing), public employee collective bargaining continues to rest on a shakier foundation than collective bargaining in the private sector.[22]

Part of the union's potential strength may be dissipated by recent moves of the Department of Corrections to sever the captains and lieutenants, who are arguably supervisors, from the rest of the guards by challenging their inclusion in the same bargaining unit with the line officers. Taking a strict interpretation of the executive order, the union has countered with the argument that the lieutenants do not strictly "hire and fire" and therefore are not supervisors. The administration has responded by issuing scores of directives urging local wardens to move the lieutenants into actual supervisory situations. Without the lieutenants and captains the union would be sapped of some of its best talent and of a group which would carry considerable weight in the event of a strike.

On the other hand it is unlikely that the captains and lieutenants would respect a picket line anyway. Recently, in hearings for promotions to lieutenant, all five of the guard applicants said that if they were promoted to lieutenant they would feel that it would be their duty to come to work even across picket lines. During the January 1973 job action, several of the lieutenants stayed on the job. More recently, lieutenants have decided among themselves that they would stay out only if the job action were over something "damn important" and that, even in such an instance, they would be available for action if "lives were in danger inside."

What will probably emerge is a series of bargaining units all within AFSCME. The captains and lieutenants may each have their own bargaining units as will the professional employees (the counselors), and the clerical employees. This may have the effect of further segmenting the different groups within the prison, although it should be pointed out that, to the degree that all employees feel some common tie to their umbrella organization AFSCME, there may be a trend away from segmentation.

The potentially most significant barrier to an effective union is the racial division among the employees. To date the blacks have not joined or participated in the union as enthusiastically as whites. Few blacks come to meetings although the present vice-president is a black guard from the Joliet Prison. Only last year the black warden of the Joliet Prison attempted to use the black guards as a counterweight to the old white guard clique that dominated the prison. He urged upon black guards the proposition that the union was racist and that there was no place in it for them. AFSCME has moved hard to establish its legitimacy as a nondiscriminatory union. However, on issues like Affirmative Action, the union and the blacks, or at least the black community, may have conflicting interests. The union is opposed to the Affirmative Action program, which sends recruitment trucks into the inner city to sign up minority guards. "They may as well ask Jeff Fort [leader of the Black P Stone Nation] to do the hiring for us." The union is also opposed to hiring men with prior criminal records to work as guards. On the issue of promotions there are also racial interests at stake. Past discrimination notwithstanding, the union's position is that promotion and assignment should come strictly with seniority.

Conclusion

Between 1970 and 1975 the guards emerged as an independent force within the Stateville organization. They were alienated from John Twomey and the reform regime which espoused an ethos of service for the inmate population. Initially the guards rallied around their traditional heroic leaders like Vernon Revis. Even up to the present, faint hope continues that the college-educated professionals will eventually turn the prison back to the traditional elite who know "how to run it."

Alienation from the reform regime, coupled with growing fear for personal safety, spurred the growth of the union movement.

The union brought the guards a voice in policy-making independent of position in the formal organization. With professional union organizers as allies, the Stateville guards became increasingly militant in their demands for greater security and a return to an authoritarian system.

Ties with the trade union movement began subtly to divide the guard subculture horizontally. Top-level guards and assistant wardens, despite their cultural affinity to many of the old-timers, were part of management. Professional union organizers and officials pressed upon the rank and file a redefinition of their work and spoke out against the military model and identification with heroic leaders. The union reinforced the demystification of the prison that was proceeding apace as the boundaries of the prison became more permeable.

The union movement articulates well with the Brierton restoration regime. The corporate model preferred some type of organization representing the rank and file. Brierton went even beyond the union in advocating better security and safety on the job. Likewise, as the union movement has become more mature, it has helped to break down the parochialism among the guards. It has also removed much of the affect from the job. Thus, the union supports the amelioration of living conditions for inmates (TV sets, recreation, school programs, etc.) as long as security needs are being met. The moral drama that once enveloped the prison may be evaporating. The union is turning its attention to raising the guard's own standard of living and assuring him a high degree of job security. Thus far Brierton's restoration regime should be able to count on support from the union.

The guard force has also been divided vertically along racial lines. The black guards are clearly more empathic to the inmates than are the white guards.[23] The culture conflict within the organization between black and white staff members would appear to be a potentially threatening issue for the future. The very empathy of the black guards for the minority prisoners is potentially antithetical to Brierton's view of the guard as a detached bureaucratic security specialist.

The division of the guards along racial lines also carries over to the union. The union cannot develop its strength without the support of the black rank-and-file guards. Yet there is a reluctance among the black guards to become active in a union that is associated with "the rednecks." The very fact that the prison, the union, and the white guards are centered in Joliet while the black guards live in and are oriented toward Chicago further reinforces the racial division.

8 Overview: Restoration and Beyond

> The position of all "democratic" currents, in the sense of currents that would minimize "authority," is necessarily ambiguous. "Equality" before the law and the demand for legal guarantees against arbitrariness demand a formal and rational "objectivity" of administration, as opposed to the personally free discretion flowing from the "grace" of the old patrimonial domination. If, however, an "ethos"—not to speak of instincts—takes hold of the masses on some individual question, it postulates substantive justice oriented toward some concrete instance and person; and such an "ethos" will unavoidably collide with the formalism and the rule-bound and cool "matter of factness" of bureaucratic administration.
>
> Max Weber, quoted in H. H. Gerth and C. W. Mills, *From Max Weber*

Between 1925 and 1975 Stateville passed through four distinct stages: anarchy, charismatic dominance, drift, and crisis. Beginning in 1975 a fifth stage is discernible: a period of restoration, in which the reforms of the past decade, as well as the redefinition of the prisoner's status, are integrated with aspects of authoritarian control. Before discussing the limits of this fifth stage it might be well to review the natural history of the prison.

Stateville Penitentiary was opened in 1925 as a reform era's effort to ameliorate the overcrowded, physically dilapidated, and scandal-ridden Joliet prison. In addition to the construction of the prison, attention of Progressive Era reformers was directed toward several other aspects of prison reform. The Progressive Merit System was established in 1920. The position of sociologist-actuary was created upon the recommendations of the academically dominated Clabaugh commission in 1928. Another foothold for reformers in the prisons was the Office of the State Criminologist, which was established in 1917. But the sum of these efforts by Progressive Era reformers amounted to no more than segmental incursions into a system that was a tool of the state political organization.

Spoils politics penetrated the prison through both the staff and the inmates between 1925 and 1936. The warden and the bulk of the guard force owed their positions to political patronage. The existence of a staff without expertise in prison management or a career commitment to the job had fateful consequences for the prison's social organization. Rules and discipline vacillated according to who was exercising authority. Between 1925 and 1932, Stateville experienced one of the most violent and unstable periods in its history. Between 1932 and 1936, the deepening Depression in the larger society was paralleled inside the prison by idleness, deterioration of discipline, and complete collapse of a daily regimen. Authority passed from the hands of the state officials into the hands of powerful inmate gang leaders. Politics also penetrated the inmate social system as is indicated in Leopold's observation about the ties between the sizable number of Jewish inmates and one of Chicago's powerful political clubs. Favoritism, lack of uniform standards and rules, and particularistic relationships all characterized the organization during this early period.

During this first decade (1925–36) the prison pursued no consistent organizational goals and developed no stable internal equilibrium. The prisoners were beyond the concern of society's elite and out of touch with its central institutional and value systems.

The year 1936 was a watershed year in Stateville's history. The convergence of an aroused press, a highly critical blue ribbon commission, and a reform governor led to Joe Ragen's appointment as warden of the Stateville/Joliet complex. At the time Ragen's appointment seemed unexceptional. Like his predecessors he was a political appointee and a former sheriff from downstate although he had also earned a good record in the several years that he had been warden of Menard.

Ragen's authoritarian system of personal dominance was first of all rooted in his ability to control the relationships between the prison and the outside. Between 1936 and 1961 he created his own independent political base by cultivating the press, the law enforcement community, and individual legislators. At the same time it is likely that during and directly after World War II public attention was completely diverted from events within the state prisons. In addition, the full-employment economy during that period erased the importance of the prison as an instrument of political patronage.

Warden Ragen created a mystique about his own invincibility and omniscience. His daily inspection of the prison, accompanied only by his two dogs, symbolized his highly personalistic rule. He alone managed all contacts with the outside thereby reinforcing his personal power. From his staff he demanded absolute loyalty, identifying his own authority with the best interests of the prison. So great was his personal prestige, charisma, and resources that his system of dominance was not weakened by the forces of politicization and bureaucratization associated with the trend toward mass society in the decade after World War II.

Ragen exercised complete domination over the guard staff. His guards were exclusively recruited from Southern Illinois. They lacked any ties to the Chicago or Joliet communities, identifying totally with the prison and the warden who personified its values. In addition, Ragen expanded the barracks and constructed a trailer court, reinforcing the staff's segregation from the surrounding community. The rigid and arbitrary discipline to which the guards were subjected generated high rates of turnover within the lower ranks. This diminished the probability that the line personnel would develop an effective counterforce. To the handpicked elite who occupied top administrative posts, Ragen offered considerable fringe benefits: food allowance, state-owned homes, and inmate servants. Such "payment in kind" Weber considered a leading characteristic of the patrimonial regime.

The inmate social system during this period conforms to what has been described by scholars who studied other prison communities in the decades before and after World War II. Criminal identities imported from the street accounted for an inmate status system. Prison sentences were long and the inmate social system tended to remain stable. A viable reward system stimulated intense competition for the few luxuries that were attainable. Many of the natural leaders among the inmates were co-opted by good jobs and the legitimate and illegitimate opportunities which were attached.

Ragen's rule was that of a totalitarian. He would not be defied even on insignificant rules. He persistently emphasized to his staff that stress upon the smallest details would prevent authority from ever being openly and collectively challenged. An inmate who challenged the system and called attention to himself as a "no good son of a bitch" would find himself on the coal pile for years, in isolation on a stringent diet, or salted away in segregation for an indefinite term. Ragen's regime typified Weber's description of pre-bureaucratic forms of administration: "All non-bureaucratic forms of domination display a peculiar coexistence: on the one hand, there is a sphere of strict traditionalism, and, on the other, a sphere of free arbitrariness and lordly grace."[1]

Particularly in the later years of Ragen's regime, the routine was systematized into a patriarchal system of administration based upon traditional authority. The latent charismatic content of the system only became explicit at infrequent moments of crisis. With Ragen's departure for Springfield, however, the charismatic aspect of the regime was greatly attenuated. Warden Pate's administration drifted into a collegial rule. Between 1961 and 1970 this system showed signs of extreme strain under pressures emanating from the outside.

The civil rights movement of the early 1960s served to politicize the prison's minority population which emerged as a solid majority by 1960. The trend toward mass society redefined the status and value of marginal groups in the polity. The demand by prisoners for fuller participation in the core culture was reinforced by the greater sensitivity of the elites to the moral worth of marginal citizens.

It was the Black Muslims who first gave expression to the heightened aspirations and expectations of the black inmates. Alone among political and religious movements in the 1960s, the Muslims defined the prison as a legitimate arena for organizing a constituency. Later, political radicals, some of whom were themselves prisoners, also attempted to transform prisoners from a group in itself to a group for itself.

The Muslims carried out collective activities which challenged the authority of the patriarchal system. The Pate administration characteristically responded to the Muslims by adopting a policy of massive resistance. Every demand of the Muslims was rejected; their leaders were thrown in segregation. The system could not tolerate any challenge to its basis of control. If it were successfully challenged at any point, authority would be fatally undermined. In order to maintain the integrity of its authority the Pate administration had no other choice than to repress the Muslims, but by doing so it made inevitable the complete collapse of authority after 1970.

The Muslims could not have sustained their challenge to the prison administration without the dramatic turn around in the orientation of the juridical system. Once again the momentum of mass society was fateful. A wide-scale legal reform movement, beginning with the leadership of the Warren Court, extended substantive and procedural rights to the indigent, the illegitimate, minors, students, servicemen, and criminal defendants. A late aspect of this extension of the rights of citizenship to marginal groups was the abandonment of the "hands off" doctrine and the recognition that prisoners were not "slaves of the state." The limited but symbolic successes of the Muslims before the courts seemed to the prison authorities a total repudiation by the central institutional system of the larger society.

Law reform also penetrated the prison through the new penal code, which expedited parole eligibility. Indirectly this reform had a powerful impact upon the social organization. By greatly increasing inmate turnover it had the effect of destabilizing the old con power structure which had subserved the authority of the system for decades and which was already undermined by rising inmate expectations and a shift from an individual to a group perspective on serving time. By 1970 the forces of bureaucratization, politicization and the penetration of juridical norms had undermined the traditional system of authority to the extent that control itself had become problematic. In the fall of 1970, Warden Pate resigned.

Between 1970 and 1975 the Stateville leadership struggled to regain its balance. The prison's boundaries had become permeable to the outside. Local control had been lost to centralized authority and the universalistic rule of law. The new emphasis on bureaucratization prescribed professional standards of preparation for a new administrative elite. Sharp conflict developed within the staff; the morale of the rank and file deteriorated. Given the weakened condition of organizational authority, politicized Chicago supergangs were able to penetrate the prison and broaden their organizational structures and prestige. Internally, the prison experienced a crisis in control that lasted until 1975.

In Springfield a young, Yale-educated businessman became

the first director of corrections in 1970. Eager to align himself with the liberal wing of American corrections, he imposed many reforms upon Stateville designed to "humanize" conditions and to extend "dignity" and "respect" to the "residents." A Unified Code of Corrections and comprehensive Administrative Regulations limited administrative discretion at the local level. The director sought the advice of reformers and academic specialists and opened the prison to representatives of minority groups.

The new Department of Corrections was far more centralized than its predecessor, the Department of Public Safety. The authority to formulate prison policy passed out of the hands of the local wardens and was exercised by a powerful, active central office in Springfield. The prison was no longer an autonomous institution.

At Stateville, Warden Pate's two immediate successors were well-educated professionals who adhered to the rehabilitative ideal and the human relations model of management. In place of the authoritarian system they attempted to establish a regime based upon consensual authority. Captains and lieutenants were urged to counsel both rank-and-file guards and inmates before resorting to formal disciplinary mechanisms. Problems in the organization were attributed to problems in communication.

The first two reform regimes failed to establish a viable equilibrium. Inmate expectations increased far more rapidly than did material benefits or the amelioration of unsatisfactory living conditions. The reformers stressed a philosophical reinterpretation of the moral implications of imprisonment at the same time that concrete physical conditions were rapidly deteriorating. Indeed, increased organizational dysfunction meant fewer showers, worse food, dirtier cells, and less regular visiting procedures. The reform regime presided over a shrinking number of programmatic opportunities but, at the same time, encouraged inmate expectations.

Finally, the first two reform regimes failed to maintain control. The number of attacks upon guards and inmates greatly increased. In addition to individual acts of violence there were also many instances of collective violence, including strikes, riots, gang fights, and the seizure of hostages. Having no other strategy to maintain control, the reform regimes periodically reverted to measures even more repressive than those of previous decades. In the years 1970–75 the greatest percentage of inmates were placed in isolation and segregation in Stateville's history. Conditions in the maximum security Special Program Unit deteriorated to a level of violence and destruction beyond anything previously seen in Illinois.

Administrators attributed the crisis in control to the liberalized court decisions as well as to the power of the supergangs. I have argued that the substance of court decisions themselves did not *cause* the crisis in control, although they did heighten inmate expectations and stimulate protest.

The most important impact of the penetration of juridical norms was to bring to bear outside pressure upon the Stateville administration to bureaucratize. The tension between the rehabilitative ideal, which prescribed the individualization of treatment, and the rule of law, which demanded universalistic criteria of decision making, was decades ago observed by Weber. The transfer of power from the patriarchal regime of Warden Pate to the professional regimes of Wardens Twomey and Cannon did not automatically transform the administration into a rational-legal bureaucracy. The reform regimes never met the demands for rational and visible decision making which were made by the courts and the department's own central office.

The reform administrations failed to develop an organization capable of maintaining control or meeting basic demands for services. They also failed to meet the demands of the legal system for visible and rational decision making or to live up to their own reform rhetoric in the opinion of various outside interest groups. And they failed to meet the crucial challenge to order and security posed by the Chicago supergangs.

After 1970 the inmate social system was dominated by four Chicago street gangs which imported their organizational structures, ideologies, and symbol systems from the streets. The very emergence of these minority "supergangs" in Chicago can be accounted for by a new relationship between secular and religious institutions and traditional youth gangs. Beginning in the early 1960s the federal government, private foundations, universities, and established churches redefined youth gangs and their leaders as legitimate indigenous grassroots organizations which spoke in the interest of the minority community. Through publicity, sizable grants, and technical assistance (as well as substantial police attention) these traditional youth gangs evolved into large proto-politicized supergangs. This transition of traditional gang boys into a potential political force was not acceptable to the political and law enforcement interests in Chicago (or to their spokesmen in Congress), and a concerted law enforcement drive against the gangs was pursued after 1968. One consequence was the massive infusion of members of the Black P Stone Nation, Disciples, Vice Lords, and Latin Kings into the state prisons.

The young gang members had assimilated a justificatory vocabulary as well as a set of rising expectations as they were growing up in the Chicago ghettos during the 1960s. The old prison reward system, which promised better jobs and the opportunity to score for "hooch," coffee, and extra food, was no longer compelling. Unlike the Muslims, the gang members had no specific issues and no concrete agenda. They brought to the prison diffuse goals and a general attitude of lawlessness and rebelliousness. The small minority of white inmates left at Stateville found themselves in grave danger, as did those blacks who were not affiliated with one of the gangs. Increasingly, inmates interrelated as blocks. For a while, the gang leaders were the organization's most stabilizing force as they struggled to reach an accommodation with one another and with the administration.

In exchange for using their services to keep things cool, the leaders continually demanded formal recognition and deference from the prison authorities. On this issue the staff was divided sharply. Lower-ranking guards and civilians found it necessary to defer to the gang leadership in order to meet their goals. The top administrators remained far more reluctant to share their power with prisoner leaders although, to be sure, certain concessions were exacted. Finally, the gangs could not be controlled. General lockups occurred in 1971, 1972, and 1973; the third occasioned by an inter-gang melee between the Black P Stones and the Disciples. In September 1973 hostages were seized at Stateville and in April 1975 hostages were seized at the Joliet prison.

The rise of professionalism, the intrusion of the courts, and the emergence of unified blocks among the inmates all contributed to a crisis in morale among the custodial staff. Guards were afraid to come to work. Rumors of riots and killings reverberated through the shifts. Many guards followed a strategy of withdrawing from the disciplinary process altogether.

Afraid for their safety and no longer in "awe" of a charismatic leader, the guards began to turn toward the union to give voice to their interests. The union had earlier begun to organize, despite Pate's protestations, under the leadership of Ross Randolph, Ragen's successor as director of public safety. The crisis in control occasioned by the gangs, and the rise of professionals, from whom the guards were alienated, made the union all the more appealing. The small local affiliated with a national union, which provided professional expertise and assistance during a period when it was scoring great organizational successes statewide and nationally in agencies throughout the public sector. In 1973, the new Democratic governor (Walker) fulfilled his campaign pledge to support collective bargaining in the public sector; the union had become a major force in Illinois prisons.

At the local level, the union continually demanded more safety and security. After the first guard in thirty years was killed at Stateville in January 1973, the local staged a walkout, taking almost the entire rank and file with them. The spirit of the trade union movement necessarily is in conflict with the paramilitary organization and *esprit de corps* that had characterized the custody staff for decades. Guards objected to the arbitrary and capricious actions of their superiors and found institutional mechanisms to ensure that they were provided with due process in charges brought against them. These changes greatly weakened the authority of the higher-echelon custody staff.

The custody staff also became increasingly heterogeneous under the combined pressures of minority groups and government Affirmative Action. By 1975, almost 50 percent of the guard force was black or Latino. The minority guards were far more empathic with the plight of the minority inmates and often found themselves alienated from the southern Illinois white guards who occupied almost all the top positions. This tension represented one more strain in an organization that was highly fragmented, factionalized, and conflict-ridden.

The years 1925–70 demonstrated the historical limits of the authoritarian system of personal dominance that depended upon the peripheral position of the prison and its inmates vis-à-vis the central institutional and value systems of society. The years 1970–75 demonstrated the incompatibility of the rehabilitative ideal and the human relations model of management with the functional requisites of maintaining control in maximum security prisons and with the demands of the courts for rational and visible decision making.

The Brierton regime suggests a fifth stage, one of restoration, in Stateville's history. The warden himself, a former chief guard of the Cook County Jail, is a physically imposing, charismatic figure. The early success of his leadership underscores the point that the maximum security prison functionally requires an imperatively coordinated administration.

Brierton has strengthened security, improved services, and rebuilt the morale of the guard staff. In the first six months of his regime he emphasized the physical reconstruction of the prison. He closed up tunnels, sealed the tiers with iron bars, placed television cameras along the cell house walls, hung tear gas cannisters from the ceilings, and instituted serious riot training. He rejected the rehabilitative ideal and the human relations model of management in favor of a highly rational, problem-oriented "corporate" model of management which is characterized as professional, detached, and cost-conscious.

The new warden has stressed the need to provide basic services through regularized procedures and has deemphasized the concern with redefinition of the inmate's status. On the other hand, Brierton has committed himself to justice; each prisoner should receive the treatment and opportunities commensurate with law and to which he is entitled. Each month the warden personally speaks to every inmate in the prison on his "call line" and provides a prompt written reply to every inquiry or grievance. He demands the same formal responsiveness of his staff. Written records have proliferated. Each time an inmate showers, the event is documented, as is every contact between a counselor and his client. Brierton has thus taken the initiative in attempting to fully bureaucratize the prison. If he is successful and can reestablish control at the same time as expanding basic services and programmatic opportunities, all without jeopardizing due process, Stateville is sure to reemerge in the next several years as a leading model of prison administration for the nation.

There are limits, however, to the degree to which the corporate model can implement a new equilibrium. The most important obstacle is resources. Will the legislature, in the face of fiscal crisis and an expanding prisoner population, provide the resources necessary to meet the needs of basic services, adequate staff, and increased security?

There may also be limits to a corporate bureaucracy's ability to be responsive to prisoner problems and needs. More prisoner complaints are being heard and "responded to," but merely because the rules have become concrete and impartial, there is no assurance that the prisoners' own conception of substantive justice will not collide with the "formalism" and "cool matter of factness" of bureaucratic administration. It is possible that the expectations engendered by the two previous reform administrations and by numerous interested parties on the outside, as well as by the courts, have created expectations that cannot be satisfied by the corporate model. Will the prisoners any longer accept a safe prison with regularized procedures, better food, regular yard time, and various (limited) programmatic opportunities? Both inmate material expectations and demands for representation in decision making may exceed the capacity of the system to provide solutions.

Third, there is potential for conflict with the media, private interest groups, and reformers. In developing the corporate model Brierton has attempted to maintain a low profile but he has already met sporadic criticism. Some reformers completely reject such security techniques as television surveillance of the cells. There are sure to be claims that Brierton is creating an Orwellian nightmare. The rehabilitative ideal still has considerable vitality among representatives of the media, reformers and academic specialists.

Related to potential criticism from reformers is a conflict over the guard's future role. Reformers cling to the idea that the guard's role can evolve into that of a quasi counselor. Brierton's system demands that the guard be a detached security specialist infused with an *esprit de corps within a paramilitary regime.* The union professional leadership is opposed to the paramilitary model. The Department of Corrections' central office itself does not seem to have moved to implement the security specialist guard role precisely because of ambivalence about completely abandoning the guard-as-counselor model.

There is the question of personnel. Can Brierton shape the kind of bureaucratic regime which he advocates with the staff which he has inherited? It is true that there has been a wholesale shake-up of staff since he became warden, yet the professional skills, particularly of management and budget, are clearly lacking except for the few very top administrative positions. The rest of the Illinois maximum security prisons are lagging far behind Stateville in becoming bureaucratized. At the Joliet prison (now under separate administration), a former guard captain without a college education and without sophisticated management skills has recently been elevated to warden. Will a change in political administrations or a reduced budget or the departure of Brierton mean that Stateville will slip back to where it was between 1970 and 1975 or earlier?

The restorational regime is also highly vulnerable to changes in the relationship of the prison to the political environment. The 1976 elections will see a change of governor in Illinois and perhaps a return to a more partisan style of administration. The Ragen legacy was a prison system well insulated from partisan politics, but that tradition is by no means immutable. It would be very difficult for any administration, no matter how partisan, to dismantle the many professional bureaucratic mechanisms built into the prison system at this point. The middle- and lower-level managers have civil service security and are in office to stay. But a partisan governor could choose to appoint a nonprofessional (like Peter Bensinger) as director of corrections, leaving it an open question whether political appointments would be made at the warden level. Even if they were not, a nonprofessional administrator could hardly provide the kind of centralized leadership that first began with Bensinger and was so substantially expanded under Sielaff.

What if the attempt to synthesize reform and control in the maximum security prison fails? What if the prison reverts to arbitrary and capricious management in a situation marked by brutality, favoritism, and staff apathy? The danger is that, in that event, the larger effort to reform our bureaucracies and basic institutions will have been dealt a mortal blow. The failure to institutionalize prison reform could reinforce more general cynicism about the capacity of our society to reform itself.

Appendixes

Appendix 1
Participant Observation among Prisoners

The first phase of my three years of discontinuous research at Stateville was a four-month participant observation study of the prison social system which began in June 1972. Many of the data reported in chapter 6, although supplemented by later documentary materials and interviews, are drawn from this fieldwork. Almost two years after the conclusion of that four-month study I reentered Stateville for a six-month period to carry out firsthand interviewing and participant observation among the administration and later the guard staff. This second study was not nearly as demanding as the earlier experience.

My attention to the problem of participant observation among prisoners is surely not meant to suggest that I place less importance on the interviewing, documentary analysis, records sampling, or survey research which were also extensively relied upon. My comments are offered simply in the hope that they will ease the path of future researchers.

The prison participant observer enters a highly unstable social setting abounding with rumor, suspicion, factionalism, and open

Much of this section has been previously published in James B. Jacobs, "Participant Observation in Prison," *Urban Life and Culture* 3, no. 2 (July 1974).

conflict. He must daily negotiate the legitimacy, content, and boundaries of his role with a society which is hostile to his presence.

What is at stake in this "how" of face-to-face interaction is the very fate of the research. The fieldworker's behavior is without clear meaning to his informants until he settles on an acceptable role. The way in which his informants come to define his role as well as their own (and the way he comes to define his role as well as theirs) will determine with whom he comes in contact, the kinds of inquiries that are permissible, the meanings assigned to the inquiries, the kinds of information communicated by informants, the meanings imputed to those communications by the researcher—ultimately, the validity and success of the project.

I entered Stateville early in the summer of 1972 through the influence of Professor Norval Morris and under the sponsorship of a Ford Foundation grant. For four months, I spent five days a week and several weekends at Stateville. For reasons of prison security and personal apprehensiveness I did no observation during the night shift, although that might have been useful. During the days I had complete freedom to walk about the prison unescorted, and I conducted interviews and observations in the prisoners' cells, in the work areas, in the isolation area, and in the prison yard.

Unlike Giallambardo,[1] whose entrance to Alderson Prison was preceded by written announcements distributed to the inmate population, I entered Stateville without a coherent definition of my role having been offered to staff or inmates. To those who inquired, I explained that I was both a law and sociology student interested in writing a book about "the way life is" in the prison. During the first several days I was thoroughly acquainted with what might be called "the institutional line." Mindful of the Sykes[2] and Giallambardo warnings, I was anxious to keep staff contacts (especially with guards) to a minimum. However, it was necessary to maintain cordial relations with staff and administration in the face of considerable skepticism about the "advisability" of this research.

The extent of factionalism and conflict within the prison could hardly be exaggerated. The most prominent division, of course, was that between staff and inmates. Scarcely less significant than the caste system were the sharp lines separating the races. At the time of the study, 70 percent of Stateville's inmates were black, 20 percent were Caucasian, and the remainder Latino.

While the inmates were divided by racial lines, there also existed substantial intraracial factionalism. About 50 percent of the black inmates aligned themselves with three large and mutually antagonistic Chicago street gangs (Black P Stone Nation, Vice Lords, Disciples). The Latino population, though relatively small, was divided between Puerto Ricans and Mexican Americans as well as between members of a Chicago street gang, the Latin Kings, and unaffiliated Latinos. Among the Caucasian inmates no formal organizational structures existed, but there were divisions into various cliques. These cliques could be characterized either as protective or nonprotective. Members of protective cliques were secure because of fighting ability, gangland ties, legal skills, or alliance with staff members. Whites within nonprotective cliques were highly vulnerable to physical assault, rape, extortion and general harassment. The prison staff was not immune from conflict and factionalism either. Sharp hostility existed between administrators and upper-echelon security officers, front-line guards, and treatment personnel.

Everyone within the prison has a reason for being there. People do not just wander in and out. Consequently, inmates as well as many staff members were from the start reluctant to accept my explanation for being allowed free access to Stateville. To my knowledge I was the first individual ever to have been granted this "privilege." Rumors that I was an agent for the FBI or the Chicago Police Department's Gang Intelligence Unit or an investigator for the governor's staff recurred throughout the research and had to be dealt with daily. As Giallambardo notes, for the researcher who chooses prison it is a formidable problem to "prove" that one is who one claims to be. The first task was to dispel the notion that I was an imposter.

With respect to this problem, my association with Professor Norval Morris was highly important. While touring a prison workshop on the second day in the field, a middle-aged black clerk introduced himself to me as a member of the inmate council (ABLE) and probed for biographical information beyond my cursory explanation. I told BD, who later became a key informant, that for several years I had worked closely with Norval Morris at the University of Chicago and had embarked upon this research upon his urging. Much to my surprise, BD was quite familiar with Morris's liberal positions on prison reform. The previous spring, Morris had addressed the high school graduation at Stateville on "the future of corrections" and had received a standing ovation. My connection with him thus located my group affiliations with a well-known university and suggested that I had access to "important" individuals in the Department of Corrections and in the prison reform movement. At one point in the research, Morris accompanied me to Stateville and met the inmate leadership informally. This immeasurably enhanced my credibility, but even this vouchsafe of my identity did not dissolve all suspicion. After all, it was not inconceivable that both Morris and myself were allied with law enforcement in some insidious venture.

The problem of establishing the validity of my claim to an independent and legitimate research identity was never fully solved. Even at the conclusion of the research there were inmates who shunned extensive conversation. Informants with whom I shared a friendly rapport frequently refused to answer questions which they felt too sensitive, incriminating, or secretive. I told inmates that they did not "have to" answer every question and that I appreciated their frankness in stating when they did not wish to pursue a particular subject. This in itself provided valuable data by sensitizing me to the limits of my acceptance in the setting and illuminating the kind of information only revealed to the most trusted insiders. Often an inmate several weeks later felt more confident about my loyalty and would reopen the previously closed topic. When it became known that I kept information confidential, inmates gradually began to speak more freely in my presence and permitted me to witness various illicit activities. One informant took me on a tour of the underground stills at Stateville. From time to time I was offered alcohol or a Marijuana cigarette. I declined them politely.

Even after my presence was accepted at the prison and my trustworthiness was reasonably well established, the success of the fieldwork was far from assured. It was most disturbing, although understandable, to find that inmates were not interested in contributing to research or in helping an aspiring scholar further his academic career. From their perspective my presence would be tolerable only if I could be helpful to them.

BD told me that I might be "useful" to the inmate leadership and that the inmate council executive committee would like an opportunity to counteract the "poison" given me by the administration and to "run down" the situation from their viewpoint. At the meeting held in a cramped office above the chapel without any staff member present, I was introduced to leaders from the Stones, Disciples, Vice Lords, and Latin Kings as well as to several articulate independents. For the next several hours I was bombarded with questions as to my loyalties, contacts, and willingness to act on behalf of inmates. Throughout this "interview" I attempted to outline my research objectives and to emphasize my concern with inmate problems. I explained that I would not write an exposé or go to the press but that I would faithfully report what I saw to Professor Morris, chairman of the Governor's Advisory Commission on the Treatment of Adult Offenders, and, through him, to the director of corrections and other senior administrators. I said it might be possible sometime in the future to arrange a meeting between the council and these individuals.

The inmate leaders at once defined my role as prison-reform advocate. They called to my attention innumerable prison conditions that demanded immediate rectification and beseeched me to take action. I expressed concern with their situation and promised to investigate abuses informally. Throughout the research I faced the constant dilemma of appearing morally committed to the inmate "cause" while pursuing interests unrelated to reform but vital to the research.

In order to demonstrate my moral commitment to the inmate "cause" and to provide some incentive for highly suspicious inmates to sustain an interactive relationship, it was necessary to carry out many favors during my months in the field. While such behavior deviates from the ideal participant observer's strict neutrality and ignores the warnings of Giallambardo and Sykes concerning role corruption, reciprocities may be necessary if the terms of the relationship are not to be considered violated.[3]

Maximum security inmates require and demand a great deal of help. Consequently, I offered legal advice, contacted families and lawyers, made suggestions for strategies in dealing with administration, served as a conduit for messages, and provided mobility from one work assignment to another for various leaders. When the daughter of one of the Stones' leaders was critically ill, I intervened with the warden in an unsuccessful attempt to arrange a furlough. More significantly I brought two University of Chicago professors to the prison to speak with the inmates about their grievances and took the case against dissolving the inmate council to senior administrators in the Department of Corrections. On another occasion I argued strenuously with the assistant director of corrections on the prison yard concerning the inappropriateness of canceling the popular inmate art show.

The difficulty implicit in such demonstrations of solidarity is in setting limits. Inmates urged me to carry letters for them out of the prison, to smuggle them "joints," and to leak information to newspapers. With respect to the newspapers I explained that the short-run shock value of an exposé (even if it were printed) would not compensate for the destructive precedent against future outside observers being allowed behind the walls that would surely result from my expulsion from the setting. Despite these arguments, requests for favors persisted and the tightrope act remained precarious until the last day in the field.

At the first meeting with the inmate council executive committee only slight indication was given of gang affiliations. Individuals were introduced by name as elected representatives of the inmate body. Within days, however, staff members approached to confide that the inmate council was dominated by gang members and warned against "falling in with this crowd." The inmate leaders themselves deflected questions concerning gangs, preferring to interact with me in their roles as inmates rather than as gang members. Where this definition of the situation prevailed, conversation was limited to issues of general inmate concern. The meeting was only the first of continuous interactions with the gang leaders in which I attempted to cast myself in the role of researcher and to cast the leaders in the role of informants, while they attempted to cast me in the role of advocate and ally and themselves in the role of aggrieved partisans. Consequently compromise had to be hammered out and renegotiated continually. At times of crises (for example when the inmate council was abolished), research had to take a back seat to advocacy, while on calmer days there was more opportunity and energy for lengthy, hair-down conversation about prison life.

While the inmate leaders' definition of my role as reform-advocate and of their own as inmate-spokesmen prevailed at all "meetings," "team performance" was not maintained in private conversation with each leader. During such occasions partisan interests and antagonisms among the gangs were aired. I learned, for example, that the Disciples felt betrayed by the Stones' alleged refusal to disipline their own members according to treaty provisions.

In addition, skilled informants were able to provide far more information privately when less sophisticated inmates were not present to misinterpret what was being said. CN, clerk for the assistant warden and articulate spokesman for the Latin Kings, quickly understood that my research posed no threat either to the Kings or to the other organizations. He met me at the gate each morning and personally undertook to orient me to Stateville. Over many weeks he gradually revealed to me the complex power relationships and social structures of the inmate organization. While GB, the younger and far less sophisticated leader of the Disciples, initially refused to enter into a relationship based upon his role as a gang leader, he eventually became an outstanding informant, providing deep insight into the organization and activities of Disciples and his own leadership position. What accounted for his acceptance of an informant role was his growing understanding of this new role set, increased confidence in my integrity, and especially my expanding knowledge about inmate society. In the early weeks, off brand inmates had been extremely helpful in describing the extent and type of power the gangs held within the prison. Gang leaders soon realized that I knew far more about the underlife at Stateville than any staff member. Once I was credited with being an insider, the amount of information to which I was exposed increased exponentially.

Initially I preferred to keep my identity vague,[4] presenting myself as a student of the prison, concerned with matters of prison reform and "telling it like it is". In order to present a student identity I carried a University of Chicago clip board, wore a beard, and dressed considerably more casually than members of the staff. At lunch I almost always sat with the clinical staff, the most tolerated members of the administration.

When it came to more narrowly defining the contours of the student role, I vacillated between the identities of lawyer and sociologist. Within the prison the identities of lawyer and sociologist have different meanings for actors and different implications for interaction. There were two thousand inmates at Stateville and at least as many legal problems. Furthermore, as a law student I was accorded special prestige. Inmates accurately perceived the administration's fear that lawyers and judges would further intrude upon prison practices and procedures. As a law student I was seen as an individual of potential power who could not be easily dismissed by the authorities. Thus, despite the danger of becoming full-time legal adviser to two thousand inmates, I was reluctant to reject this role because of its high exchange value and its tendency to place me in a position of receiving information on a great diversity of issues.

The role of sociologist was more ambiguous for inmates. Most confusing was that within the prison "sociologist" is a clinical position whose incumbents are responsible for writing up diagnostic classifications and parole evaluations which often evoke inmate resentment. While hostility on the part of inmates toward prison sociologists is considerably less than that directed toward guards, the former are still defined as control agents to be duped and exploited. When asserting claim to sociologist status it was necessary for me explicitly to disassociate myself from prison sociologists.

Excessive role clarity would have been extremely restrictive. As a law student it seemed appropriate to inmates that I be interested in disciplinary hearings and administrative discretion but not the involvement of gangs in the distribution of contraband. As a sociologist all my inquiries were permissible but all suspect to the extent that this role was seen to be integrated within the prison's formal organization. Neither identity was alone entirely satisfactory, but by manipulating the two it was possible to structure a research role of sufficient breadth to make legitimate my concern with a wide variety of prison matters.

Prison is a pervasive institution. Actors are deeply committed to their prison roles. Where individuals define their roles as crucial to their identities, it may be seen as morally impermissible for a newcomer to remain neutral and aloof. Had I assumed a "balanced" attitude toward matters of inmate concern, I would certainly have been shut off from any meaningful interaction with inmates. In this setting to be neutral is to be allied with the enemy.

On the other hand, with respect to competing factions among inmates the best strategy was strict neutrality, while emphasizing concern over matters pertinent to all inmates. This convenient stance was not always successful in the face of strong pressures to commit oneself.

I felt, for example, that the vulnerability of young white inmates to sexual pressure and "rip-offs" (rapes) was quite important in adequately assessing what appeared to be an increasingly anarchic situation. Despite careful explanation of my purposes within the prison, white inmates imputed to me a sentiment of racial solidarity with whites and a motive to work on *their* behalf to improve *their* position. When they concluded that I was unwilling to be their advocate and that I would continue to maintain my relations with black gang members, our rapport deteriorated rapidly, culminating with the following note:

> Mr. Jacobs: Hey, you Super Liberal Piece of Shit. So far this week two white guys have been jumped on and beaten by groups of Afro-Americans.* The next time you go over to "B" house lock-up to let some jackoff ripoff artist know who told on him for raping some white kid so he can get even later on why don't you tell him about yourself too. Also instead of doing your bull shit research from an armchair, why didn't you come in as an inmate so you could find out what it's all about, you phoney cock sucker.
>
> *human nigger scum.

What had been a shaky working agreement between this faction of the prison community and myself had utterly dissolved. Now I was redefined as a "nigger lover" and racial traitor. No longer was there enough common agreement on social identities and social tasks to support more than the most superficial communication. Perhaps this demonstrates that neutrality itself is a role enactment subject to interpretation?

Because of the frequent tension between the Disciples and the Stones, the best strategy was to cultivate closest ties with the Latin Kings and the Vice Lords. From informants within these groups I received a valuable perspective on the nature of gang organization and activity within the prison without being pulled into a possible conflict situation. It was not long, however, before a black inmate informed me that rumors were circulating throughout the prison that I was actually Puerto Rican—that although I tried to conceal it I was propelled into close contact with my Latin people. Once again imputed identification (with the Latino faction) was damaging for my "neutral" role, since the interests of the Spanish and black gangs were not wholly coincident. It is no easy task to maintain the confidence of all partisan groups. If research is to be carried out for a long period of time in such a conflict-ridden society, it may eventually be necessary to focus primary attention on one faction.

Even with respect to a single faction it is important for the researcher to honor status hierarchies and local arrangements lest he unwittingly get pulled into an intraorganizational dispute. Failure to observe this principle ultimately led to the loss of meaningful communication with the Black P Stone Nation.

A cooperative clinical counselor introduced me to an inmate gang member he thought would be especially insightful. I explained to LB that I was interested in understanding what life was like in the prison and asked him several questions about how the presence of the gangs had "changed things" since prisons were described in decades past. LB told me that he was a lieutenant in the Stones and vaguely described some of the obligations which this position entailed while in the prison. Not long after this conversation I was "summoned" to the cell of one of the Stones' top leaders. There I was warned that I was to stop asking questions about the Stones' organization to anyone other than to BJ himself. BJ reminded me of another serious breach of protocol that had occurred a week before. As I recalled that incident, three women had approached me in the prison parking lot one rainy afternoon after the day shift had been relieved. They explained that their car had broken down and asked for a ride to Chicago. During the ride I told them about my research, and they volunteered that they were related to various Black P Stone Nation members. I asked further questions about prison and the history of the Stones until they reached their destination. In the prison the next day several Stone leaders interrogated me concerning that conversation. At the time I felt that my explanations had satisfied them. Apparently it had not satisfied everyone, because BJ's insistence that I had delved too deeply into the activities of the Stones led him, on behalf of the Stones, to break off all but superficial relations with me during the remainder of the fieldwork.

Participant observers are often concerned with the objective accuracy of informants' statements of fact and interpretation. Some have abandoned the search for objective reality in favor of "getting into the head" of the actors in order to discover the subjective reality of various positions in the social setting.[5] The prison researcher faces this epistemological problem and a more practical one as well. In this highly balkanized and conflict-ridden society the known observer must be especially sensitive to being "duped"—this term being reserved for those instances when informants consciously falsify or distort information because they believe that they have a stake in having the researcher accept a definition of the situation which they "know" to be untrue in order to stimulate some impression or action.

The researcher needs to be sensitive to those issues with respect to which it is likely that he is being duped. Once these issues are identified he can proceed to investigate the interests perceived to be at stake. By recognizing the positions of various informants in the social organization it may be possible to check and recheck information so that ideology and interpretation can be analytically distinguished.

During the summer of 1970 a melee was touched off at Stateville's ball diamond. In the course of the melee several guards were seriously injured and the entire prison was consequently placed on "lockup" (inmates confined to their cells) for four months. In order to understand the impact of the gangs on prison social organization, I felt it crucial to reconstruct that event. But I was unsuccessful even after several months of interviewing. The staff held to the point of view that the fight between the two inmates which touched off the conflict had been "staged" by the gangs in order to draw line officers into a conflict.

The gang leadership denied this, claiming that the participants in the fight were unaffiliated with gangs and that the administration used this insignificant incident as a pretext to lock up the entire prison and transfer gang leaders to a new super segregation unit (the Special Program Unit). Independent inmates were somewhat divided in their account of the incident. Some adhered to each of the above interpretations while others volunteered alternate versions. After checking and counterchecking stories for weeks, I was unable to satisfy myself either as to objective facts (e.g., were the two individuals members of gangs?) or as to whether informants actually believed the interpretations they were offering.

The existence of the gangs within Illinois prisons was a sensitive issue for everyone. Staff members were committed to an anti-gang ideology and attributed all disorders at Stateville to their presence. Whoever I was and whatever use would be made of my research, the staff was interested that the gang leaders be defined as troublemakers and that the administrative decision to segregate the leadership at SPU be interpreted as necessary and legitimate.

Gang leaders, of course, wanted to present their ideology and activities in the light they perceived would be most favorable to the researcher. Thus, in discussing their grievances they constantly stressed their commitment to social and political action programs on the streets and to progressive prison reform behind the walls. When questioned closely about racial assaults, extortions, and other illicit activities which most whites attributed to them, they explained that the gang leadership opposed all these activities, that accounts of them were highly exaggerated, and that they were powerless to police their soldiers when they could offer them nothing by way of administrative concessions for adherence to institutional rules.

Several of the thoughtful "old cons" at Stateville were among my most cooperative informants. They readily grasped the purpose of the research and helped introduce me to veteran inmates who could provide perspective on the changes in prison life over the past several years. Even the old cons and independents, however, were not without vested interests in the setting. The old con power structure dominated by clerks, runners, and knowledgeable old-timers had been destroyed as the gangs solidified power. For the first time old cons no longer enjoyed a secure existence at Stateville. Not wishing to antagonize the powerful gang hierarchy and risk physical harm, these informants spoke cautiously about the gangs. Often there was implicit in their conversation disapproval of "gang-bangers" (young gang members) and their methods.

Inmates who have had long experience in duping representatives of the establishment may provide information other than that which they believe to be true, even where vested interests are not perceived as threatened. Inmates may exaggerate simply for reasons of self-aggrandizement. This was true of some whites, who denigrated other factions. Informants from this small group stressed their "connections" (to organized crime) inside and outside the prison, boasting that they, not the gang leaders, could obtain steak and a bottle of scotch any time they desired.

Furthermore, inmates may fabricate information in order merely to sustain an interaction that they find intrinsically satisfying. Giallambardo reports that on many occasions she had to put her research aside in order to provide a sounding board and emotional outlet for an inmate who had had a "bad day." This was no less true at Stateville. Many inmates found conversing with me in private offices or around the prison yard a pleasant break from the boredom and stress of prison life. In the researcher they found a polite and sympathetic listener. One "wise" inmate suggested to me that various individuals sought out my company only in order to pass time with a young male.

The known observer should never be insensitive to the impact he is having on the setting. Individuals may believe that there is something to gain by allying with the researcher. For example, being seen locked in serious conversation with the researcher served to validate and reinforce the status of leadership at the expense of potential and actual rivals. Few days passed at Stateville without at least one inmate flagging me down on the yard or interrupting an ongoing conversation in order to ask when I was coming to interview him.

The deprivations and pains of imprisonment have been documented over the years. The gravity of the prison setting was dramatically impressed upon me at the initial meeting with the executive committee of the inmate council. My field notes from that meeting recount the gang leaders' interpretation of the situation at Stateville.

Since Professor Morris' speech last spring things have been continuously deteriorating. Everything will be coming to a head soon because Revis is coming back to Stateville which means a return to the old order. He thinks of inmates as scum and is an admirer of the repressive system of Warden Joe Ragen. For weeks the guards have been telling inmates that the inmate council will be destroyed, that it is their turn to get even. Weapons are being stockpiled up front and the inmate leadership fears that an incident will be provoked or staged in order to carry out an Attica-like genocide. Over and over again the inmate leaders urged me to take them seriously and not to consider their fears paranoid. They are convinced that a riot is imminent and complain that they can no longer control the rank and file. All this was summed up by one gang leader who said, "The whole place could blow any day."

To be sure, prison is neither a pleasant place to live, to work, or to carry out fieldwork. It is depressing to enter the din of the cellhouse, to observe men shouting to you while gripping the bars of their steel cages. Despite one's sincere concern for those inmates one knows personally as well as for inmates in general, it is scarcely possible not to be hounded by the feeling that one does not care enough. The daily return home to Chicago was a constant reminder that for the researcher prison is merely a field setting.

According to Lofland, one of the gravest problems in maintaining the observer role through the fieldwork situation is the experience of marginality often felt by the observer. Although he is so close to the participants that he can empathize with their joys, pains, and boredoms, he is never really one of them. Very often during the experience it was pointed out to me that when the day ended I was going home, while the deprivations attending incarceration persist inexorably. Often inmates asked why I didn't become an inmate for a week or two in order to experience the totality of their world. During such questioning it seemed to me that my self-conception was severely threatened. It has been said that the marginality of one's position in the field often initiates introspection into the ethics of that position.[6]

The known observer can never really belong. Perhaps this is best discussed in terms of role strain. When, because of faulty role enactment, moral qualms, or marginality, the gap between self and role widens, one's role playing becomes more self-conscious and the performance consequently more problematic. The individual increasingly feels more frustrated and is more likely to withdraw from the scene to repatch the damaged role. This is a tactic I found necessary throughout the research.

As one wanders about the prison pursuing research hypotheses and preparing field notes, one cannot help but wonder if this is not the part of the voyeur. Consistently deflecting comments from complaints and accounts of suffering in order to steer conversation toward tentative hypotheses, one sometimes questions whether this type of research should be done at all.

I think the best answer is that such research must be continued. Not only is the prison an important setting in which to study individual and group behavior, but prisons too long have been isolated from the scrutiny of neutral observers. Even where the researcher's avowed purpose is not prison reform, it is important that prisons be open to social scientists who can bear witness to what occurs within. Observing the prison disciplinary committee or pursuing administrative channels to check out inmate grievances, I found the staff anxious to follow written procedure and due process. The presence of outside observers may have the desirable effect of encouraging all actors within the setting to adhere to the rules.

It might well be argued that all field researchers have some moral debt to the individuals who have made their research possible. These obligations can perhaps be fulfilled through individual reciprocities (e.g., parole recommendations, help in finding employment) or through more diffuse contributions. Giallambardo reports that she told inmates at Alderson that, though her research could not be expected to help them personally, it was aimed at helping "women in trouble everywhere."

This may be the consequence if those of us who have had the extraordinary opportunity to look at life behind the walls have the courage and desire to make known our feelings as well as our more technical research. Academics to date have played a not unimportant role in the prison reform movement, and that role should become more significant in the future.

Appendix 2
Tables

Table 1
Population of Stateville Penitentiary, 1919–73

Year	Count	Year	Count	Year	Count
1919	242	1934	3,857	1961	3,616
1920	400	1935	3,952	1962	3,527
1921	444	1941	3,565	1963	3,272
1922	665	1942	3,261	1964	3,169
1923	711	1944	3,491	1966	2,854
1924	920	1945	3,006	1967	2,448
1927	1,226	1948	3,219	1969	2,517
1929	2,030	1955	3,069	1970	2,270
1930	2,607	1956	3,036	1971	2,043
1931	2,685	1957	2,987	1972	1,931
1932	3,014	1959	3,285	1973	1,785
1933	3,506	1960	3,365		

The count was arrived at by averaging the daily counts for thirty random days in each year. No figures were available for the years not included.

TABLE 2
Escapes from Stateville/Joliet Complex, 1929–75

Year	Escapes	Year	Escapes	Year	Escapes
1929	14	1940	3	1954	0
1930	8	1941	0	1955	0
1931	6	1942	7	1956	0
1932	12	1946	3	1957	0
1933	12	1947	4	1963	0
1934	11	1948	0	1965	0
1935	18	1949	0	1969	7
1936	6	1950	1	1973	3
1937	9	1951	2	1974	5
1938	5	1952	0	1975	2
1939	4	1953	1		

TABLE 3
Civil Suits Filed Against Stateville/Joliet Administration, 1954–75

Year	Lawsuits	Year	Lawsuits	Year	Lawsuits
1954	1	1962	7	1969	66
1956	6	1963	33	1970	100
1957	10	1964	21	1971	123
1958	1	1965	17	1972	111
1959	3	1966	34	1973	104
1960	0	1967	52	1974	69
1961	3	1968	42	1975	101

*No data available for 1955.

TABLE 4
Transfers from Stateville/Joliet Complex to Menard Psychiatric Division, 1954–72

Year	Transfers	Year	Transfers
1954	41	1964	95
1956	98	1966[b]	72
1958	105	1968	53
1960	134	1970[c]	88
1962[a]	116	1972	40

[a]Frank Pate becomes warden; Ragen is director.
[b]Menard's Ross Randolph replaces Ragen as director.
[c]John Twomey becomes warden; Peter Bensinger is director.

TABLE 5
Appointments and Separations for Stateville/Joliet Complex, 1960–74

Year	Appointments	Separations	Total Guard Positions Authorized	Ratio of Separations/ Authorized Positions
1960	335	340	—	—
1961	379	339	—	—
1962	336	357	—	—
1963	651	471	—	—
1964	345	366	508	.72
1965	374	451	—	—
1966	560	505	554	.91
1967	557	632	—	—
1968	511	529	601	.88
1969	611	550	—	—
1970	416	340	608	.56
1971	341	323	630	.51
1972	415	437	607	.72
1973	444	485	622	.78
1974	435	396	622	.64

TABLE 6
Approximate Total Sales of All Prison Industries 1948–72

Year	Sales ($)	Year	Sales ($)	Year	Sales ($)
1948	1,550,000	1957	1,850,000	1965	2,700,000
1949	1,100,000	1958	2,300,000	1966	2,750,000
1950	1,300,000	1959	2,100,000	1967	2,650,000
1951	1,400,000	1960	2,350,000	1968	2,500,000
1952	1,750,000	1961	2,250,000	1969	2,350,000
1953	1,450,000	1962	2,600,000	1970	2,300,000
1954	1,400,000	1963	2,950,000	1971	2,100,000
1955	1,550,000	1964	3,050,000	1972	1,600,000
1956	1,750,000				

Figures are correct to the nearest fifty thousand.

TABLE 7
Inmate Turnover for Stateville/Joliet Complex, 1944–73

Year	Total Admissions (A)	Total Discharges (D)	Total A + D	Average Prison Population	Ratio (A + D)/ APP
1954	2091	1914	4005	4290	.93
1955	2164	2164	4328	4440	.97
1956	2016	2119	4135	4451	.93
1957	2167	2149	4416	4322	1.02
1958	2461	2176	4637	4549	1.02
1959	2423	2402	4825	4649	1.04
1960	2836	2602	5438	4848	1.12
1961	2909	2611	5520	5102	1.08
1962	2597	2911	5508	5074	1.09
1963	3092	3208	6300	4814	1.31
1964	2679	2825	5504	4781	1.15
1965	2984	3147	6131	4628	1.32
1966	2790	3113	5903	4262	1.39
1967	2825	3194	6019	3865	1.56
1968	3569	3501	7070	3953	1.79
1969	—	—	—	—	—
1970	3569	3691	6917	3730	1.85
1971	3226	3526	6635	3412	1.94
1972	3547	3902	7449	2874	2.60
1973	3277	3825	7102	2665	2.66

TABLE 8
Prison Racial Composition for Stateville/Joliet Complex, 1953–74

Year	White[a]	Percent	Black	Percent	Total
1953	2,281	53	1,984	47	4,265
1954	2,188	51	2,102	49	4,290
1955	2,146	48	2,294	52	4,440
1956	2,103	47	2,348	53	4,451
1957	2,013	47	2,309	53	4,322
1958	2,026	45	2,523	55	4,549
1959	2,007	43	2,642	57	4,649
1960	2,043	42	2,805	58	4,848
1961	2,210	43	2,892	57	5,102
1962	2,168	43	2,906	57	5,074
1963	2,056	43	2,758	57	4,814
1964	1,861	39	2,920	61	4,781
1965	1,862	40	2,746	60	4,628
1966	1,747	41	2,515	59	4,262
1967	1,599	41	2,266	59	3,865
1968	1,633	41	2,328	59	3,953
1969	1,567	41	2,274	59	3,841
1970	1,464	39	2,266	61	3,730
1971	1,266	37	2,146	63	3,412
1972	983	34	1,891	66	2,874
1973	752	28	1,913	72	2,665
1974[b]	407	25	1,202	75	1,609

[a]Note that Latinos are carried as white, which would not be consistent with the inmates' definition of Latinos as a separate race. When given the option of considering themselves black or white, the Latinos at Stateville invariably prefer to be identified with the blacks. It should be pointed out that the whites are probably somewhat underrepresented at Stateville and Diagnostic Depot and overrepresented at Joliet and the Honor Farm.

[b]Stateville only.

TABLE 9
Assaults on Officers and Direct Challenges to Authority, 1946–70

Year	Assaults	Challenges
1946	0	264
1954	1	255
1958	3	481
1962	0	467
1966	31	521
1970	5	460

TABLE 10
Inmates under Special Confinement, 1941–73

Year	Total Inmates	Average Isolation	%	Average Segregation	%	Average Detent. Hosp.	%	Total % in Confinement
1941	3,565	—	—	21	.58	45	1.26	1.85
1942	3,261	—	—	23	.70	54	1.65	2.36
1944	3,491	34	.97	—	—	39	1.17	2.09
1945	3,006	21	.70	—	—	28	.93	1.68
1948	3,219	37	1.15	16	.50	30	.93	2.58
1955	3,069	30	.98	34	1.10	29	.96	3.03
1956	3,036	33	1.09	36	1.19	29	.94	3.23
1957	2,987	33	1.10	36	1.20	28	.94	3.25
1959	3,285	40	1.21	38	1.15	26	.79	3.16
1960	3,365	41	1.22	40	1.18	21	.62	2.76
1961	3,616	37	1.02	33	.91	24	.66	2.60
1962	3,527	37	1.05	33	.94	19	.54	2.52
1963	3,272	41	1.25	35	1.06	21	.64	2.96
1964	3,169	41	1.29	35	1.10	23	.72	3.12
1966	2,854	30	1.05	36	1.26	28	.98	3.29
1967	2.448	30	1.22	36	1.47	31	1.26	3.96
1969	2,517	52	2.06	48	1.90	38	1.50	5.48
1970	2,270	40	1.76	41	1.80	36	1.58	5.15
1971	2,043	33	1.62	34	1:66	34	1.66	4.94
1972	1,931	39	2.02	39	2.02	32	1.66	5.70
1973	1,785	48	2.69	33	1.85	27	1.51	6.05

Table 11
Average Time Served in Isolation, 1946–72

Year	Days	Year	Days
1946	5.14	1966	5.7
1954	6.7	1970	8.0
1958	7.98	1971	6.84
1962	7.76	1972	8.33

TABLE 12
Offenses Resulting in Inmates' Serving Isolation Time, 1946–70

(1) 12 day sample (2) 50 day sample	1946 (N = 308) (N = 1,238)	1954 (N = 199) (N = 838)	1958 (N = 350) (N = 1,314)	1962 (N = 322) (N = 1,288)	1966 (N = 351) (N = 1,191)	1970 (N = 353) (N = 1,371)
Direct challenges to authority	19% 21%	30% 30%	34% 36%	36% 36%	34% 43%	34% 34%
Offenses against other inmates	9% 10%	18% 18%	11% 10%	22% 19%	11% 14%	13% 13%
Failure to comply with order maintenance rules	51% 47%	28% 31%	31% 29%	22% 23%	17% 21%	30% 32%
Possession of contraband	18% 21%	22% 19%	20% 19%	16% 19%	23% 20%	20% 20%
Miscellaneous	0% 0%	0% 0%	0% 0%	0% 1%	0% 0%	2% 1%

See chapter 5, note 25, for details of the samples.

TABLE 13

Age at Admission to Stateville, 1934–73 (by Percentage)

Year	15–19	20–24	25–29	30–34	35–39	40–44	45–49	50–54	55–59	60
1934	22.5	30.5	19.1	10.4	7.0	4.0	2.6	1.4	1.2	1.3
1935	26.6	31.0	16.3	9.9	6.5	4.0	2.3	1.2	.7	1.5
1936	23.2	31.0	16.2	11.0	7.3	3.2	3.0	1.2	1.2	2.7
1937	20.3	25.5	19.5	10.1	8.3	5.7	3.6	2.2	1.5	3.3
1938	21.8	28.2	15.6	11.3	8.7	5.0	4.5	1.6	1.3	1.9
1939	19.5	29.2	17.3	12.2	6.5	5.7	3.2	2.6	1.2	2.6
1940	18.1	32.7	16.0	10.0	8.0	4.1	3.0	2.3	2.2	.9
1941	19.5	31.0	18.7	12.7	7.2	5.2	3.1	2.7	1.1	1.5
1942	22.9	29.5	16.7	10.5	6.9	5.6	3.6	2.1	1.5	.7
1944	30.0	25.8	14.7	9.6	6.8	5.3	3.4	1.7	1.9	1.0
1945	18.0	26.0	16.0	12.0	9.0	7.0	5.0	3.0	2.0	2.0
1946	28.9	23.4	16.3	10.8	6.9	5.8	3.2	1.9	.9	1.4
1947	20.5	26.8	18.5	11.7	7.8	6.1	4.1	1.8	1.4	1.3
1948	19.1	30.8	16.9	11.5	8.6	5.2	2.7	2.1	1.8	1.3
1949	18.7	32.7	20.4	10.7	6.9	4.0	2.3	2.3	1.1	.9
1950	18.8	32.1	18.9	9.8	7.8	4.0	2.9	2.3	1.1	1.4
1951	16.7	32.9	22.2	10.5	6.2	4.2	3.4	2.3	.8	.8
1952	15.6	30.9	22.3	10.8	7.1	5.5	3.4	2.1	1.3	1.0
1953	20.3	31.2	22.5	9.8	6.9	4.2	2.3	1.4	1.0	.4
1954	17.4	31.4	22.5	11.2	7.0	4.8	2.3	1.7	.9	.6
1955	13.9	28.0	24.9	15.3	7.4	4.5	2.5	1.9	.9	.7
1957	15.0	31.0	23.0	13.0	8.0	5.0	2.0	3.0		
1963	10.4	28.0	22.9	17.0	10.3	5.9	5.6			
1965	10.5	26.8	20.9	15.7	12.2	7.0	6.9			
1969	12.9	32.9	20.6	13.6	7.9	6.2	5.9			
1970	7.4	20.7	27.2	19.3	12.9	6.6	2.8	3.2		
1973	6.6	18.7	24.2	20.9	13.7	10.9	2.9	2.1		

TABLE 14
Offenses Committed by Inmates Admitted to Joliet Diagnostic Depot, 1942–73 (*by Percentage*)

	1942	1953	1957	1963	1967	1969	1970	1973
Robbery	32.1	31.7	31.6	31.0	27.4	23.8	28.1	26.4
Burglary	18.3	20.8	22.5	26.1	27.4	28.5	23.5	19.9
Larceny	20.0	19.4	12.7	7.8	9.4	8.7	4.2	4.1
Fraud	6.8	5.9	6.4	5.4	5.2	4.1	6.5	6.4
Murder	10.4	6.5	9.6	8.4	9.3	11.6	12.4	11.4
Sex offenses	10.4	9.7	9.4	6.5	7.5	4.8	10.6	10.81
Miscellaneous	.2	1.3	1.3	2.4	5.1	5.3	5.8	6.8
Narcotics		4.7	6.5	12.2	8.7	9.4	8.9	13.4
Battery						4.4		2.2

Table 15
Common Subcategories of Robbery, Murder, and Sex Offenses

	Armed Robberies as % of Total Robberies	Murders as % of Total Homicide	Rapes as a % of Total Sex Offenses
1942	64.1	58.1	53.8
1953	65.7	46.9	47.6
1957	67.1	45.7	38.2
1963	Subcategories not listed		—
1967	Subcategories not listed		—
1969	Subcategories not listed		—
1970	71.8	62.7	45.3
1973	65.5	63.6	42.0

For 1963, 1967, and 1969, consult table 14 for total figures.

Table 16
Admissions by County, 1955–73 (by Percentage)

	Cook County	All Others
1955	81.0	19.0
1957	75.0	25.0
1966	80.5	14.5
1968	82.5	17.5
1970	82.3	17.7
1973	86.6	13.4

TABLE 17
Injuries to Stateville/Joliet Employees Due to Inmate Aggression, 1966-74

Year	Type of Injury
1966	Multiple stab wounds; struck with shovel
1967	Slashed with razor
1968	Struck in face
1969	Sprained ankle
1970	Assault; struck on left ear
1971	Hurt when pushed into bars; stabbed with razor (3 occurrences); stabbed in neck; cut with spear fashioned from fluorescent bulb; punched and kicked; hurt restraining inmate; tripped and hurt leg; hurt by inmate assault
1972	Hit with baseball bat; hit with pipe (2 occurrences); punched by inmate; attacked and knocked out (2 occurrences); assaulted (5 occurrences); kicked (2 occurrences); twisted wrist in scuffle; attacked; hit by salt shaker; hit with iron bar; struck with earphones; knifed; scratched; punched in jaw
1973	Killed; psychological disorder after being held hostage (3 occurrences); hurt back; punched; hit with stick; struck in the eye; strained back trying to break up fight; assaulted (2 occurrences); table shoved into shoulder; beaten with mop handle
1974	Strained neck; assaulted (3 occurrences); chipped bone in hand; struck in right eye; struck in face (2 occurrences); slapped (2 occurrences); punched in jaw; hurt subduing inmate

The data are taken from accident reports and include only those "accidents" resulting from conflict with inmates.

TABLE 18
Appointment of Black Guards, 1943–74

Year	Total Appointed	Median Yrs of Tenure	Percent Terminated within first year	Percent Remaining Two Years or More
1943-62	30	10.6	—	—
1963	34	1.7	58	21
1964	30	1.4	33	37
1965	23	.87	48	26
1966	30	1.5	67	17
1967	28	.75	61	14
1968	24	.87	71	7
1969	40	.53	70	10
1970	38	2.2	42	52
1971	49	1.2	43	30
1972	146	.80	56	22
1973	200	.87	45	29
1974	195	—	40	—

TABLE 19
Absenteeism of Guards

	Discharged		Resigned		Total	
	White	Black	White	Black	White	Black
I. OUR RESPONDENTS: Employees who left Stateville within 6 months. (N = 55)						
Median days docked per month	4.00	.95	.13	1.50	.25	1.17
Median days absent	.67	.46	.82	1.00	.80	.62

	White (N = 9)	Black (N = 15)	Total (N = 24)
II. CONTROL GROUP: Employees who started working at Stateville between January 1 and May 1, 1974, and who are still employed as of February 25, 1975.			
Median days docked per month	.12	.20	.16
Median days absent per month	.90	.30	.61

Notes

Introduction

1. Charles Perrow points to an "institutional school of organizational analysis" whose three main contributions are: (1) emphasis upon organization as a whole; (2) suggestion of the real possibility that at least some organizations do take on a life of their own, irrespective of the desires of those presumably in control; and (3) emphasis upon the environment. For Perrow the institutional school is noteworthy for its attention to organizational history. Sociologists contributing to the development of this perspective have shown that organizational structures and decision making are constrained by previous policies, decisions, and institutionalization of values as well as by drift and value displacement. The emphasis upon a holistic and organic approach to the study of organization has indicated that, methodologically, "the forte of the institutional school is the carefully documented case study." Charles Perrow, *Complex Organizations* (Chicago: Scott, Foresman, and Company, 1972).

2. Morris Janowitz, *The Professional Soldier* (New York: Free Press, 1960; 2d ed., 1971).

3. Philip Selznick, *T.V.A. and the Grass Roots* (New York: Harper and Row, 1966).

4. George Rusche and Otto Kirchheimer, *Punishment and Social Structure* (New York: Columbia University Press, 1939).

5. David Rothman, *The Discovery of the Asylum: Social Order and Disorder in the Republic* (Boston: Little, Brown, 1971).

6. Donald Clemmer, *The Prison Community* (New York: Rinehart, 1958).

7. Ibid., p. xi.

8. Gresham Sykes, *The Society of Captives* (Princeton, N.J.: Princeton University Press, 1958; repr. New York: Atteneur, 1966), p. 8.

9. Richard McCleery, "Communication Systems as Bases of Systems of Authority and Power," in Richard A. Cloward et al., *Theoretical Studies in Social*

Organization of the Prison (New York: Social Science Research Council, 1960).

10. David Street, Robert Vinter, and Charles Perrow, *Organization for Treatment* (New York: Free Press, 1966).

11. John Irwin, *The Felon* (Englewood Cliffs, N.J.: Prentice-Hall, 1970); Eric Wright, *The Politics of Punishment* (New York: Harper and Row, 1973); Theodore Davidson, *Chicano Prisoners: The Key to San Quentin* (New York: Holt, Rinehart and Winston, 1974).

12. Leo Carroll, *Hacks, Blacks, and Cons* (Lexington, Mass.: D. C. Heath and Company, 1974), p. 10.

13. Edward Shils, *The Logic of Personal Knowledge* (London: Routledge and Kegan Paul, 1961); repr. in *Selected Essays of Edward Shils* (University of Chicago, Department of Sociology, n.d.).

14. Edward Shils, "The Theory of Mass Society," *Diogenes* 39 (1962); repr. in *Center and Periphery: Essays in Macrosociology* (Chicago: University of Chicago Press, 1975).

15. Ibid., p. 99 (Chicago ed.).

16. Lou Harris and Associates, *The Public Looks at Crime and Corrections* (Washington: Joint Commission on Correctional Manpower and Training, 1968).

17. William S. Mathias, "Higher Education and the Police," in Arthur Niederhoffer and Abraham Blumberg, *The Ambivalent Force* (New York: Dryden Press, 1976), pp. 377–84.

18. *Ruffin* v. *Commonwealth* 62 Va. (21 Gratt.) 490, 796 (1971); *Price* v. *Johnson* 334 U.S. 266 (1948).

Chapter 1

1. For an exhaustive discussion of the reform efforts responsible for the Juvenile Court, see Anthony Platt, *The Child Savers* (Chicago: University of Chicago Press, 1969).

2. Illinois Prison Inquiry Commission, *The Prison System in Illinois* (Springfield, 1937), p. 591.

3. Bentham wrote two essays on the panopticon: "Panopticon: or the Inspection-House" (1791), and "Panopticon vs. New South Wales" (1802), in *The Works of Jeremy Bentham*, ed. John Bowering (Edinburgh: William Tait, 1838–43), vol. 4, pp. 37–172, 173–248.

4. In practice the panopticon did not function so ideally. Warden Ragen was fond of pointing out that the design which allowed the tower guard in each cell house to see into the cells also permitted the inmates to see when the guard's back was turned.

5. In *Fifty Year History of the Division of the Criminologist* (Springfield: State of Illinois, 1968), p. 10, we read: "The social approval, without which progressive legislation in corrections could not have become operative, seems to have had impetus during the early decades of the century in a number of interrelated conditions. One important condition was an equitable public opinion, which at the time seems to have regarded offenders of the law as persons who were more in need of treatment and help than severe punishment. This condition may have had reference to the rising humanitarianism and nationalism of a people who were at war, as it frequently is contended that a state of war welds a nation together, creating sympathy for fellow nationals and unity toward opponents. So, as the first World War was raging at the time, the legislation creating the Division became law, criminals were regarded with less revengeful feeling insofar as the popular feeling was directed towards the Central Powers who were, we thought, menacing democracy."

6. I have elsewhere discussed the way in which a classification system can

be corrupted by the tendency to transform a multi-institutional "differentiated" prison system into a "hierarchical" prison system, where social control is maximized by the distribution of prisons along a reward/punishment continuum. Eric Steele and James Jacobs, "A Theory of Prison Systems," *Crime and Delinquency* 21, no. 2 (April 1975): 149–62.

7. Nathan Leopold, *Life Plus Ninety Nine Years* (New York: Doubleday, 1957).

8. The report of the commission was published in 1928 as: *The Workings of the Indeterminate Sentence Law and the Parole System in Illinois,* ed. Andrew Bruce, Ernest Burgess, and Albert Horno.

9. Selznick argues that formal co-optation takes place when the group which requires neutralization is weak. Philip Selznick, *Leadership in Administration* (Evanston, Ill.: Row-Peterson, 1957), p. 21.

10. *Prison System* (see n. 2 above), p. 16.

11. Clemmer, in *The Prison Community* (see Introduction, n. 6, above), discusses the tension between the spoils system and prison administration as it affected Illinois's downstate maximum security prison at Menard. Illinois was not alone among states in the 1930s whose prisons were pervaded by partisan politics. John Bartlow Martin, in *Break Down the Walls* (New York: Ballentine Books, 1951), p. 22, points out that prisons all over the country were a pork barrel for spoils politics in the thirties and forties.

12. Bruce et al. (see n. 8 above), p. 62.

13. Personal interview with Father Elegius Weir. Father Weir was Stateville's Catholic Chaplain between 1916 and 1948. He holds several advanced degrees and is the author of a textbook in criminology. His recall of names, facts, and events going back almost fifty years is nothing short of remarkable.

14. *Prison System* (see n. 2 above), p. 496.

15. Bruce et al., *Workings* (see n. 7 above), p. 62.

16. Ibid., pp. 167–68.

17. There is no better illustration of Perrow's point that organizational participants pursue multiple goals simultaneously. He argues that organizations are tools used by actors to achieve influence and power. Perrow, *Complex Organizations* (see Introduction, n. 1, above), chapter 4.

18. Father Weir recalls "that they had one husky Jew chained up for seventy days."

19. With respect to the corruption of the professional's role in prison, see Harvey Powelson and Reinhard Bendix, "Psychiatry in Prisons," *Psychiatry* 14 (February 1951): 73–86.

20. Leopold, *Life* (see n. 7 above). Leopold dedicates this autobiographical account of his more than thirty years in the Stateville/Joliet prisons to Father Weir; Donald Clemmer describes the same kind of status hierarchy at Menard during the same years in *The Prison Community*. (See Introduction, n. 6, above).

21. Gladys Erickson, *Ragen of Joliet* (New York: Dutton, 1957), p. 57.

22. Ibid., p. 42.

23. Leopold, *Life* (see n. 7 above), p. 115.

24. Erickson, *Ragen* (see n. 21 above), p. 46.

25. It seems remarkable that Superintendent Vernon Revis recounts almost exactly the same incident as occurring at the Joliet Prison in 1970, when a leader of the Black P Stone Nation simply "refused" to "accept" any punishment and was released to his cell house. A similar incident of intimidation stimulated a walk-out and subsequent violence in Eastern Correctional Institution (pseudonym). See Carroll, *Hacks, Blacks and Cons* (see Introduction, n. 12, above).

26. The *Chicago Tribune* (18 March 1931, p. 6) reported that "Capt. George L. Whitmeyer who resigned under pressure from his prison post [at the old prison]

said that he was going to tell the legislative investigating committee when it meets on Friday that guards deliberately trapped and killed three men who attempted to escape on February 22nd. 'I warned prison officials of that break. The brutality shown in that affair led to the weekend riot.'"

27. According to the *Chicago Tribune* (15 March 1931, p. 1), Warden Henry Hill attributed the rioting of 14 March to "overcrowding, unemployment and to sentimentality on the part of so-called reformers." Hill stated that public support for the inmates over the Washington's Birthday incident encouraged the inmates to continue in rebellion.

28. Leopold, *Life* (see n. 7 above), p. 214.

29. Both Father Weir and Nathaniel Leopold identify the tough and arbitrary decisions of the parole board as the underlying cause of the riot of 1931. Perhaps during the next several years the deepening Depression changed the comparative attractiveness of release from prison.

30. An excellent early history of the Illinois State Penitentiary was prepared by a long-term Stateville inmate, R. F. Johns, entitled "A Short History of the Illinois State Penitentiary" (undated). This point about the labor contracts appears on p. 42. I am indebted to Hans Mattick for lending me his copy of this manuscript.

31. *Prison System* (see n. 2 above), p. 179.

Chapter 2

1. The gang activities, escapes, and other lurid incidents occurring at Stateville finally (after the killing of Richard Loeb) led the governor to appoint a blue ribbon commission in 1936 (discussed in chapter 1). The extent to which the situation at Stateville before Ragen's appointment had deteriorated is not precisely clear. While all reports are agreed that inmate bosses had taken over, Gladys Erickson's and the Tribune reporters' (1955) descriptions, wherein they speak of the inmate golf course, shanty town, vegetable gardens, and truck hijackings, seem somewhat exaggerated when compared with the accounts of Nathan Leopold and Father Eligius Weir.

2. Gladys Erickson reports that, at the outset, Ragen "took a beating in the press." *Ragen* (see chap. 1, n. 21, above), p. 72.

3. Ragen had been warden of Menard for three years prior to taking the job at Stateville. His tenure at Menard overlapped with Donald Clemmer's. About Ragen, Clemmer, in *Prison Community* (see Intro., n. 6, above), p. 62, noted: "The second warden, a younger man, was 39 years of age when appointed early in 1933. He had attended high school and was in the Navy during the World War. Prior to assuming the wardenship, he had served as deputy sheriff for four years, as a sheriff for four years, and had been county treasurer for three years before his appointment. While his appointment was essentially political, the governor considered him suitable material to administer the lives of 2300 inmates and 230 employees living and working in an institution valued at two and a half million dollars. Soon after taking office, the warden gave evidence of possessing a humanitarian point of view. He allowed inmates who were assigned to indoor shops to have the freedom of the athletic field for an hour each noon. While he insisted on strict discipline, he demanded that brutal punishment be stopped, and in one case discharged a senior officer, who belonged to the same political party as he, for kicking an inmate. He stopped much needless waste and reduced operating costs. He initiated football and boxing. He cooperated with all employees, and for the first time gave some prestige to the Mental Health Staff. The new warden was a marked improvement over his predecessor and when one considers the confusing complexities of penal administration, one can but wonder that prison officials operating in a society such as ours handle the situation as well as they do."

4. Daniel Glaser explains (in personal correspondence) that Ragen was an active

leader of the conservative Warden's Association. Within the American Correctional Association there was an understanding that liberals and conservatives would alternate in the presidency from year to year.

5. One of the characteristics of prebureaucratic forms of administration is the leader's monopoly over all specialized skills and knowledge. See Max Weber, "Bureaucracy," in *From Max Weber: Essays in Sociology*, trans H. H. Gerth and C. Wright Mills, 2d ed. (New York: Oxford University Press, 1946), pp. 235–39.

6. Joseph Ragen and Charles Finstone, *Inside the World's Toughest Prison* (Springfield, Ill.: C. C. Thomas, 1962). This volume combines the Inmate Rule Book, the officer's Manual, and statements of the duties and responsibilities of each position in the organization along with interspersed statements of the Ragen philosophy. Citations to this book throughout the chapter refer to rules of one kind or another under which the prison was operating.

7. Ibid., pp. 162–63.

8. Clemmer, *Prison Community* (see Intro., no. 6, above), p. 54.

9. See Philip Selznick's distinction between an organization and an institution, in *Leadership* (chap. 1, n. 9, above), p. 21: "As an organization acquires a self, a distinctive identity, it becomes an institution. This involves the taking on of values, ways of acting and believing that are deemed important for their own sake. From then on self-maintenance becomes more than bare organizational survival; it becomes a struggle to preserve the uniqueness of the group in the face of new problems and altered circumstances."

10. Gladys Erickson points out that prior to Ragen's resignation after Governor Greene's election, "unknown to him, the professional and business people of Joliet had prepared a petition and circulated it throughout the state, requesting the new governor to retain Ragen as warden. When he announced his resignation, this petition was just about to be mailed. . . . At the same time, he received telephone calls from prominent citizens all over the state, who insisted that they would do everything in their power to see that he was reinstated, if he would consent to their efforts." Erickson, *Ragen* (see chap. 1, n. 21, above), p. 151.

11. Ibid.

12. Ragen and Finstone, *Inside* (see n. 6 above).

13. For example, Ragen wrote in the Preface to one of his many public relations pamphlets on Stateville (early 1950s): "Illinois was one of the first states to classify prisoners according to age, past criminal history, mentality and the possibilities for rehabilitation. This method of classification has proven to have a stabilizing effect on the inmates' adjustment."

14. *Annual Report of the Department of Public Safety* (1 July 1952–30 June 1953), p. 81.

15. Neither Daniel Glaser nor Lloyd Ohlin received this treatment, although they too report consistent shakedowns of their offices.

16. According to Mattick, after seventeen months at Stateville he was required to write a parole report on the notorious Major Price, a rebellious prisoner whom Ragen kept in segregation for eleven years. When Mattick approached the gate to the yard and reported that he was going to "the corner" (the segregation unit), he was asked whom he intended to interview. When he replied that he had to see Major Price, the guard said the warden's permission was required for that. Mattick had interviewed other prisoners in segregation before, but Price was, apparently, a "sensitive case." When Mattick went to Ragen's office to ask why he was being prevented from preparing a report on Price for the Parole Board, Ragen replied, "Well, we don't know you people." Mattick had to threaten to make a formal report about this incident before Ragen reluctantly conceded in order to avoid a showdown with Joseph Lohman, chairman of the Parole Board.

17. According to Stateville administrator Vernon Revis as well as former

Stateville sociologist-actuary Hans Mattick, Joe Ragen once threatened to lock Parole Board chairman Joe Lohman out of Stateville because of a disagreement over parole policy. Lohman in turn made Ragen back down by threatening to call the National Guard to aid him in carrying out his legislative duties.

18. Leopold describes the impact of this ground-breaking decision in *Life* (see chap. 1, n. 7, above), p. 301: "I had lots of free time, but I didn't get to use very much of it for my own reading and study, for Federal Judge Barnes of Chicago had just ruled that every inmate of the penitentiary must be allowed free access to the courts and be given the right to file a writ whenever he pleased. This had not previously been allowed. The joint promptly went writ-crazy. . . . I was deluged with requests to write writs for the fellows."

And gangster Roger Touhy described the impact of the same decision in his autobiography *The Stolen Years* (Cleveland: Pennington Press, 1959), p. 280: "The U.S. Supreme Court discovered that convicts in the Illinois penitentiaries were being stopped from mailing out petitions for writs of *habeas corpus*. Regardless of the circumstances of their convictions, the development of new evidence or other extenuating circumstances, the convict had no right to appeal. The high court held that hundreds of Illinois convicts were on a legal merry-go-round and 'at the end of blind alleys' in violation of their constitutional rights. The Supreme Court asked Judge Barnes to do something about the situation and he did. He threatened to send to jail any prison warden who refused to allow an inmate to mail a petition for a writ."

19. *Siegel* v. *Ragen,* 180 F.2d 785 (1950). Inmate Harp complained that: (1) he was beaten on numerous occasions, (2) his personal property was confiscated, and (3) that he was denied due process at disciplinary hearings where he was maneuvered into the offense of calling a guard a liar if he chose to dispute the ticket. Maurice Meyer, Stateville's most famous jailhouse lawyer, argued that: (1) Ragen had no right to prevent him from providing legal assistance, (2) it was unconstitutional to put him in segregation for being a jailhouse lawyer, and (3) it was unconstitutional to punish him for trying to set up the Prisoners' Welfare League. Siegel complained that: (1) he was unconstitutionally punished for his part in trying to establish the Prisoners' Welfare League, (2) Ragen stole $20,000 out of the inmate amusement fund. The inmates also, on behalf of all other inmates similarly situated, complained of arbitrary enforcement of the rules, illegal expenditures from the inmates' benefit fund, and poor medical and dietary facilities.

20. *U.S. ex rel. George Atterbury* v. *Ragen* 237 F.2d 153 (1956).

21. *U.S. ex rel. Wagner* v. *Ragen* 213 F.2d 294 (1954).

22. *Joseph Ortega* v. *Ragen* 216 F.2d 561 (1954).

23. Some feeling for the military discipline enforced upon the staff can be obtained from passages like this in Ragen and Finstone, *Inside* (see chap. 2, n. 6, above), p. 151: "In the opinion of the administration, there is no cause for a riot unless some employee weakens. United, the employees of a prison can be compared to a forged chain of security and a chain is as strong as each link. It is an employee who is not following the rules—one who is not properly supervising the inmates who are assigned to his division, who is not reporting violations of the rules; one who is too weak to speak up, not giving proper application to his job; who is not supervising the use of tools and equipment; who is permitting inmates to connive and organize; and last, but not least, is fraternizing and trafficking with inmates or failing to report an employee who is doing these things."

24. Even today, eight of nine guards at the captain's level and above are not originally from Northern Illinois. The trailer court adjacent to the prison has yet to be integrated by a nonwhite family.

25. Payment in kind, according to Weber, is a hallmark of the prebureaucratic regime. "Every sort of assignment of usufructs, tributes, and services which are due to the lord himself or to the official for personal exploitation, always means a surrender of the pure type of bureaucratic organization. The official in such a position has a personal right to the possession of his office. This is the case to a still higher degree when official duty and compensation are interrelated in such a way that the official does not transfer to the lord any yields gained from the objects left to him, but handles these objects for his private ends and in turn renders to the lord services of a personal or a military, political, or ecclesiastical character." This passage applies equally well to Warden Ragen and his top underlings. Weber, "Bureaucracy" (see n. 5 above), p. 207.

26. Personal correspondence.

27. I am indebted to Bob Brown of the Fortune Society for the observation that Stateville's rules on contraband were different than those in other prisons. While most prisons listed contraband, Ragen listed all permitted items; everything else was contraband.

28. In a vivid account of life at Stateville in the early 1940s, Paul Warren explains in *Next Time Is For Life* (New York: Dell Publishing Co., 1953), p. 137: "I watched the captain's big red, well fed face and smelled the talcum powder. He read from some papers before him, then looked up at me. 'The officer says you were talking and laughing in the dining room and when he called your attention to this, you argued with him. What do you have to say?' 'I was whispering for the salt. I wasn't talking and laughing, sir.' 'Do my officers lie?' He had me both ways. I remained silent."

29. *Annual Report of the Department of Public Safety* (1 July 1954–30 June 1955), p. 40.

30. Note Weber's observation that "All non-bureaucratic forms of domination display a peculiar co-existence: on the one hand there is a sphere of strict traditionalism and on the other, a sphere of free arbitrariness and lordly grace." "Bureaucracy" (see n. 5 above), p. 217.

31. Personal interview.

32. Personal correspondence.

33. Inside Stateville—World of Its Own," *Chicago Tribune*, 3 July 1955, p. 18.

34. Roger Touhy "Stateville Prison and Warden Ragen," in Erickson, *Ragen* (see chap. 1, n. 21, above), p. 192.

35. Paul Warren himself went through such an experience. *Next Time* (see n. 28 above), chap. 17.

36. I have no statistics on the rate of *requests* for transfer, but am assured by former sociologist-actuary, Hans Mattick, and former Menard warden, Ross Randolph, that voluntary transfer to the more relaxed Menard Penitentiary was a frequent aspiration of Stateville inmates. (Menard Penitentiary has both a general population and a Psychiatric Division).

37. Ragen and Finstone, *Inside* (see n. 6 above), p. 695. I am assured by one long-time Stateville employee and admirer of Warden Ragen that this fluent passage was far beyond the warden's limited literary skill. Since the book was written with Ragen's cooperation and close participation, I offer the quotation as indicative of the type of statement about the causes of crime and the need for rehabilitation that Ragen would have approved.

38. Personal correspondence from Daniel Glaser.

39. Erickson, *Ragen* (see chap. 1, n. 21, above), p. 71.

40. See Glaser's contrary view, at n. 38 above.

41. In his very perceptive unpublished manuscript "We Send the Wrong Men to Prison" (1954) former inmate R. F. Jahns estimates that "less than 20% of the

total inmate population is employed in the several state-operated industries permitted by labor law." The 20 percent estimate corresponds with estimates provided by several informants.

42. Personal correspondence.

43. Warren (see n. 28 above), p. 130.

44. This is according to "Characteristics of State Prisoners," (Federal Bureau of Prisons, 1962.) While it is exceedingly difficult to find a way to express average time served by an inmate population, there is no doubt that before the new sentencing provisions of 1961 Illinois prisoners were serving very long sentences. The pre-1961 laws provided that an offender sentenced to life must serve twenty calendar years before being eligible for parole. Those inmates sentenced to a definite term of years had to serve one-third before parole eligibility, i.e., an offender sentenced to ninety-nine years had to serve thirty-three calendar years at the minimum.

A letter to the editor in the June 1955 issue of the *Joliet-Stateville Time* (a prisoner-published newsletter) reported, "Since I'm a resident of Cell House C and celling in 328, I figured out one for Dave. In casually glancing around the cell house, I got a total number of years equal to my cell number: CH 34 yrs., EM 29 yrs., GT 27 yrs., FF 26 yrs., WB 26 yrs., WP 25 yrs., MF 23 yrs., JB 21 yrs., JB 21 yrs., FB 20 yrs., LC 20 yrs., LE 19 yrs., RK 19 yrs., AD 18 yrs. Total: 328 yrs.

45. An interesting fictional account of the influence of John Ditto, a big shot and the editor of an inmate newspaper, based upon a prison experience at Stateville, was presented in J. E. Webb, *Four Steps to the Wall* (New York: Bantam Books, 1948).

46. Gresham Sykes, *The Society of Captives: A Study of a Maximum Security Prison* (Princeton: Princeton University Press, 1958). Sheldon Messinger and Gresham Sykes, "The Inmate Social System," in Cloward et al., *Theoretical Studies* (see Intro., n. 9, above).

47. Ragen and Finstone, *Inside* (see n. 6 above), p. 190.

Chapter 3

1. Pappy Dort had come to Stateville in 1933, even before Ragen arrived, and had been an assistant warden since 1950. William Burris began his career at Stateville during World War II and was appointed as assistant warden in the mid-1950s. The third assistant warden, Vernon Revis, entered Stateville in 1951, became the youngest lieutenant in its history, and was appointed assistant warden when Pate became warden.

2. Weber speaks of the "routinization of charisma." "It is the fate of charisma, whenever it comes into the permanent institutions of a community, to give way to powers of tradition or of rational socialization. This waning of charisma generally indicates the diminishing importance of individual action." Weber (see chap. 2, n. 5, above), p. 253.

3. John Twomey, Stateville's warden between 1970 and 1973, recalls that upon assuming his duties he was stunned to learn that the "old boss" with whom he was frequently (and unflatteringly) compared was Joe Ragen and that "there was practically no mention of the man who had been my predecessor for 10 years" (private interview).

4. James D. Thompson speaks of an organization's ability to neutralize environmental encroachments as the basic principle of organizational action. Thompson, *Organizations in Action* (New York: McGraw-Hill, 1967).

5. Ragen is said to have discouraged his staff from becoming involved in local community affairs. No doubt he saw community involvement as competitive with the absolute identification with and loyalty to the prison which he demanded. In

the Southern Illinois prisons, local folkways and the political tradition have never allowed a prison warden to maintain such an aloof and independent position.

6. The very fact that Stampar, a close Ragen protégé in Springfield, was (according to his own report) considered a complete outsider at Stateville is excellent evidence of the complete homogeneity of the staff. Stampar recalls that in his first few years he was constantly fighting to liberalize the old rules which had been in force for decades. Consistent with the whole theme of this chapter is Stampar's recollection that "in those days they wouldn't relent at all; they wouldn't give the inmate anything."

7. So often has the story of the insurance agent who volunteered to teach at Stateville been brought to my attention that it would be an oversight to neglect its mention. Several staff informants explain that in 1967 or 1968 an ambitious young insurance salesman obtained government funding to teach a course on investments to inmates at Stateville. The staff say that he rarely showed up for the course and used it merely as a publicity gimmick for his own aggrandizement. It was experiences like this that led Warden Pate frequently to reiterate that "Stateville is one of the most over-programmed institutions in the world."

8. Because this statement might seem self-serving had it come from union organizers, I should point out that the information comes from one of the staff people who participated in the monitoring of union activities.

9. Ill. Rev. Stat. 1961 ch. 38 par. 801 states "every person sentenced to the penitentiary regardless of the length of such sentence shall be eligible for parole at the end of twenty years."

10. *Kubala* v. *Kinney*, 25 Ill. 2d 491, 185 N.E. 2d 337 (1963) held that the 1961 section on parole eligibility for those serving determinate sentences of life must be interpreted to apply retroactively to those sentenced before 1 January 1962, the effective date of the act.

11. In a 1962 letter to the Illinois attorney general, Pate stated that there were forty-four inmates at Stateville/Joliet who at the time had already served more than twenty years.

12. The amount of money sent to Stateville/Joliet prisoners between 1 July 1964 and 30 June 1965 was $731,407 for an average population of 3,169. Eight years later a prisoner population which was only 60 percent as large received $822,986 from outside sources.

13. The Black Muslims are undoubtedly the largest and most organized group ever to reside in American prisons. Their impact upon American prisons, particularly on prisoners' rights litigation, has yet to be adequately assessed. Under the direction of Elijah Muhammad, the Black Muslims throughout the 1950s and 1960s strove to become a broad-based mass movement in the United States. Prisoners, alcoholics, dope addicts, and prostitutes were not excluded. On the contrary, they were from the beginning seen as particularly embittered and frustrated and therefore a potentially important source of recruitment. When C. Eric Lincoln published *The Black Muslims in America* (Boston: Beacon Press) in 1961, there were three temples behind prison walls. For discussions of some of the early confrontations between the Muslims and prison authorities see: "Black Muslims in Prison: Of Muslim Rights and Constitutional Rights," *Columbia Law Review* 62 (1962): 1488; Brown, "Black Muslim Prisoners and Religious Discrimination: the Developing Criteria for Judicial Review," *George Washington Law Review* 32, 112 4 (1964. See also James B. Jacobs, "Stratification and Conflict among Prison Inmates," *Journal of Criminal Law and Criminology* 66, no. 4 December 1975.

14. The prison had arrived at a cozy accommodation with the traditional religions and their ministers. The Catholic chaplain since 1947 had been both

formally (since he sat on committees) and informally, a member of the administration. The traditional religions, like latter-day group psychotherapy, urged upon prisoners a definition of themselves as morally tainted. The chaplains would carry out favors for inmates but only within very limited bounds.

15. For similar occurrences at other prisons see *Fulwood* v. *Clemmer* 206 F. Supp. 370 (1962); *Pierce* v. *LaVallee* 212 F. Supp. 865 (1962).

16. *Cooper* v. *Pate* 324 F. 2d 165 (1963). Speaking for the Court of Appeals, Judge Duffy said: "A prisoner may not approve of prison rules and regulations, but under all ordinary circumstances that is no basis for coming into a federal court seeking relief even though he may claim that the restrictions placed on his activities are in violation of his constitutional rights."

17. *Cooper* v. *Pate* 378 U.S. 546 (1964). Cooper was represented before the Supreme Court by Alex Elson and Bernard Weisberg.

18. *Cooper* v. *Pate* 382 F. 2d 518 (7th circuit) 1967.

19. Depending upon whose estimates one accepts, between 33 and 50 percent of the segregation inmates were Muslims. In a 9 March 1965 memorandum from the disciplinary captain to Pate (obviously written with an eye toward building a record for litigation), each inmate in segregation was identified as "White," "Colored Muslim," or "Colored, not known to be a Muslim." There were nine listed in each category. At the trial, Cooper claimed that twelve of the segregation inmates were Muslims.

20. The disciplinary captain documented the Muslim challenge to the social order of the prison in the following memorandum to the warden on 23 July 1966, which was passed along to the Attorney General: " . . . of an approximate population of 3,000 inmates, we have knowledge of approximately 100 self professed followers of the black Muslim Sect which roundly speaking, is 3% of the total population of the institution. During the past eleven months, there has been 134 disciplinary cases, a total of 57 were inmates claiming to be Muslims. This amounts to approximately 42%. . . . A review of disciplinary reports regarding disrespect to and disobedience of officers and officials has revealed the fact that approximately 80% of these reports can be attributed to this same 3%."

Also worth mentioning is the fact that due to the converting efforts of these Muslims, which includes agitating, preaching of race hatred, and in some cases physical force, has led to several incidents where other inmates, who did not want to be converted to the Muslim doctrine, have had to be transferred from their assignments and cell houses for their own safety."

21. Consider the following administrative reply (dated 8 September 1972) to Cooper's request to maintain possession of a medallion: "Regarding your grievance and our follow-up interview, I have been able to discuss this situation with Warden John J. Twomey. I showed him the paper work that we had on this issue of returning to you the Islamic medallions that you had fashioned in the institution and which were now being kept by Captain M. B. Hall. I showed him the court case and the number that you had sent to me dated August 31, 1972. Mr. Twomey does not feel that he can change the basic policy of the Adult Division of the Department of Corrections. Religious medals are allowed to the men if they are presented to them by the Chaplains who in turn receive these from interested friends and relatives. If a medallion is not received by the resident from the Chaplain, then it is considered contraband and contrary to the rules of the institution. Warden Twomey considers then that the medallions in question in the possession of Captain Hall are to be considered contraband unless the department changes its basic rules. Therefore, I am afraid that I cannot help you with your grievance in this matter insofar as my assistance would be contrary to the departmental regulations."

22. In spring 1975, 147 Stateville inmates listed themselves as Muslims. I counted 127 subscriptions to *Mohammad Speaks,* but the card list of journal subscriptions is not kept up to date.

23. This practice persisted until Judge Will ordered it discontinued in 1966. By that time, however, the inmates maneuvered to segregate themselves.

24. Several inmates, black and white, have told me about a small number of Klan. The long and bloody history of the KKK in Southern Illinois lends some credence to these reports. See Paul M. Angle, *Bloody Williamson* (New York: Alfred A. Knopf, 1952).

Chapter 4

1. The 1965 figure includes the entire central office of the Department of Public Safety which also had responsibility for other state agencies like the state police. Thus, the actual increase in the size of the central office is even greater.

2. Perhaps the height of Bensinger's success with the media came in the October 1972 issue of *Reader's Digest* in an article entitled "Prison Reform: Illinois Shows the Way." The introductory blurb stated: "In three years, one of the worst correctional systems has been transformed into a national showcase by an imaginative businessman who wanted to serve his state." The article was condensed from Earl and Minan Selby, "Prison Reform: Illinois Shows the Way," *Christian Herald,* October 1972.

3. In 1975 Bensinger was defeated in his campaign for the office of Cook County sheriff. In early 1976 he was appointed by the president to head the Federal Drug Administration.

4. *Illinois Revised Statutes,* chap. 38 §§ 1001–8.

5. Ibid., § 1003-2-6.

6. Ibid., § 1003-5-2.

7. Bensinger expressed shock when I informed him that the mail room employees were continuing to read (and return) outgoing mail despite clear directives and regulations to the contrary.

8. "Ragenite" is a term with which many of the long-term employees identify positively.

9. Revis recalls that during the middle sixties dozens of warden positions around the country were offered him, but that none were tendered after 1969. The process of professionalization had caught up with Corrections.

10. Fogel studied under the noted criminologist Leslie Wilkens.

11. Sielaff holds degrees both in law and in social work. In August 1976 he left Illinois to become director of the Wisconsin prison system.

12. I have been told by reliable sources that at the time Sielaff took over the department there was a memorandum on file from the demoralized Twomey to Acting Director Coughlin, recommending that Stateville be left on "continual lock-up" inasmuch as "there was no way to ensure the safety and security of the institution."

13. Sielaff and Brierton appointed a separate warden for the Joliet prison, a reform suggested in the 1966 Galvin report and also pressed unsuccessfully on Peter Bensinger by Norval Morris. The Galvin report was a more or less routine survey of the Illinois prisons in the mid-1960s. See John J. Galvin, "Correctional Services (Preliminary and Confidential Draft for Commission consideration—May 2, 1966)," *Commission on State Government—Illinois;* Staff Memorandum no. 14, 1966. Here as elsewhere I am indebted to Professor Hans W. Mattick for bringing obscure documents to my attention.

14. Cannon had studied at Ohio State under noted criminologist Walter Reckless.

15. During this period, I spent four months (September–December, 1974) of

daily observation at Stateville, attending staff meetings, interviewing, and observing the Cannon administration.

16. The two assistant wardens were illustrative of the trend toward professionalization of correctional administration. Robert Kapture (age thirty), assistant warden of programs, had completed all requirements except the dissertation for his Ph.D. in sociology at the University of Illinois, where he had studied under Daniel Glaser. Kapture had for several years worked as an administrator at the Reception and Diagnostic Unit in Joliet, and viewed himself as a correctional professional. Daniel Bosse, assistant warden of operations, was also young (twenty-eight) and college-educated. He was a graduate of Michigan State University (in law enforcement) and was studying for his master's at Chicago State University (where Kapture was a part-time instructor). Bosse had been a schoolteacher at Stateville, then administrative assistant to Pate (who drafted him as an aide to the Bensinger task force) and to Twomey, then warden of the Minimum Security Unit, before becoming assistant warden of operations.

17. Brierton seems to attract high praise from all who come in contact with him, further suggesting that Stateville may be entering a period of restoration. The *Reader's Digest* article (see n. 2 above) gave praise to Brierton for his successes in the juvenile division equal to that given Bensinger. Brierton has also received favorable comment from Patrick J. Murphy, formerly chief attorney of Chicago's Juvenile Legal Aid Society and a man with few kind words for institutional administrators. See Murphy, *Our Kindly Parent, the State* (New York: Viking Press, 1974), p. 72.

18. Ibid., chap. 5.

19. One of the more important changes is the appointment of Arthur Wallenstein as clinical services director. Wallenstein had completed all but the dissertation toward his Ph.D. degree at the University of Pennsylvania—another example of the new young professionals.

20. The chief guard left Stateville in the spring to become assistant warden of the Psychiatric Division at Menard.

21. Consider the fact that in 1958 there were sixty-seven prisoners assigned to the administration building. The largest number worked in the mail and censor's offices (16) and as porters (15).

22. Much of this material on the Stateville counselors had been separately reported in James B. Jacobs, "The Stateville Counsellors: Symbol of Reform in Search of a Role," *Social Service Review* 50, no. 1 (March 1976).

23. Perhaps the prison is one of the last communities where one can witness at first hand the transition from a Gemeinschaft to a Gesellschaft.

24. It is interesting to note that this has become a somewhat generalized phenomenon in American society. The tremendous increase in the percentage of appellate cases has been a frequent subject of comment by lawyers and judges.

25. For the last seven months of 1974, there were 259 appeals to the Inquiry Board from a Stateville inmate population of approximately 1,450. In other words, for that period approximately 30 percent of all grievances were appealed to the second stage. Inmates also did better in getting relief at the second stage. Roughly 23 percent of the appeals to the Inquiry Board for this period were successful as compared with about 10 percent success on first-level grievances.

26. Ma Houston, long-time prison reform crusader and currently affiliated with Operation PUSH, often sits on the Administrative Review Board—to the horror of the Stateville staff.

27. Between 6 September 1973 and 31 December 1974, the Administrative Review Board heard 240 third-step appeals from Stateville, Of these, 123 were resolved "totally favorable" to the inmate. Of the remaining, 85 were resolved "totally unfavorable" to the inmate and 32 with mixed results.

Chapter 5

1. Across the country, prison administrators reacted to the demise of the "hands off" doctrine with apprehension, resentment, resistance, and predictions of organizational disintegration. See, for example, article by a former director of the Federal Bureau of Prisons, James Bennett, "Who Wants to be a Warden?" *New England Journal of Prison Law* 1, no. 1 (1974): 69–79.

2. Ibid., p. 73. Bennett has written: "Let me point out the importance of developing an objective, unruffled, and dispassionate system of dealing with prisoners' complaints, petitions and suggestions. The day when the Warden or his deputy was a czar and his arbitrary and capricious word was final is no more." Time and again the courts were frustrated by being unable to ascertain how decisions at Stateville were made.

3. See *Haines* v. *Kerner* 404 U.S. 519 (1972), in which the Supreme Court held that "prisoners' allegations in *pro se* complaints should be held to less stringent standards than formal pleading drafted by lawyers in determining whether it appears beyond a reasonable doubt that the plaintiff can prove no set of facts in support of his claim which would entitle him to relief." The consequence is that prisoners more often will be allowed to offer proof of their allegations at a hearing rather than having their suits dismissed on the pleadings.

4. *Johnson* v. *Avery* 393 U.S. 483 (1969).

5. *Adams* v. *Pate* 445 F.2d 105 (1971).

6. *Adams* v. *Pate* 445 F.2d 105, 108 (1971).

7. *State of Illinois Department of Corrections, Five Year Plan: Adult Division* (1970).

8. *Manual of Operation for Special Program Unit,* p. 7.

9. Ibid., p. 9.

10. *Armstrong* v. *Bensinger* 71 C. 2144 (1972). For a detailed history of this litigation by the American Civil Liberties Union lawyer who managed it, see David Goldberger, "Court Challenges to Prison Behavior Modification Programs: A Case Study," *American Criminal Law Review* 13, no. 37 (1975).

11. There is a widespread belief among the guards that the courts abolished SPU. While technically the courts refused to accept therapeutic justification for SPU, they have never objected to the existence of maximum security wings of maximum security prisons. Sometimes court decisions can be used by the administration to bring about changes that it cannot itself sponsor; for example, the administration may blame the courts for losing SPU, but disassemble it for its own reasons.

12. These were essentially the due process guarantees mandated by the U.S. Supreme Court for parolees at revocation hearings in *Morrissey* v. *Brewer* 408 U.S. 471 (1972).

13. *Miller* v. *Twomey* 479 F.2d 701 (1973).

14. *Morrissey* v. *Brewer* 407 U.S. 471 (1972).

15. *Miller* v. *Twomey* at p. 712. In *Morales* v. *Schmidt* 494 (1974), the Seventh Circuit sitting *en banc* held that a three-judge appellate panel had acted incorrectly in reversing a district court which enjoined the prison authorities from interfering with Morales' right to correspond with his sister-in-law. The Seventh Circuit *en banc* recognized that the prisoner is not a slave of the state. Most interesting from our perspective is the fact that the state felt that the issue of whether an inmate should be free to correspond with a relative was a crucial enough question to appeal through the federal courts. Inmate Morales had long since been released.

16. *Miller* v. *Twomey* at p. 716.

17. *Wolff* v. *McDonell* 418 U.S. 539 (1974).

18. *Labatt* v. *Twomey* 16 Cr.L. 2351 (1975).

19. *Labatt* v. *Twomey* said: "Accordingly, where a sufficiently extended deprivation of prisoners' rights occurs, notice of the cause of the deprivation, the reason for its continuance, and an opportunity to respond must be provided within a reasonable period of time after the emergency decision has been effectuated and while its extraordinary effects continue."

20. *Murphy* v. *Wheaton* 381 F.Supp. 1252 (1974), still pending 74 C 405.

21. There has been no written decision in this case, 74-1106 (7th Cir. 1974), cert. denied 43 U.S.L.W. 3528 (1975).

22. William Bailey points out that after *Miller* v. *Twomey* there was no slackening in the number of inmates' claims in the Northern District of Illinois alleging that they had been placed in punitive segregation without due process, although there were fewer claims alleging denial of notice and a hearing, "Realities of Prisoners' Cases under 42 U.S.C. §1983: A Statistical Survey in the Northern District of Illinois," *Loyola University Law Journal* 6 (Summer 1975): 527–39.

23. The Harvard Center for Criminal Justice carried out a comprehensive evaluation of the impact of judicial intervention on the processing of prison disciplinary cases at the Rhode Island Adult Correctional Institution. The due process requirements placed upon the disciplinary hearings were similar to those extended to Stateville prison disciplinary hearing in *Miller* v. *Twomey.* The Harvard group concluded that the efforts to bring due process to the disciplinary hearings had little, if any, effect. Various organizational dynamics eroded the formal requirements so that the substantive outcomes remained unchanged. The Harvard group concluded, as I do, that without the good faith efforts of the administration, the court decisions cannot be effective. The Harvard group goes further and questions whether the judicial process should be extended into the prison setting at all, in light of the peculiar nature of prison society. Harvard Center for Criminal Justice, "Judicial Intervention in Prison Discipline," *Journal of Criminal Law and Criminology* 63, no. 2 (June 1972): 200–228.

24. The figures were taken from the captain's logbooks, which include the daily count, broken down by various locations. Unfortunately, the 1968 logbook could not be found. Thirty days were chosen at random, and the figures were computed by surveying the isolation, segregation, and detention populations on those thirty days in each year.

25. Two samples were chosen. First fifty days were sampled for each of the sample years in order to determine those offenses for which isolation time was being served. The offenses were then collapsed into the categories presented in table 11. In order to avoid contaminating the results by differences in length of sentence in the various sample years, a second sample of twelve days was chosen so that each day sampled was more than fifteen days (the maximum isolation time) from every other day. The results are indistinguishable.

26. The inmates who were summarily thrown into segregation in connection with the commissary boycott have initiated a lawsuit (for money damages) against the prison administration (*Arsberry* v. *Sielaff* 74 C 1918). Plaintiffs charged that written and clear requirements for a disciplinary hearing provided for under section 804 of the department's Administrative Regulations were totally ignored. Arsberry claims that he was taken from his cell on 3 June 1974 and placed in the segregation wing on a tier known as "behavioral adjustment." Plaintiff claims that at no time was he given a formal statement of the charges against him or any type of hearing whatsoever.

27. See, for example, U.S. ex. rel. *Knight* v. *Ragen* 337 F.2d 425 (1964), where the petitioner alleged that "prison officials arbitrarily placed him in isolation, deprived him of adequate nourishment, comfort and liberty without due process

of law and denied him medication and drugs." The Seventh Circuit rejected these complaints: "Except under exceptional circumstances, internal matters in state penitentiaries are the sole concern of the states and federal courts will not inquire concerning them."

28. In a recently published article, William S. Bailey reports that there were 218 civil rights complaints in the Northern District of Illinois, Eastern Division in 1971 and 192 in 1973. See Supra. n. 22.

29. In the 1973 sample of prisoner civil rights cases Bailey found that 20 percent of the cases survived a motion to dismiss; of these 36 cases 22 advanced to the hearing stage. Ibid., p. 535.

30. Prison Legal Services administrator Keith Davis writes: "This writer has stood at the gates of the prison serving summons on prison guards being sued by prisoners. He has watched the confusion and fear ripple through the ranks of security officers as they gather around in clusters trying to understand the legal language and harsh rhetoric of the complaints." "The Prison Legal Services Project: History and Evaluation" (unpublished paper) p. 31.

31. The following statement made by a reform administrator at the Rhode Island Adult Correctional Institution (ACI) perfectly articulates the tension between the rehabilitative ideal and the demands of the courts for rational decision making: "The court decrees work against the inmate. It is too formal, too rigid. It dehumanized the ACI. We have tried to humanize the ACI by abolishing the use of prison numbers. The new regulations work in the opposite direction." Quoted in "Judicial Intervention" (see n. 23 above), p. 223.

32. The gate house sign-in sheets for fifty days chosen at random were examined for each of the sample years.

33. Personal interview with Gerald Solvay, the Jenner and Block partner who supervises *pro bono* service.

34. Prison Legal Services is not the only legal aid group to provide legal services to Stateville prisoners. The State Appellate Defender provides representation in criminal appeals, and a group of Northwestern law students has also provided assistance on postconviction relief for some years.

35. Keith Davis (see n. 30 above) has pointed out that "while it is said that more than 95% of the cases presented to Prison Legal Services did not concern institution related problems, nearly 90% of the time of the majority of the staff was delegated to addressing institutional abuses."

36. This demand called the attorneys' attention to the legal success of a Rhode Island prisoner group in *National Prisoners Reform Association* v. *Sharkey* 347 F. Supp. 1234 (1972).

37. *Falconer* v. *Bensinger* 71 C 2255 (1974).

38. Sometimes the lack of organizational efficiency served the interest of prisoner advocates. Davis (see n. 30 above) encountered the same disorganized situation at Stateville that I did: "The prison was in absolute chaos—we were able to use the prison organization against itself. For example, I'd call a lieutenant or a guard and tell him to bring an inmate up front to see me now! The guard might ask, "By whose authority?" I would reply, "Never you mind, just bring him." It never failed to work. They never checked anything out.... In the beginning we were very aggressive. If I had to wait 20 minutes at the gate I would threaten to call Fogel or the Governor's office. Guards didn't know what authority I had or where I should be allowed to go. Onc time the guard at Gate 1 handed me the key to lock people in and out while he went off to check something for us in the record office."

39. See, for example, the Chief Justice's speech at the National Conference of Christians and Jews (Philadelphia, 16 November 1972); Burger Report on the Federal Judicial Branch, 1973, *American Bar Association Journal* 59 (1973): 1125.

40. E.g., Federal District Court (and liberal) judge, James Doyle, in *Morales* v. *Schmidt* 340 F. Supp. 544 (W.D. Wisc, 1972) at p. 547.

41. Donald Liebentritt, "The Making of a Prison Guard: 1974" (Center for Studies in Criminal Justice, University of Chicago Law School, 1974, unpublished).

42. Since 1970 there has been a Department of Corrections long-range planning unit at Stateville on the fourth floor of the administration building, but this unit has departmental responsibility and is not a part of the Stateville organization.

43. Hampton was one of the two counselors fired in August 1972 because of his participation in the protest over participation in the disciplinary process.

44. There have been two black wardens (Pontiac and Old Joliet) appointed by Sielaff. Neither is still with the department.

45. Donald Cressey, *Other People's Money* (Glencoe, Ill.: Free Press, 1953).

46. Personal correspondence.

47. The Joliet factories have resisted unionization, and so the manufacturers perhaps saw in the prisoners a potential pool of future nonunion labor.

48. See James B. Jacobs, "Prison/Town Relationships as a Crucial Determinate of Prison Reform," *Social Service Review* 50, no. 4 (December 1976).

49. For an interesting study of ex-convict self-help groups in Chicago, see Patrick McAnany, Dennis Sullivan, William Kaplan, and Edward Tromanhauser, "Identification and Description of Ex-Offender Groups in the Chicago Area," Final Report to the Center for Research in Criminal Justice, University of Illinois, Chicago Circle (August 1974, unpublished).

50. In a personal interview, former state legislator Peggy Smith Martin explained that many of her constituents who have friends or relatives in the prisons are embarrassed openly to admit their associations with convicted felons but have asked her confidentially to look out for various prisoners' interests.

51. Several of the gang leaders have expressed privately to me strong reservations about the Reverend Jesse Jackson. They view him as competing with themselves for leadership in the black community.

52. Quoted in a report of the speech by Wayne Hearn, "Are the Inmates at Stateville Mistreated?" *Champaign-Urbana News Gazette,* 11 April 1974.

53. An individual with a background quite similar to Ma Houston's is the lay minister, Ann Rubalaca. A black woman in her middle years, Rubalaca, like Houston, has been in constant conflict with the administration for the past several years about whether she can claim ministerial visiting privileges. Many members of the staff consider Rubalaca and Houston serious adversaries, working to undermine the system. The precise content of their ministries is not clear to me, but I believe it involves small favors, like contacting families or employers.

54. Personal interview.

55. The article appeared in *Chicago Today* on 10 September 1974. It quoted a guard as saying, "We fear for our lives." It insinuated that George Carney, who burned himself to death in his cell in B house in the fall of 1973, had actually been murdered. In addition, it attacked the racial composition of the guard force, and stated that while the inmates ate food that was barely edible, the warden and his staff were served food prepared by Swiss cooks. One of the top administrators responded to the article in my presence by saying, "that dirty bitch, this almost encourages a riot."

56. Personal interview.

57. That the guards from whom she received cooperation were the young blacks on the staff was not made explicit in the report but was expressed to me in a personal interview.

58. There are a few other less important groups with contact at the prison.

Operation Reconciliation, a program developed by a Joliet businessman, brings citizens into the minimum security unit "to work with" inmates. Currently the program is suspended while the administration is seeking a more stringent definition of its content. At various times in the last few years drug rehabilitation groups like DARE (Direct Action for Rehabilitation and Employment) and group therapy groups like CHANCE have been given access to the prison.

The John Howard Association, Illinois's oldest and most established prison watchdog organization, enjoyed a harmonious relationship with the prison people until the late 1960s. After that time and under different leadership, John Howard became more of an adversary. On 2 March 1970, JHA released an "Illinois Penitentiary Survey and Progress Report" which called for immediate implementation of the full liberal-rehabilitation agenda: teachers, counselors, more psychologists, more programs, better pay for guards, more relevant job training, etc. On the whole, however, the report was not unfavorable to the new Bensinger administration. On the synoptic press release it was stated: "Joseph R. Rowan, Executive Director of JHA, said, "I have been involved in a number of reform movements in various states and I must say that more changes for the better have been made here in the past several months than I have ever seen before."

Since 1970 the John Howard Association has had only intermittent contact with Stateville. It has particularly turned its attention to the Cook County Jail. In the fall of 1974, John Howard released a scathing report about alleged brutalities in Illinois's youth facilities, which are administered by the Department of Corrections. The Department of Corrections branded the report "irresponsible" and banned the JHA from all Illinois penal institutions.

59. The Illinois Prison and Jail Project received funding from several of the foundations which gave financial support to the Chicago Street gangs in the late 1960s—the Wieboldt Foundation, Playboy Foundation, Field Foundation, Cummins Engine Foundation, the Woods Charitable Fund, and Chicago Community Trust. This is discussed in chapter 6.

60. The recent U.S. Supreme Court case of *Pell* v. *Procunier* 94 S.Ct. 2800 (1974) appears to give inmates unrestricted access to the press.

61. Recently, however, Director Sielaff has taken a beating in the press over the issue of furloughs.

62. When we look at the coverage of the 6 September 1973 cell house B takeover in the *Chicago Tribune* and *Chicago Today*, we can see the degree to which the establishment press remains dependent upon the definition of the situation presented by the prison administration.

The *Chicago Tribune* printed thirteen articles concerning the taking of hostages at B house; two of these were letters to the editor. Of the eleven news articles only two were written about the inmates and their grievances. The other nine articles discussed Warden Cannon, Governor Walker, and the prison's guards. There were seventeen sources either directly quoted or to whom comments were attributed. Three of the sources were inmates; the rest were either officials or guards. The only editorial the *Tribune* printed on the matter was a statement of praise for Governor Walker.

Chicago Today (now defunct) printed ten articles about the B house takeover; no letters to the editor. Of the ten articles, three were about the inmates and their grievances. Of fifteen sources either directly quoted to to whom comments were attributed, five were inmates. The single editorial printed by *Chicago Today* praised Governor Walker's efforts to settle the riot. Noting Peggy Smith Martin's criticisms of the prison system, the editorial called for amelioration of the conditions that led to riot, but argued that inmates who riot must be punished if order is to be preserved.

63. In early 1975 I counted the following number of journal subscriptions: *Rising Up Angry*—73; *Up against the Bench*—49; *On Ice*—57. Since each copy may be circulated to other inmates, the influence of these papers may be substantial.

64. See David Fogel, *We Are the Living Proof: A Social Justice Model for Corrections* (Cincinnati: W. H. Anderson, 1975).

Chapter 6

1. For the Blackstone Rangers see John Fry, *Fire and Blackstone* (Philadelphia: J. B. Lippincott, 1969); R. Sale, *The Blackstone Rangers* (New York: Popular Library, 1971); J. McPherson, "Almighty Black P Stone and What Does that Mean?" *Atlantic Monthly* 223 (May and June, 1969). For the Devil's Disciples see J. Laing, "The Black Disciples," *Wall Street Journal*, 12 September 1969, p. 1. For the Vice Lords see Lincoln Kaiser, *The Vice Lords: Warriors of the Street* (New York: Holt, Rinehart, and Winston, 1969); David Dawley, *A Nation of Lords* (New York: Anchor Books, 1973). See also Irving Spergel, "Youth Manpower Project: What Happened in Woodlawn" unpublished, University of Chicago, School of Social Service Administration, 1969).

2. As far as I can tell the term "supergang" was invented by Lawrence Sherman, in "Youth Workers, Police, and the Gangs: Chicago 1956-1970" (master's thesis, Division of Social Sciences, University of Chicago, 1970). It has been used by James Short, "Youth, Gangs, and Society: Micro and Macrosociological Processes," *The Sociological Quarterly* 15 (Winter 1974): 3-19. Malcolm Klein has argued that to characterize groups the size of the Black P Stone Nation or Disciples as "gangs" sacrifices any meaningful definition of the term. Malcolm Klein, *Street Gangs and Street Workers* (Englewood Cliffs, N.J.: Prentice Hall, 1971), p. 79.

3. James Short, "Gangs, Politics and the Social Order" (paper delivered at the McKay symposium at The University of Chicago Department of Sociology in the fall of 1972).

4. Fry, *Fire;* McPherson, "Black P Stone"; and Dawley, *Lords* (see n. 1 above).

5. Office of the Mayor of Chicago, "Organized Youth Crime in Chicago" (mimeo February 1970).

6. R. Cloward and F. Piven argue that national politics effected a change in the approach to the gangs after the Kennedy victory of 1960. In order to assuage the black neighborhoods concerned about juvenile violence and to placate ethnic whites concerned about integration, the federal government committed itself to various kinds of crime control through social welfare measures on the streets of the ghettos. Cloward and Piven, *Regulating the Poor* (New York: Pantheon Books, 1971).

7. Sherman, "Youth Workers" (see n. 2 above), p. 24.

8. Ibid., p. 26.

9. I was often amazed by the Stones' grandiose vision of controlling the entire city of Chicago. Spergel, in *Manpower* (see n. 1 above), p. 58, reported the same vision several years earlier.

10. OEO had come to believe that many of their job corps and vocational training programs of the mid-sixties had not succeeded in reaching hard-core ghetto youth. A romanticism, shared by private foundations and some in the federal government, apparently including Vice-president Humphrey, promoted belief in the potential of indigenous community gang leaders to solve their own problems. This romanticism reached its height in 1967 and 1968. Gang leaders were flown in and out of Washington, D.C., as the federal government attempted to forge a national alliance (YOU) of inner city street gangs. The Youth Manpower

Project was another effort to "reach" the hard-core inner city youths by allowing them a great degree of autonomy and control in planning and carrying out an antipoverty program.

For the history of the New York gang "The Real Great Society" and the success of its leaders in convincing government leaders of its potential to effect constructive change in the minority ghettos, see Richard W. Poston, *The Gangs and the Establishment* (New York: Harper and Row, 1971).

11. Spergel, "Manpower" (see n. 1 above), p. 165.

12. U.S., Congress, Senate, Permanent Subcommittee on Investigations of the Committee on Government Operations, *Hearings on Riots, Civil and Criminal Disorders,* 90th Congress, 2d session, 1968, part 10.

13. Lincoln Kaiser notes that the Vice Lord Nation originated in 1958 at the Illinois State Training School for Boys at St. Charles. *Vice Lords* (see n. 1 above), p. 1.

14. Dawley, *Lords* (see n. 1 above), p. 11.

15. Between 1967 and 1969 the following Vice Lord programs were undertaken: (1) Teen Town—an ice cream parlor converted from a gutted storefront with funds from Alderman Collins and Sears Roebuck; (2) African Lion—a soul shop which was aided in a management training program by a grant from the Field Foundation; (3) Tastee Freeze—an ice cream franchise established with a loan from American National Bank; (4) Simone—a business venture, involving the marketing of black cosmetics, carried out with Sammy Davis, Jr.; (5) West Side Community Development Corporation—a coalition of neighborhood groups attempting to build a viable economic community on the West Side, aided by loans from the First National Bank of Chicago; (6) Management Training Institute—a twenty-week program that taught black history, self-awareness, and business skills, funded by a Coalition for Youth Action in the Department of Labor; (7) Street Academy—an alternative educational program for community dropouts; (8) Partners—in 1968 the Ford Foundation gave $130,000 to improve the executive skills of Vice Lord leaders; (9) House of Lords—two neighborhood "hang'ins" created with Vice Lords money for community youth; (10) Beautification—a program to clean up Lawndale given impetus by an administrative grant from the Field Foundation and a donation of one hundred Youth Corps positions from the Catholic School Board; (11) Tenant's Rights Action Group—organized to help local people with legal services in disputes with landlords; (12) Art and Soul—two unoccupied storefronts were converted into a studio and gallery to develop the talent of local youth with a grant from the Wieboldt Foundation and with the assistance of Circle Campus.

16. Dawley, *Lords* (see n. 1 above), pp. 107–36.

17. Sherman, "Youth Workers" (see n. 2 above), p. 34. Captain Buckney of the Gang Intelligence Unit maintained that the Blackstone Rangers were paid to conduct the no-vote campaign.

18. Since June 1972, when I began studying Stateville, the most consistent estimate of gang membership is 50 percent. A few independents have estimated gang membership as low as 33 percent and a few guards as "at least 80 percent." It is quite remarkable that, even though the gangs have been the gravest problem affecting Illinois corrections for six years, there is no accurate method of compiling information on them. A random sample of the disciplinary cards of all inmates whose inmate number ended in "3" revealed twenty-five cards with a notation of gang membership (16 Stones, 7 Disciples, 1 Latin King, 1 Vice Lord), which would indicate a total of 250 gang members in the entire inmate population. This figure is not given credence by informants. It is a more illuminating statement of the record keeping at the prison than it is of gang membership. A

separate census of the 86 inmates in segregation on 1 January 1975 revealed that 34 of them were in the gangs. When the total number of disciplinary tickets is compared for the sample of 25 gang members with the 144 non-gang members, we find that the gang members average 34.0 disciplinary reports as compared with 13.3 for non-gang. For the segregation inmates the 34 gang members (19 Stones, 15 Disciples) averaged 43.0 disciplinary reports, while the 52 non-gang members averaged 35.2.

19. See William Davidson, "The Worst Jail I Have Ever Seen," *Saturday Evening Post,* 13 July 1968, p. 18.

20. "Organized Crime" (see n. 5 above).

21. Involvement of youth street gangs in urban politics is hardly a modern phenomenon. In Frederick Thrasher's classic work, *The Gang* (Chicago: University of Chicago Press, 1927), he pointed out that "political alliances with members of gangs have become so common in recent years that there has been a disposition to regard gangsters as "inlaws" rather than "outlaws." See also Gerald Suttles and Stephen Kalberg, "Inarticulate Protests: Gangs, the Police, and Politicians in Chicago during 1964–1970" (unpublished paper) delivered by Suttles at the dedication of the Burgess papers, University of Chicago (Spring 1974).

22. Walter B. Miller, "American Youth Gangs, Past and Present," in Abraham S. Blumberg, *Current Perspective on Criminal Behavior* (New York: Alfred A. Knopf, 1974), pp. 210–37, at p. 232.

23. Ibid., p. 235.

24. In his evaluation of the Youth Manpower Project (see n. 1 above, p. 59), Spergel also pointed out that the Stones were an alternative to politicization. "There was also some interest in Black Power and black culture activities by both groups, particularly among the Blackstone Rangers. Nevertheless, neither of the organizations appears to have had a strong civil rights commitment or to have engaged significantly in local or citywide civil rights and Black Power efforts. There were frequent attempts by representatives of these other organizations to involve the Rangers and Disciples; and the Rangers, on several occasions, participated, on a limited basis, in Black Power meetings and civil rights demonstrations, *but both Rangers and Disciples clearly avoided commitment or systematic engagement in race-related issues and activities. They were primarily concerned with their power, not with Black Power.*"

25. Some of the materials in this section have been previously reported in James B. Jacobs, "Street Gangs behind Bars," *Social Problems* 21, no. 4 (winter 1974). That article reported a participant observation study carried out at Stateville between June and September 1972. Many more data have been collected since then and appear throughout the text.

26. It seems inaccurate to speak of these gangs as "organizations" as the term is used sociologically. Lewis Yablonsky argues that the violent gang stands midway between a mob and a group and has coined the term "near group" to refer to that organizational form. Yablonsky, *The Violent Gang* (Baltimore: Penguin Books, 1970), chap. 14. I feel that "near group" is not a very helpful analytical term. It might be more useful to think of the supergangs as proto-organizations of the "normative" type suggested by A. Etzioni, *A Comparative Analysis of Complex Organizations* (London: Collier-Macmillan, 1971).

27. I have reproduced the inmate documents with their original spelling and syntax in order to describe more accurately the prison situation which includes the linguistic styles of the gang members.

28. In this section, some of which is based upon participant observation in 1972,

I have used fictitious initials in place of the real names of informants in order to protect their confidences.

29. Thrasher distinguished three levels of involvement in the street gangs which he studied: (1) the inner circle, including the leader and his lieutenants; (2) the rank and file, including members in good standing; and (3) the fringers, or the nebulous ring of hangers-on who cannot be counted on to go to the full length in any exploit. *The Gang* (see n. 21 above). In his study of violent gangs in the Morningside Heights area of Manhattan, Lewis Yablonsky also sought to delineate levels of membership but tied his categories of core and marginal membership to personality types rather than to organizational role. Yablonsky, *The Violent Gang* (see n. 26 above), pp. 248–257.

30. McCleery observed that the key concern of the convicted man is lack of information about institutional policies and decisions. *Theoretical Studies* (see Introduction, n. 9, above).

31. The Sielaff administration, which took office in 1973, eliminated all inmate clerk jobs and thus speeded up the disintegration of the old inmate social system. Communication between front and back was slowed down.

32. Whether one subscribes to the theories of Albert K. Cohen, *Delinquent Boys: The Culture of the Gang* (New York: Free Press, 1955), or of Walter B. Miller, "Lower Class Subculture as a Generating Milieu of Gang Violence," *Journal of Social Issues* 14 (Summer 1958): 5–19, with respect to the origins of delinquent gangs, the important point here, is, as Thrasher has emphasized, that the gang serves as a membership and reference group which provides the delinquent youth with status and a favorable evaluation of self.

33. Robert Johns, "Civil Rights and Prison Violence" (unpublished paper, undated).

34. For parallel examples of secondary group organization inside prison see James B. Jacobs, "Stratification and Conflict Among Prison Inmates," *Journal of Criminal Law and Criminology*, vol. 66 no. 4 December 1975.

35. Warden John Petrilli at Pontiac Penitentiary did extend formal recognition to the gangs. The gangs were given separate cell houses, proportional representation on assignments, and open access to the warden, who declared that "everything is negotiable." The inmates were organized in various committees and met with the warden frequently. Each gang was allowed to use the chapel for a full assembly each month. While the young gang members spoke highly of Warden Petrilli, they were unable to keep the peace among themselves. Part of this may be explained by the absence of any of the older or higher-ranking gang leadership. In any case, two gang rumbles at Pontiac, which left several dead and seriously injured, led to the repudiation of this policy and ultimately to the removal of Warden Petrilli.

36. See. n. 35 above.

Chapter 7

1. The telephone questionnaire was designed by this author and administered by a law student, Mary Grear. The results have been separately reported in "Drop Outs and Rejects: An Analysis of Turnover Among Stateville Prison Guards" (unpublished, Center for Studies in Criminal Justice, University of Chicago Law School, 1975).

2. See *Chicago Sun Times*, 11 August 1971.

3. *The Task Force on Corrections* of the President's Commission on Crime and the Administration of Justice concluded: "In contrast with the traditional system, a new concept of relationships in correctional institutions, the "collaborative

regime," has been evolving during the past few decades. An outstanding feature of this trend is increased communication between custodial staff, inmates and treatment staff. Custodial staff, by virtue of their close contact with all aspects of an inmate's life, have a great potential for counselling functions, both with individual inmates and in group discussions" (p. 11).

The same call for a redefinition of the guard's role was set forth in a John Howard report, "Adult Correctional Facilities and Programs in Illinois" (released 2 March 1970).

4. E.g., Morris Janowitz and R. Vinter, "Effective Institutions for Juvenile Delinquents: A Research Statement," *Social Service Review* 33 (June) 1959: 118–130.

5. Donald Cressey, "Limitations on Organization of Treatment in the Modern Prison," pp. 77–104 in *Theoretical Studies in Social Organization of the Prison*, ed. R. Cloward et al. (New York: Social Science Research Council, 1960).

6. This point is made in the mental hospital context by A. Stanton and M. Schwartz, *The Mental Hospital* (London: Tavistock, 1954).

7. Note the following sober warning presented as a model for guard training by the American Correctional Association, *Correction Officers Training Guide* (n.d.), p. 23. "Bribery usually begins as a result of being too intimate with inmates. They offer a cigar, cigarettes, or some trivial article. Each time this is done a closer contact is made and finally they come through with what they really want the officer to do. They may work the officer into a compromising position by securing information from him which may make it appear to his superiors that he has been passing on confidential or department information. Or it may be that an inmate is a witness to some incident involving the officer, and which, if known, would not add to his reputation for efficiency and reliability. Self-protection being a powerful instinct, the officer, might ask the inmate to keep quiet or to falsify his testimony when questioned. This is the beginning of bribery, and it may get the officer on the inmate's payroll from that time on."

8. The figure varies slightly depending upon whom one wants to count as a guard, since recent Department of Personnel changes have transformed some guards into "prison clerks" and various other positions. A recent lawsuit brought by the University of Chicago's Mandel Legal Aid Clinic, *Greer* vs. *Sielaff* (No. 75C247), charges that a black guard was discriminatorily discharged from his position at Stateville. The suit has been brought as a class action and charges that "at all times, the Defendants acting individually and in concert have maintained policies, practices and customs of limiting the employment opportunities of past, present and prospective black prison guards, including plaintiff, by such acts as: (a) selecting and hiring guards on the basis of race, (b) discharging and disciplining guards on the basis of race, (c) distributing work assignments on the basis of race, (d) promoting guards on the basis of race.

9. See James B. Jacobs and Mary P. Greer, "Drop-outs and Rejects: An Analysis of Turnover among Stateville Prison Guards" (unpublished paper, Center for Studies in Criminal Justice, University of Chicago Law School, 1975).

10. The Model Employer Program carried out by the State of Illinois Department of Personnel began in July 1974, when the first minority recruits were hired to become prospective prison guards. Unlike the usual recruit, the "Affirmative Action group" (as they have come to be called) is given a three-week orientation program *before* beginning recruit training at the academy. To date (June 1975), seventy-five Stateville/Joliet guards have been hired in this way.

11. This version of the events is consistent with Randolph's own recollection.

12. In 1961 the Illinois legislature passed a statute providing "that any employee of the state may authorize the withholding of a portion of his salary,

wages and annuities for any one or more of the following purposes . . . (3) For payment to any labor union." *Ill. Rev. Stat.*, chap. 127, sec. 351–60 (1965).

13. In 1969 Stateville/Joliet employees collectively accumulated 289 pink slip warnings, 171 suspensions, and 107 probationary discharges and requests to resign. Soon after Bensinger came into office, the "pinkies" were abolished.

14. During the early years of local 1866 there was considerable debate whether the lieutenants would be allowed to join because of fear that that would create a company union. One of the bylaws stated that lieutenants and above could not join, but AFSCME representatives explained to the local that such a clause was illegal.

15. Similar demands were made by the union in March 1971 after an incident in which an inmate threatened guards with a razor blade.

16. The guards did implement a job action at Pontiac several weeks later.

17. From what I can tell, the three guards were not at the prison at the time of the escape but were fired for not *discovering* the escape sooner.

18. "Stateville Dissension: Prison Lock-up Angers Inmates," *Chicago Daily News*, 6 July 1972, p. 27.

19. Governor Walker early in 1973 made good on a campaign promise to initiate public employee bargaining. Executive Order No. 6 created the Office of Collective Bargaining and established the right of state employees to bargain collectively.

20. The question of what issues are bargainable is a crucial and particularly difficult one in the context of the public sector, where there are no well-established inherent management prerogatives. In other states, particularly New York, the guard union has gone far in encroaching upon what the Department of Corrections has traditionally viewed as its prerogatives. Similar issues are sure to arise in Illinois within the next several years.

21. Consider the following bulletin signed by Frank Pate (Bulletin No. 231, 2 December 1965): "I would like to take this opportunity to thank all the employees who are helping to carry the tremendous load at the institution during the shortage of help. It is very gratifying to one to know that people think enough of the institution to work their days off and also double shifts when necessary. Everyone who has been requested to work overtime will eventually get compensatory time off for his extra work."

22. The crucial question is likely to be answered on some question of a strike. Quite recently in *City of Pana* v. *Crowe* 57 Ill. 2d 547 (1974) the Illinois Supreme Court held that Illinois legislation prohibiting court injunctions of unions did not apply to public employee unions. Thus the state could move for an injunction against union leaders if the guards went out on strike. Of course the political ramifications, at this late date, of any politician moving against labor unions might make the whole question quite hypothetical.

23. Incomplete results of a survey that I have been administering to all in-service prison guards in Illinois as they pass through the Illinois Correctional Academy shows that for a sample of 160 Stateville/Joliet guards, including 109 whites and 51 blacks, there is a highly significant (at .001 level) difference in factor scores constructed from a series of questions measuring the guard's social distance from the prisoners.

Chapter 8

1. Weber, "Bureaucracy" (see chap. 2, n. 5, above), p. 217.

Appendix

1. Rose Giallambardo, "Interviewing in the Prison Community," *Journal of*

Criminal Law, Criminology, and Police Science 7, no. 3 (September 1966).

2. Sykes, *Society of Captives* (see Introduction, n. 8, above).

3. In *Analyzing Social Settings* (Belmont: Wadsworth, 1971) John Lofland observes that "at the practical level of maintaining the role and one's acceptability to the participants, it is probably necessary for one to perform services in the setting. In terms of "exchange of services"—the pure observer role involves a highly imbalanced relation to the participants. They let him watch but he does nothing for them in return. More immediate reciprocities are necessary. Indeed in a wide range of emergent circumstances, it will seem peculiar if the observer does not volunteer his help" (p. 98).

4. See Arthur Vidich, "Participant Observation and the Collection and Interpretation of Data," in *Issues in Participant Observation*, ed. G. McCall and J. Simmons (Reading: Addison-Wesley, 1969), pp. 78-86.

5. Howard Becker, "Problems of Inference and Proof in Participant Observation," *American Sociological Review* 23 (1958): 652-60.

6. Vidich, "Observation" (see n. 4 above), p. 81. Vidich has said it well: "In avoiding commitments to political issues, [the participant-observer] plays the role of political eunuch. He is socially marginal to the extent that he measures his society as a non-involved outsider and avoids committing his loyalties and allegiances to segments of it. This is not hypocrisy but rather, as Howe has noted of Stendhal, 'it is living a ruse.' Being both a participant and an observer is 'the strategy of deceiving the society to study it and wooing the society to live in it.'"

Index